FRED BIRD

(203) 966-8466

OPTION EMBEDDED BONDS

Price Analysis, Credit Risk and
Investment Strategies

OPTION EMBEDDED BONDS

Price Analysis, Credit Risk and Investment Strategies

ISRAEL NELKEN
Editor

IRWIN
Professional Publishing®
Chicago • London • Singapore

Times Mirror
Higher Education Group

Library of Congress Cataloging-in-Publication Data
Option-embedded bonds / edited by Israel Nelken.
        p. cm.
    Includes index.
    ISBN 0–7863–0818–4
    1. Bonds. 2. Options (Finance). 3. Derivative securities.
    I. Nelkin, Israel.
    HG4651.068   1997
    332.63'23—dc20   96–25710

Printed in the United States of America
1 2 3 4 5 6 7 8 9 DO 0 3 2 1 0 9 8 7

This book is dedicated to my wife, Lisa,
with much love and affection.

P R E F A C E

When one party borrows money from another, a debt is created. Many times this debt is in the form of a bond. When a bond is initially purchased, the buyer of the bond lends money to the issuer who promises to pay back at maturity. In the case of a coupon-bearing bond, the holder also gets to receive the intermediate cash flows generated by the coupons.

Many bonds include options that may take effect during the life of the contract. For example, if a bond is callable and interest rates decline during its life, the issuer may choose to call the bond, prepay the holder, and terminate the outstanding debt. In other cases, the holder has the right to put bonds, or sell them back to the issuer at predetermined prices on specific dates. If interest rates rise during the life of the bond, it will probably be advantageous to the holder to do just that. Some bonds include both call and put options.

Many other types of options can be embedded in a bond. Obviously, all of these options must be accounted for when analyzing a bond. Lenders who have the ability to correctly assess complex bonds will typically earn higher returns on their capital. Conversely, issuers who have this ability will be able to borrow at lower rates.

The book is divided into three parts. In the first part, we cover several issues relating to yield curve models and forecasting interest rates. In the second section, we discuss measures of risk. The third and most comprehensive section describes some of the more interesting instruments and their applications.

This book brings together the work of some of the world's leading experts on the topic. We are very grateful to all of the authors for their time, energy, and dedication to this project. We also thank the people at Irwin Professional Publishing for their efforts.

Finally, I would like to thank Robert Klein and Jess Lederman for their enthusiasm and support.

—*Israel "Izzy" Nelken*

PREFACE

When one party borrows money from another, a debt is created. Many times this debt is in the form of a bond. When a bond is initially purchased, the buyer of the bond lends money to the issuer who promises to pay back at maturity. In the case of a coupon-bearing bond, the holder also gets to receive the intermediate cash flows generated by the coupons.

Many bonds include options that may take effect during the life of the contract. For example, if a bond is callable and interest rates decline during its life, the issuer may choose to call the bond, prepay the holder, and terminate the outstanding debt. In other cases, the holder has the right to put bonds, or sell them back to the issuer at predetermined prices on specific dates. If interest rates rise during the life of the bond, it will probably be advantageous to the holder to do just that. Some bonds include both call and put options.

Many other types of options can be embedded in a bond. Obviously, all of these options must be accounted for when analyzing a bond. Lenders who have the ability to correctly assess complex bonds will typically earn higher returns on their capital. Conversely, issuers who have this ability will be able to borrow at lower rates.

The book is divided into three parts. In the first part, we cover several issues relating to yield curve models and forecasting interest rates. In the second section, we discuss measures of risk. The third and most comprehensive section describes some of the more interesting instruments and their applications.

This book brings together the work of some of the world's leading experts on the topic. We are very grateful to all of the authors for their time, energy, and dedication to this project. We also thank the people at Irwin Professional Publishing for their efforts.

Finally, I would like to thank Robert Klein and Jess Lederman for their enthusiasm and support.

—*Israel "Izzy" Nelken*

BRIEF CONTENTS

ix

CONTENTS

Chapter 11

Pricing Derivatives on Risky Bonds as Applied to Emerging Markets   231
P. Calderini, V. Finkelstein, and B.Y. Gelfand

Chapter 12

Interest Rates and Life Insurance   257
J. P. Hunziker and P. Koch-Medina

Chapter 13

Options on Volatility   273
Menachem Brenner and Dan Galai

AUTHOR BIOGRAPHIES

KERRY BACK

Dr. Back is professor of finance at the Olin School of Business of Washington University. His early research was in mathematical economics and mathematical programming. His research in finance has been acknowledged with a Batterymarch Fellowship in 1991–92 and with the best paper award in the *Review of Financial Studies* in 1993. He is currently editor of the *Review of Financial Studies* and serves on the editorial boards of several other economics and finance journals.

Dr. Back received his PhD in economics from the University of Kentucky in 1983. He has held appointments at Northwestern University, the University of Pennsylvania, and Indiana University.

ALAIN BENSOUSSAN

Dr. Bensoussan has been president of Institut National de Recherche en Informatique et Automatique (INRIA), since December 1984, and he is on the boards of several industrial companies.

Dr. Bensoussan has followed an acadmic career as a professor at the University Paris-Dauphine, Ecole Polytechnique, and Ecole Normale Superieure. He holds a PhD in mathematics, and is a graduate of Ecole Polytechnique and ENSAE in France. He has published 13 books and more than 300 articles in academic journals in the areas of stochastic differential equations, filtering and control of stochastic distributed systems, optimal stopping, impulse control, variational and quasi-variational inequalities, regulation of nonlinear systems of elliptic parabolic PDE and applications, robust control, exact controlability, homogenization, regular and singular perturbations, and specific problems in operations management and finance. He is also on the editorial boards of many scientific journals including Applied

Mathematics and Optimization, Mathematical Finance, RAIRO, and Advanced Series in Management (with North Holland). Dr. Bensoussan is a member of the scientific council of EDF, France Telecom, and SNCF as well as of the French Defense Scientific Council and the French Academy of Sciences. Dr. Bensoussan was granted the Legion d'Honneur in 1991.

MENACHEM BRENNER

Dr. Brenner is a professor of finance at the Leonard N. Stern School of Business at New York University.

Dr. Brenner has served as a consultant to leading stock exchanges, banks, and other financial institutions. He is an organizer and speaker at the annual American Stock Exchange Options Colloquium, and he has been a floor trader in futures and options on the New York Futures Exchange. Dr. Brenner was a member of the board of directors and chairman of the new products committee and the index maintenance committee of the Tel Aviv Stock Exchange. He is a member of the advisory panel on emerging markets investable indexes at the International Finance Corporation.

Dr. Brenner has published numerous papers and has edited a book on option pricing. His most recent work, coauthored with Subrahmanyam and Uno, deals with arbitrage opportunities in the Japanese futures markets. He holds MA and PhD degrees in finance and economics from Cornell University and a B.A. degree in economics from Hebrew University.

PABLO E. CALDERINI

Mr. Calderini is in charge of risk management for emerging market derivatives at J. P. Morgan. He holds a Masters degree in economics from the Center for Macroeconomics Studies of Argentina (CEMA).

DAIZHAN CHENG

Dr. Cheng is a research associate at Gifford Fong Associates. His expertise is system sciences and mathematics.

Dr. Cheng was a full professor at the Chinese Academy of Sciences and a visiting assistant professor at Texas Tech University.

He holds a PhD in system sciences from Washington University in Missouri.

LES CLEWLOW

Dr. Les Clewlow is a senior research fellow with the Financial Options Research Centre, University of Warwick. He also works as a financial consultant implementing pricing and hedging models and numerical/computational techniques for major organizations and software companies which develop risk management systems. Dr. Clewlow has been published in trade and academic journals, has presented papers at leading academic and practioner conferences, and has taught advanced courses in Euorpe, the United States, and Australia.

Dr. Clewlow has a first class honours degree in physics with astrophysics (Birmingham), and a PhD in computer science (Warwick).

MICHEL CROUHY

Dr. Crouhy is vice president of global analytics in the market risk-management division at Canadian Imperial Bank of Commerce (CIBC). Prior to joining CIBC, he was a professor of finance at the HEC School of Management, where he was also director of the MS in International Finance, a unique program that prepares engineers from the best engineering schools in Europe to become investment bankers. He has been a visiting professor at the Wharton School and at UCLA.

Dr. Crouhy holds a PhD from the Wharton School and is a graduate of Ecole Nationale des Ponts et Chaussées, France. He has published extensively in academic journals in the areas of banking, options, and financial markets, and he is editor of the book collection Banque & Bourse at Presses Universitaires de France.

Dr. Crouhy is associate editor of the *Journal of Derivatives*, the *Journal of Banking and Finance*, and *Financial Engineering and the Japanese Markets*. He is a board member of the European Institute for Advanced Studies in Management (EIASM) in Brussels. He has also served as a consultant to major financial institutions in Europe and in the United States in the areas of quantitative portfolio management, risk management, valuation and hedging of derivative products, forecasting volatility term structure, and correlations.

CHRISTIAN L. DUNIS

Dr. Dunis is the head of quantitative research and trading (QRT) at Chemical Bank. He is a vice president with Chemical's global trading division based in London, where he is responsible for developing the bank's quantitative research capabilities and managing the development of computer models for generating proprietary trading revenues.

Dr. Dunis is the organizer, with Imperial College, of an annual international conference held in London on forecasting financial markets that covers advances for exchange rates, interest rates, and asset management. He is the editor of Chemical's "Working Papers in Financial Economics" and a member of the editorial board of The European Journal of Finance. Dr. Dunis is the coauthor of *Exchange Rate Forecasting*, the editor and coauthor of *Forecasting Financial Markets*, and the coeditor and coauthor of *Nonlinear Modelling of High Frequency Financial Time Series* to be published in early 1997.

Dr. Dunis holds a Diploma in Higher Studies in economics and international finance and a PhD in economics from the University of Paris. He is a member of the Securities and Futures Authority in London, of the French Association of Corporate Treasurers (AFTE) in Paris, and of the International Institute of Forecasters in the United States.

RAVIT EFRATY

Dr. Efraty is a vice president of Salomon Brothers. She is a trader in the fixed-income derivatives department. Dr. Efraty originally joined Salomon Brothers as an analyst in the derivatives research group.

Dr. Efraty received a BSc in mathematics and physics from Tel Aviv University, and a PhD from Columbia University in theoretical physics.

VLADIMIR FINKELSTEIN

Dr. Finkelstein is a vice president in the derivatives research group of J. P. Morgan in New York. He is in charge of the group responsible for model development for all interest-rate derivatives, including swap, hybrid, and emerging-markets products.

Dr. Finkelstein studied physics in Moscow, earned his PhD at New York University, and was an assistant professor in the department of physics at New York University before joining J.P. Morgan.

H. GIFFORD FONG

Mr. Fong is president of Gifford Fong Associates, a firm specializing in fixed-income, asset-allocation, and derivative-product analysis. He is on the editorial boards of *The Journal of Portfolio Management* and *The Financial Analysts Journal;* is a contributor to *Managing Investment Portfolios: A Dynamic Process;* and serves as a member of the Institute for Quantitative Research in Finance, The Research Foundation of the Institute of Chartered Financial Analysts, the Association for Investment Management and Research (AIMR) Council on Education and Research (CER), the Fixed Income Analysis and Portfolio Management Specialization Curriculum Committee, and the editorial advisory board for the *Handbook of Fixed-Income Securities.*

In addition, Mr. Fong is coauthor of *Fixed-Income Portfolio Management* and coauthor of *Advanced Fixed-Income Portfolio Management.* He is the author of numerous trade journal publications and has received several honors, including the Institute for Quantitative Research in Finance Award. Mr. Fong is a graduate of the University of California where he earned his BS, MBA, and law degrees.

DAN GALAI

Dr. Galai is the Abe Gray professor of finance and business administration at the Hebrew University School of Business Administration in Jerusalem. He was a visiting professor of finance at INSEAD and has also taught at the University of California, Los Angeles, and the University of Chicago.

Dr. Galai holds a PhD from the University of Chicago and undergraduate and graduate degrees from the Hebrew University. He has served as a consultant for the Chicago Board of Options Exchange (CBOE) and the American Stock Exchange as well as for major banks. He has published numerous articles on options, financial assets, and corporate finance in leading business and finance journals. Dr. Galai was a winner of the First Annual Pomeranze Prize for excellence in options research presented by the CBOE. Dr. Galai is a principal in SIMGA P.C.M., which is engaged in portfolio management and corporate finance.

BORIS Y. GELFAND

Dr. Gelfand is a risk manager in emerging markets derivatives at J.P. Morgan. He received a PhD in physics from Harvard University in 1994.

PAUL GRAVER

Mr. Graver is managing director of the Financial Risk Strategy Practice. He consults on valuation (including modeling), policies, programs, and procedures involving financial derivative products to financial establishments. Derivative products include, but are not limited to, collateralized mortgage obligations, pass-throughs, governments, corporates, futures, and swap base transactions.

Previously Mr. Graver was director of KPMG Peat Marwick's financial risk strategy group; president of P. A. Graver & Associates, Inc.; and senior vice president at Drexel Burnham Lambert.

Mr. Graver has a BS in finance from Marquette University and an MBA from Loyola University.

J.P. HUNZIKER

Dr. Hunziker is a vice president with Winterthur Insurance Group, where he is responsible for central risk management in the finance department. He has been instrumental in the development of the equity-linked life insurance market in Switzerland and has coauthored several articles on the topic. Previously, he worked for Swiss Re and Ecofin, a research and consulting company based in Zurich. Dr. Hunziker holds a degree in physics from the Swiss Federal Institute of Technology and a PhD in economics from the Univeristy of Zurich.

DUNMU JI

Dr. Ji is vice president and director of research at Gifford Fong Associates (GFA). He specializes in mortgage-backed securities, futures valuation, Treasuries, and other fixed-income security valuation. He is an expert in object-oriented programming and mathematical modeling. His research has resulted in the expansion of the traditional contingent claims model to more accurately value fixed-income securities. His work has also improved term structure determination at GFA. Dr. Ji has been instrumental in the development of Treasury futures valuation with a full contingent claims treatment.

Dr. Ji is a native of Beijing, China, where he obtained a Masters degree in system science from the Academy Sinica in 1982. He also holds a PhD in applied mathematics from Brown University in Rhode Island, which he received in 1987.

GUNNAR KLINKHAMMER

Dr. Klinkhammer is vice president of quantitative research at Capital Management Sciences. Previously he was with McKinsey & Company, where he conducted change management programs for large corporations in the United States and Europe.

Dr. Klinkhammer received his PhD in Theoretical Physics from the California Institute of Technology. Building on his expertise in mathematical modeling and his business experience, Dr. Klinkhammer manages the CMS Analytics Group, a team responsible for the analytical integrity of all valuation and simulation tools as well as the continued innovation and expansion of CMS's analytics. Dr. Klinkhammer is a frequent speaker at industry conferences.

P. KOCH-MEDINA

Dr. Koch-Medina is an assistant vice president with Winterthur Insurance Group, where he is in charge of the development of insurance products involving derivatives at Winterthur-Life. He has been instrumental in the development of the equity-linked life insurance market in Switzerland and has coauthored several articles on the topic. Previously, Dr. Koch-Medina worked for J. P. Morgan. He holds a PhD in mathematics from the University of Zurich.

JOHN ANDREW MCQUOWN

Mr. McQuown is a founding partner of Kealhofer, McQuown, Vasicek, and is a director of KMV Corporation. He cofounded Diversified Corporate Loans. He is also a cofounder and director of

Dimensional Fund Advisors, Chalone Wine Group Ltd., Micro-Source, and Mortgage Information Corporation. Currently an entrepreneur in financial services, Mr. McQuown began his business career in 1961 in the corporate finance department of Smith, Barney & Co., New York. Between 1964 and 1974 he was with Wells Fargo Bank, serving as director of management sciences.

Mr. McQuown received his BS in Mechanical Engineering from Northwestern University and an MBA from the Harvard Business School.

ROBERT NAVIN

Dr. Navin is currently engaged in building financial models of convertible bonds at Swiss Bank Corporation. Prior to this he was a consultant to Capital Management Sciences.

He previously worked as a research theoretical physicist in the central research laboratories of a company in the nuclear energy industry after completing a PhD in theoretical particle physics at the California Institute of Technology.

IZZY NELKEN

Dr. Nelken is the founder of Super Computing Consulting Corporation, which provides services to the financial community. He has developed new methodologies and software for pricing and evaluating exotic options, convertible bonds, option-embedded securities, and structured notes. Previously, Dr. Nelken served on the faculty of the Department of Computer Science at the University of Toronto. He has published numerous articles, and he is a frequent lecturer on topics such as credit derivatives, exotic options, and equity swaps. Dr. Nelken is a lecturer at the financial mathematics program at the University of Chicago.

Dr. Nelken received his BSc in mathematics and computer science from Tel Aviv University and his PhD in computer science from Rutgers University.

TERM STRUCTURE MODELS AND FORECASTING

1

⑥ YIELD CURVE MODELS: A MATHEMATICAL REVIEW

Kerry Back*

Vernon W. and Marion K. Piper Professor of Financial Economics
Olin School of Business
Washington University in St. Louis

The yield curve is the set of yields of default-risk-free discount (i.e., zero coupon) bonds of various maturities. The yield curve defines the prices of discount bonds and also of coupon bonds, since a coupon bond is simply a portfolio of discount bonds. To price other interest-rate-sensitive claims requires a model for how the yield curve may evolve over time. Of course, modeling the yield curve is equivalent to modeling the set of discount bond prices or modeling the forward rate curve, and we can focus on one or the other as a matter of convenience.

YIELDS AND THE SHORT RATE

Letting t denote the current date and $u > t$ the date at which a discount bond matures, so that $u - t$ is the number of years remaining until maturity, the (continuously compounded) yield $r(t, u)$ of the bond is related to its price $P(t,u)$ by[1]

---

*I thank Donald Aucamp for reading and commenting upon parts of this chapter. Of course, all errors are my own.

1 P(t,u) denotes the price per $1 face value. Henceforth, the face value will be taken to be $1, so that there is no need to repeat this phrase. The qualifier "default risk free" will also not be repeated, since default risk is not considered anywhere in the chapter.

$$P(t,u) = e^{-r(t,u)\{u-t\}} \Leftrightarrow r(t,u) = -\frac{\log P(t,u)}{u-t} \tag{1}$$

For the purposes of modeling, it is convenient to assume that discount bonds of all maturities exist. In particular, I will assume that at each date t there is a bond that is just maturing, the yield of which is

$$r(t) \equiv \lim_{u \downarrow t} r(t,u).$$

Because the bond pays its face value with certainty when it matures, this short bond is riskless, and its rate of return equals its yield. The rate of return is called the short rate.

CONTINUOUS-TIME MODELS

As the preceding discussion suggests, this chapter will survey continuous-time models of the yield curve.[2] Continuous-time models are simpler than discrete-time models in some respects because there is a calculus that can be applied to functions of continuous time. The numerical solution of continuous-time models often involves some discretization of time; however, solving the "obvious" discrete-time analogue of a continuous-time model is usually not the most efficient procedure. Therefore, continuous-time models are of considerable interest even if numerical solutions are necessary. The drawback of continuous-time models is that the requisite mathematics is more involved.

The next section provides an introduction to the mathematics of continuous-time models. The key results are Itô's Formula (also called "Itô's Lemma") and Girsanov's Theorem. Readers familiar with these results can skip to the section on risk-neutral pricing.

STOCHASTIC CALCULUS

Brownian Motion

The first objective is to explain what *Brownian motion* means. I will use this term only for what is sometimes called a *standard Brownian motion*, also referred to as a *Wiener process*. I will begin with the notion of a ran-

---

2 For an exposition of common discrete-time (lattice) models, see the recent monograph by Tuckman (1995).

dom walk. Consider a random walk that steps either up or down by one unit at each discrete time $t = 1, 2, \ldots$, with up and down being equally likely. The position of the random walk at time t, which I will denote by $X(t)$, is the sum of the steps up to and including time t. The position depends on the "state of the world" (i.e., it is random), though the notation $X(t)$ does not indicate this dependence. This is a convention that I will follow throughout the chapter. Such a random walk X has several important properties:

1. It is a Markov stochastic process: given the history $(X(s)$, $s \leq t)$, the position $X(t)$ is a sufficient statistic for the purpose of forecasting $X(u)$ for $u > t$; i.e., the past $(X(s), s < t)$ is irrelevant.

2. It is a martingale: the mathematical expectation of $X(u)$ given the history $(X(s), s \leq t)$ is $X(t)$.

3. The quadratic variation (sum of squared changes) through any jump date t is equal to t. This is true for every possible path.

These properties are retained when we allow jumps at noninteger times, provided the jump size is the square root of the amount of time between jumps (this square-root relation is needed for property 3).

This is perhaps not a bad starting place for building a security price model. Of course, we might want to use a random walk as a model of the logarithm of the stock price rather than the stock price itself (so as to ensure that prices are nonnegative) and we might want to allow expected changes to be nonzero (for example, by attaching more probability to an up jump than to a down jump). Another variation on a random walk, on which I will focus now, is to assume that prices change continuously rather than discretely. The purpose of this assumption is to make the model more tractable.

If we require

1. Continuous paths: i.e., the function $t \mapsto X(t)$ is continuous in each state of the world,

2. The stochastic process X is a martingale, and

3. The quadratic variation[3] through each date t equals t,

then the distribution of the stochastic process X is uniquely determined. It must be a Brownian motion.

---

3 This will be defined below.

A Brownian motion can be constructed by taking the limit of the random walk with jumps equal to plus or minus the square root of the time between jumps, as the time between jumps converges to zero. Heuristically, a Brownian motion "jumps" by $\pm\sqrt{dt}$ in each instant dt (this interpretation can actually be made rigorous in nonstandard analysis).

In addition to properties 1–3, a Brownian motion is a Markov process and the changes $X(u) - X(t)$ for $u > t$ are normally distributed with variance $u - t$. These properties come "free" from assuming 1–3. The normality can be viewed as a consequence of the Central Limit Theorem, thinking of $X(u) - X(t)$ as a sum of i.i.d. random variables with values $\pm\sqrt{dt}$.

Property 3 seems somewhat special and indeed there is no particular reason to assume it for stock prices (or for the logarithms of stock prices). However, it is really just a normalization. Any other continuous martingale can be converted to a Brownian motion just by deforming the time scale. It is also possible to represent many continuous martingales as stochastic integrals with respect to Brownian motions. Thus, in one way or another, the Brownian motion is the basic building block for continuous martingales.

Itô's Formula

One reason for being interested in martingales is what Dybvig and Ross (1989) term the *Fundamental Theorem of Asset Pricing*. This theorem says that, if there are no arbitrage opportunities, then properly normalized security prices are martingales under some probability measure. The reason for being interested in continuity is, as mentioned earlier, that it leads to greater tractability. In particular, there is a calculus for continuous martingales. This calculus was developed by K. Itô. Its key tool is the change-of-variable formula for differentiation, which is called Itô's Formula.

Quadratic Example
I will introduce Itô's Formula by means of a standard example. Let X be some function of time, and define $Y(t) = X(t)^2$. One can think of Y as a composite function, namely $Y(t) = f(X(t))$ where f is the "square" function. Consider a discrete partition

$$0 = t_0 < t_1 < t_2 < \cdots < t_N = T$$

of the time interval $[0, T]$. We can write

$$Y(T) = Y(0) + \sum_{i=1}^{N} \Delta Y(t_i),$$

where $\Delta Y(t_i) \equiv Y(t_i) - Y(t_{i-1})$. For any real numbers a and b,

$$b^2 - a^2 = 2a(b-a) + (b-a)^2;$$

therefore,

$$\Delta Y(t_i) \equiv X(t_i)^2 - X(t_{i-1})^2 = 2X(t_{i-1})\Delta X(t_i) + \left[\Delta X(t_i)\right]^2.$$

Hence,

$$Y(T) = Y(0) + 2\sum_{i=1}^{N} X(t_{i-1})\Delta X(t_i) + \sum_{i=1}^{N} \left[\Delta X(t_i)\right]^2. \tag{2}$$

If we let $N \to \infty$ and the time intervals $t_i - t_{i-1}$ shrink to zero, then in the limit, we should get

$$Y(T) = Y(0) + 2\int_0^T X(t)dX(t) + \langle X, X \rangle(T), \tag{3}$$

where $\langle X, X \rangle(T)$ is the quadratic variation mentioned earlier and is defined to be the limit of

$$\sum_{i=1}^{N} \left[\Delta X(t_i)\right]^2 \text{ as } N \to \infty.$$

Let's compare the above to the usual chain rule. If X is a continuously differentiable function of time, then the chain rule states that

$$dY(t) = f'\big(X(t)\big)dX(t) = 2X(t)dX(t).$$

When we integrate both sides we get, from the Fundamental Theorem of Calculus,

$$Y(T) = Y(0) + \int_0^T dY(t)dt \tag{4}$$

$$= Y(0) + 2\int_0^T X(t)dX(t).$$

The difference between (3) and (4) is obviously the presence of the quadratic variation term in (3). Equation (3) is correct even for continuously differentiable functions, because the quadratic variation of a continuously differentiable function is zero. Thus, (3) and (4) say the same thing for continuously differentiable functions. However, (3) is valid more generally.[4]

---

4 This statement should be qualified by noting that the limit defining the integral in (3) may only exist in probability, and X must be a sufficiently regular stochastic process.

One might ask why we don't stay within the realm of continuously differentiable functions, so we can use the usual calculus. After all, it was good enough for Newton! The reason is that there simply aren't any martingales with continuously differentiable paths, except for the trivial ones that are constant. As we have already noted, we need to study martingales if we are to study asset prices, so we cannot assume continuous differentiability and we must use the more general formula (3).

General One-Dimensional Formula
In terms of the square function f, we can write (3) as

$$Y(T) = Y(0) + \int_0^T f'\big(X(t)\big)dX(t) + \int_0^T \frac{1}{2}f''\big(X(t)\big)d\langle X, X\rangle(t), \qquad (5)$$

because $f'(x) = 2x, f''(x) = 2$ and $\int_0^T d\langle X, X\rangle(t) = \langle X, X\rangle(T)$. Equation (5) is the general form of Itô's Formula for functions of a real variable X. Its differential form is

$$dY(t) = f'\big(X(t)\big)dX(t) + \frac{1}{2}f''\big(X(t)\big)d\langle X, X\rangle(t). \qquad (6)$$

Itô's Integral
For (5) to be valid, the first integral in (5) must be defined in a particular way. If X were continuously differentiable, it would not matter whether we computed the limit of

$$\sum_{i=1}^N X\big(t_{i-1}\big)\Delta X\big(t_i\big) \qquad (7)$$

as in (2) or the limit of

$$\sum_{i=1}^N X\big(t_i\big)\Delta X\big(t_i\big).$$

However, it does matter in general. Itô chose the first version, evaluating the integrand $X(t)$ at the left-hand side of each time interval $[t_{i-1}, t_i]$. Stratonovich suggested the midpoint (leading to the Stratonovich integral), and it is also possible to use the right-hand side (leading to the belated Itô integral). However, Itô's choice is exactly the right one for finance applications. Replacing the integrand in (7) by a more general function of time, say $\theta(t)$, the sum

$$\sum_{i=1}^{N} \theta(t_{i-1})\Delta X(t_i)$$

can be viewed as a model for the gain on a trading strategy, where θ denotes the number of shares of an asset and ΔX the price change. Using the left-hand side t_{i-1} of the time interval and requiring $\theta(t_{i-1})$ to depend only on information available at time t_{i-1} implies that the number of shares to hold must be chosen before the price change is known. This is obviously an essential characteristic of any model of security trading.

Multidimensional Formula

Itô's Formula (5) also applies to n-dimensional vectors $X = (X_1, \ldots, X_n)$ provided we interpret

$$f'(X(t))dX(t) = \sum_{i=1}^{n} \frac{\partial f(X(t))}{\partial X_i} dX_i(t), \tag{8}$$

and

$$f''(X(t))d\langle X, X \rangle(t) = \sum_{i=1}^{n} \sum_{j=1}^{n} \frac{\partial^2 f(X(t))}{\partial X_i \partial X_j} d\langle X_i, X_j \rangle, \tag{9}$$

where $\langle X_i, X_j \rangle$ is defined as the limit of the sum of the products $\Delta X_i(t) \cdot \Delta X_j(t)$. In order to apply the formula, we need to know how to calculate the differentials of the "sharp bracket processes" $\langle X_i, X_j \rangle$. Motivated by the fact that the sharp bracket process is defined as the limit of sums of products of discrete changes, it is common to write

$$d\langle X_i, X_j \rangle = dX_i dX_j \, ,$$

and we will follow that convention here. The rules we need to know are:

1. If B is a Brownian motion, then $dB(t)dB(t) = dt$ (because the quadratic variation through date t is t, as already stated).

2. More generally, if B_1 and B_2 are two Brownian motions, then the product of the $dB_i(t)$ equals $\rho(t)\, dt$ for some function p called the instantaneous correlation.

3. For any Brownian motion B, $dB(t)dt = 0$. Furthermore, $dt\, dt = 0$.

We are now prepared to compute the sharp bracket processes of any processes

$$X_i(t) = \int_0^t \phi_i(s)ds + \sum_{j=1}^n \int_0^t \theta_{ij}(s)dB_j(s), \tag{10}$$

given Brownian motions B_j, simply by multiplying out the differentials

$$dX_i(t) = \phi_i(t)dt + \sum_{j=1}^n \theta_{ij}(t)dB_j(t)$$

and following rules 1–3. Processes of the form (10) are called Itô processes and are the most general usually encountered in asset pricing models.

Time-Dependent Functions
A special case of the general Itô's Formula that is frequently encountered is the case $Y(t) = f(t,Z(t))$, where Z is one-dimensional. In this case, we have[5]

$$dX_i(t) = \frac{\partial f(t,Z(t))}{\partial t}dt + \frac{\partial f(t,Z(t))}{\partial Z}dZ(t) + \frac{1}{2}\frac{\partial^2 f(t,Z(t))}{\partial Z^2}d\langle Z,Z\rangle(t). \tag{11}$$

Example 1: Compounding/Discounting Let

$$Y(t) = e^{\alpha t}Z(t)$$

for a constant α. Then $f(t,Z) = e^{\alpha t}Z$. Applying Itô's Formula (11) gives

$$dY(t) = \alpha e^{\alpha t}Z(t)dt + e^{\alpha t}dZ(t),$$

which we can write as

$$\frac{dY(t)}{Y(t)} = \alpha dt + \frac{dZ(t)}{Z(t)}.$$

Note that this is the same as in the usual calculus.

Example 2: Exponential Martingale Let

$$Y(t) = e^{-\sigma^2 t/2 + \sigma B(t)}$$

for a constant σ, where B is a Brownian motion. Then $f(t,B) = e^{-\sigma^2 t/2 + \sigma B}$, and Itô's Formula is

---

5 This follows by applying the n-dimensional version with $n = 2$ and $X(t) = (t,Z(t))$.

$$dY(t) = -\frac{\sigma^2}{2}Y(t)dt + \sigma Y(t)dB(t) + \frac{1}{2}\sigma^2 Y(t)d\langle B, B\rangle(t) \quad (12)$$

$$= \sigma Y(t)dB(t).$$

Thus,

$$\frac{dY(t)}{Y(t)} = \sigma dB(t). \quad (13)$$

If B were a continuously differentiable function rather than a Brownian motion, then the last term on the right-hand side of (12) would be absent and hence could not cancel the first. We can understand this cancellation by observing that Y is a martingale. This follows immediately from the fact that, for $u > t$, $B(u) - B(t)$ is normally distributed with mean zero and variance $u - t$, leading to

$$E\big[Y(u) - Y(t)|Y(t)\big] = E\left[e^{-\sigma^2 u/2 + \sigma B(u)} - e^{-\sigma^2 t/2 + \sigma B(t)}\,\Big|\,B(t)\right]$$

$$= e^{-\sigma^2 u/2 + \sigma B(t)}E\left[e^{\sigma(B(u)-B(t))} - e^{\sigma^2(u-t)/2}\,\Big|\,B(t)\right]$$

$$= 0.$$

This helps to explain (13), which can be interpreted as saying that the expected rate of change in Y is zero.

Girsanov's Theorem

As we will explain in the next section, Girsanov's Theorem is the key to risk-neutral pricing in continuous time. It shows how to change the drift of an Itô process by changing the probability measure.

A heuristic explanation of Girsanov's Theorem is as follows. Let λ be a constant, and let B be a Wiener process relative to a probability P. Let $B^*(t) = B(t) + \lambda t$. Then B^* has the drift (expected change) of λdt in each instant dt. Girsanov's Theorem shows how to change the drift of B^* to zero, that is, how to make B^* a martingale. Think of dB as being $\pm\sqrt{dt}$. Then $dB^* = \lambda dt \pm \sqrt{dt}$. If we change the probability of the up move to $(1 - \lambda\sqrt{dt})/2$ and the probability of the down move to $(1 + \lambda\sqrt{dt})/2$, then the expected change in B^* will be

$$\left(\frac{1 - \lambda\sqrt{dt}}{2}\right)\left(\lambda dt + \sqrt{dt}\right) + \left(\frac{1 + \lambda\sqrt{dt}}{2}\right)\left(\lambda dt - \sqrt{dt}\right) = 0.$$

Therefore, B^* is a martingale under these revised probabilities.

So far, we have only discussed the probabilities at a particular branch of the tree. The probability of a path through the tree is the product of the probabilities of the branches, so, letting P^* denote the revised probabilities and P the original probabilities ($1/2$ probability of up or down at each time), we have

$$\frac{P^*(\text{path through time } t)}{P(\text{path through time } t)} = \frac{P^*(\text{path through time } t - dt)}{P(\text{path through time } t - dt)}$$

$$\times \frac{P^*(\text{branch at } t)}{P(\text{branch at } t)}.$$

Note that for both the up and down branches

$$\frac{P^*(\text{branch at } t)}{P(\text{branch at } t)} = 1 - \lambda dB(t).$$

Therefore,

$$\frac{P^*(\text{path through time } t)}{P(\text{path through time } t)} = \frac{P^*(\text{path through time } t - dt)}{P(\text{path through time } t - dt)} \times \left(1 - \lambda dB(t)\right).$$

If we let $Y(t)$ denote the ratio of path probabilities through time t, this shows that the percent change in Y at time t is $- \lambda dB(t)$, that is,

$$\frac{dY(t)}{Y(t)} = -\lambda dB(t).$$

The solution of this equation (with $Y(0) = 1$) is the exponential martingale

$$Y(t) = e^{-\lambda^2 t / 2 - \lambda B(t)}. \qquad (14)$$

We conclude from the above heuristic argument that the process (14) defines a ratio of path probabilities, P^* to P, such that B^* is a martingale under P^*. Since B^* is continuous and its quadratic variation through each date t is equal to t (because the addition of λt to B does not alter the quadratic variation of B), B^* must in fact be a P^* – Brownian motion.[6] This is the content of Girsanov's Theorem. Its formal statement makes no reference to ratios of path probabilities

---

6 One lesson from this is that there is more than one way to represent a Brownian motion in terms of infinitesimal changes. We have argued that both $\pm \sqrt{dt}$ with equal probabilities and $\lambda dt \pm \sqrt{dt}$ with the P^*–probabilities define a Brownian motion.

because individual paths actually have zero probabilities under either P or P^*. Instead, the theorem states that B^* is converted to a Wiener process by multiplying the P probability of any event (set of paths) by the conditional expectation of Y, given the event.

There is no need to assume λ is a constant, provided the stochastic process λ is sufficiently regular that the general form of (14), that is,

$$Y(t) \equiv \exp\left\{-\frac{1}{2}\int_0^t \lambda^2(u)du - \int_0^t \lambda(u)dB(u)\right\},\qquad (15)$$

is a martingale.[7]

Girsanov's Theorem

Let $(B(t), 0 \le t \le T)$ *be a Brownian motion relative to the probability measure* $P,$ *and let* λ *be a stochastic process such that* Y *defined by (15) is a martingale. Define*

$$B^*(t) = B(t) + \int_0^t \lambda(u)du,$$

and define a new probability measure P^* *by setting, for any event A with* $P(A) > 0,$

$$P^*(A) = E\big[Y(T)\big|A\big]P(A).$$

Then $(B^*(t),0 \le t \le T)$ *is a Brownian motion relative to* $P^*.$

RISK-NEUTRAL PRICING

It is very convenient in pricing securities to act as if all expected returns equal the risk-free rate, which is the same as acting as if all investors are risk neutral. This is called the principle of risk-neutral pricing. To price risk neutrally, one must change the probability measure to what is called, naturally, a risk-neutral probability. A risk-neutral probability exists if there are no arbitrage opportunities in the market, which is of course a very mild assumption and much

---

7 The process (15) is always a "local martingale." A sufficient condition for (15) to actually be a martingale is that

$$E\left[\exp\left\{\frac{1}{2}\int_0^T \lambda^2(u)du\right\}\right] < \infty.$$

This is called Novikov's condition. See, for example, Karatzas and Shreve (1987).

more reasonable than actually assuming investors are risk neutral.[8] Risk-neutral probabilities are very closely related to "state prices."

State Prices and Risk-Neutral Probabilities

We can view any contingent claim or cash-flow stream as a portfolio of what are called *Arrow securities* in recognition of the seminal paper by Arrow (1964). An Arrow security pays \$1 at a particular date if a particular event has occurred at that date and pays 0 at all other dates and in all other states of the world. The prices of the Arrow securities are called *state prices*. Assuming there are no arbitrage opportunities in the market, the price of the contingent claim must equal the sum of the prices of the constituent Arrow securities. This means that a stochastic process ρ (which specifies the prices per unit probability of the Arrow securities) exists such that the price at date 0 of a contingent claim X that pays at any date $t < T$, where T is a fixed horizon, is $E[\rho(t)X]$. As is customary, we have not explicitly indicated the dependence of the cash flow X on the state of the world, nor have we indicated the similar dependence of the price on the state. The stochastic process ρ is called the "state price density process."[9]

Define

$$Y(T) = \exp\left\{\int_0^T r(t)dt\right\}\rho(T) ,$$

and for any event A, define, as in Girsanov's Theorem,

$$P^*(A) = E\left[1_A Y(T)\right] , \tag{16}$$

where 1_A denotes the random variable that takes the value 1 if the true state of the world is in the event A and is 0 otherwise. I claim

---

8 This method of pricing was first proposed by Cox and Ross (1976) and later refined by Harrison and Kreps (1979) and Harrison and Pliska (1981). To be somewhat more precise, if there are an infinite number of possible states of the world, the existence of a risk-neutral probability depends on a somewhat stronger assumption than absence of arbitrage opportunities as usually defined. See Back and Pliska (1991) for an example and Schachermayer (1994) for a recent review of the literature on this issue. As is customary, I will ignore this fine point and simply mean the stronger assumption when I say "no arbitrage opportunities exist."

9 The term *density* refers to the fact that it is the price *per unit probability*. This is analogous to the meaning of *density* in the statistical phrase "probability density function" (which means probability per unit Lebesgue measure).

that P^* is a risk-neutral probability. The only issue pertaining to P^* being a probability that is not obvious is that the P^*–probability of the sure event is one. To see this, consider the contingent claim X defined by investing $1 at the short rate at time 0 and continuously rolling over the investment. The value of this claim at time T is

$$X = \exp\left\{ \int_0^T r(u)du \right\} \equiv \frac{Y(T)}{\rho(T)}.$$

Since the price of this claim at time 0 is $1, we must have

$$1 = E[\rho(T)X] = E[Y(T)].$$

This implies that the P^*–probability of the sure event is 1, as it should be for a probability. To show that P^* is a risk-neutral probability, we should show that the date–0 price of any contingent claim X that pays at date $t \leq T$ is the expected value of X discounted at the rolled-over short rate, that is,

$$E^* \left[\exp\left\{ -\int_0^t r(u)du \right\} X \right],$$

where E^* denotes expectation relative to the probability P^*. This follows directly from the definition of P^* in terms of the state price density process ρ.

Discount Bond Prices

The price at date t of any contingent claim paying X at date $u \in [t, T]$ is the expectation, under a risk-neutral probability, of the payoff X discounted at the rolled-over short rate, i.e.,

$$E_t^* \left[\exp\left\{ -\int_t^u r(s)ds \right\} X \right],$$

where E_t^* denotes expectation relative to P^* conditioned on time-t information. In particular, the price $P(t,u)$ of a date–u maturity discount bond at time t is

$$P(t,u) = E_t^* \left[\exp\left\{ -\int_t^u r(s)ds \right\} \right]. \tag{17}$$

Thus, a model of the yield curve is a model of these risk-neutral expectations.

Price of Risk

Suppose an asset pays no dividends and its price is X satisfying

$$\frac{dX(t)}{X(t)} = \mu(t)dt + \sigma(t)dB(t) \tag{18}$$

for some stochastic processes μ and σ and a Brownian motion B. For example, if μ and σ are constants, then X is a geometric Brownian motion. One interprets $\mu(t)$ as the expected instantaneous rate of return and $\sigma(t)$ as the standard deviation of the instantaneous rate of return.

Define

$$\lambda(t) = \frac{\mu(t) - r(t)}{\sigma(t)}.$$

This $\lambda(t)$ is known as the *price of risk*, because the risk premium $\mu(t) - r(t)$, which is what one is "paid" for accepting the risk in the asset, is equal to the amount of risk $\sigma(t)$ times the price-per-unit-risk $\lambda(t)$.

The price of risk is intimately related to the risk-neutral probability. We can see this from Girsanov's Theorem. Defining B^* as in the statement of Girsanov's Theorem, we can write the rate of return as

$$\frac{dX(t)}{X(t)} = \mu(t)dt + \sigma(t)dB^*(t) - \sigma(t)\lambda(t)dt$$

$$= r(t)dt + \sigma(t)dB^*(t). \tag{19}$$

Assuming the price-of-risk process is such that (15) defines a martingale, the process B^* is a Brownian motion relative to the probability measure P^* defined in Girsanov's Theorem. Thus, (19) implies that the P^*–expected rate of return of the asset is the riskless rate $r(t)$. Therefore, we have risk-neutral pricing under P^*—it is the risk-neutral probability.

We can relate the risk-neutral probability and the price of risk in terms of the original Brownian motion B as follows: under the risk-neutral probability, the expectation of $dB(t)$ is $-\lambda(t)dt$.

In a more general setting with m asset prices X_i and n independent Brownian motions B_j, we can write the m–vector of rates of return as

$$\mu(t) + \sigma(t)dB(t),$$

where $\mu(t)$ denotes the m–vector of expected rates of return, B is the n-vector of Brownian motions, and $\sigma(t)$ is an $m \times n$ matrix. In this case, a price of risk should be associated to each of the sources of risk B_j. The price-of-risk process is an n-vector defined by

$$\mu(t) - r(t) = \sigma(t)\lambda(t), \tag{20}$$

where here we interpret $r(t)$ as the m-vector with each element equal to the short rate. Equation (20) can be interpreted as saying that the risk premium of each asset is the sum of the asset's risk exposures multiplied by the prices of the risks.

If there are no arbitrage opportunities, there is at least one solution λ to (20). Furthermore, there is a solution such that the multivariate analogue of (15), namely

$$Y(t) \equiv \exp\left\{-\frac{1}{2}\sum_{j=1}^{n}\int_0^t \lambda_j^2(u)du - \sum_{j=1}^{n}\int_0^t \lambda_j(u)dB_j(u)\right\}$$

is a martingale. This process Y defines a risk-neutral probability just as in the univariate case discussed above. If there are more sources of risk than there are assets (more precisely, if there are more sources of risk than there are linearly independent rows of σ), then there may be multiple solutions of (20) and multiple risk-neutral probabilities. In this case, there are contingent claims that are not spanned and hence cannot be priced by arbitrage.

Notice that the variance of the rate of return is the same under the actual and risk-neutral probabilities. Only the means are different. This fact is important for portfolio choice or to compute value at risk, because these activities are done under the actual probability.

Derivative Security Pricing

To price a security the value of which depends on another variable X, we must compute the expected discounted value of the derivative security under the risk-neutral probability. To do this, we need to know the distribution of X under the risk-neutral probability. If X is the price of a traded asset, then the expected instantaneous rate of return is the riskless rate, so we only need to know the variance. In particular, there is no need to know the prices of risks.

The situation is different if X is not the price of a traded asset. This is the case in particular when X is the yield of a bond—for example, the short rate of interest. In this case, we can deduce the mean and variance of the instantaneous change in X under the risk-neutral probability from the mean and variance under the actual probability and the prices of risks. For the purposes of pricing, we can ignore the actual probability and prices of risks and work entirely with the distribution of X under the risk-neutral probability. If we also make assumptions about the distribution of X under the actual probability—for example, to compute value at risk—then we have implicitly made assumptions about the prices of risks.

Arbitrage versus Equilibrium Approaches

A distinction is often made between the arbitrage approach to security pricing and the equilibrium approach or between arbitrage models and equilibrium models. There seems to have been some change over time in the meaning of this distinction, which can easily lead to confusion.

Brennan and Schwartz (1979), Dothan (1978), Richard (1978), and Vasicek (1977) introduced the arbitrage approach to bond pricing. Their analyses are based on the assumption that risk premia are sums of exposures to risks multiplied by prices of risks. As explained above, this is true if there are no arbitrage opportunities. The existence of prices of risks does not quite imply the absence of arbitrage opportunities, however, because of the need to ensure that the process Y appearing in Girsanov's Theorem is actually a martingale. Thus, the arbitrage approach can lead to models in which there are actually arbitrage opportunities.[10] This point was made by Cox, Ingersoll, and Ross (1985), hereafter CIR.[11] CIR give an equilibrium foundation for a class of yield curve models, meaning a specification of endowments and preferences of traders which, through clearing of competitive markets, generates the proposed yield curve model. There can be no arbitrage opportunities in equilibrium, so CIR's approach is superior to the arbitrage approach in this respect.

An equally good approach is to simply assume there are no arbitrage opportunities. In fact, this is equivalent to the equilibrium approach because there are no arbitrage opportunities in equilibri-

---

10 In fact, it seems to be an open question whether there are arbitrage opportunities in the Brennan-Schwartz model. See Hogan (1993). (I thank Hal Pedersen for this reference.)

11 CIR do not explain the situation in exactly the same way it has been explained here. In particular, they do not refer to Girsanov's Theorem.

um, and, conversely, if there are no arbitrage opportunities, then the model is an equilibrium for some specification of endowments and preferences.[12] The equivalence of these assumptions seems to have been missed by some authors, who perhaps have focused on the distinction between equilibrium and arbitrage approaches made by CIR, without understanding the fine distinction between the arbitrage approach and absence of arbitrage opportunities.

As explained above, absence of arbitrage opportunities is equivalent to the existence of a risk-neutral probability, so the equilibrium approach to asset pricing is the same as risk-neutral pricing.

The recent literature makes a distinction between arbitrage (or "arbitrage-free" or "no-arbitrage") models and equilibrium models, in which the term *arbitrage model* refers neither to the arbitrage approach of Brennan and Schwartz, Dothan, Richard, and Vasicek nor to absence of arbitrage opportunities, as we have used that term in this chapter. This distinction began with the paper of Ho and Lee (1986), even though Ho and Lee use the term *arbitrage-free* to mean absence of arbitrage opportunities (equivalently, equilibrium) in the same way as do earlier authors. Notwithstanding Ho and Lee's use of the term *arbitrage-free*, subsequent authors have identified it with a model of the Ho-Lee type, namely, a model that fits the actual yield curve when the model is initiated.[13] Essentially, what this means is that an arbitrage model has a large number of free parameters.

I would argue that this distinction between equilibrium models and arbitrage models is not very useful, because one can add parameters to any model so as to be able to fit the current yield curve.[14] In fact, CIR already demonstrated this in connection with their equilibrium model. This issue will be discussed further below.

FACTOR MODELS

We can either assume that the yield curve is determined by a finite number of variables (factors) and model the evolution of these variables or directly model the evolution of the entire yield curve. The

---

12 For one demonstration of this fact, see Harrison and Kreps (1979). This is part of the Fundamental Theorem of Asset Pricing mentioned earlier. See Dybvig and Ross (1989).

13 For example, Tuckman (1995, p. 107) states that "equilibrium models ... do not constrain the model's zero-coupon prices to match the market's ... Equilibrium models do not take bond prices as given whereas arbitrage-free models do."

14 This point is made forcefully by Dybvig (forthcoming).

former approach has obvious computational advantages, though the latter approach, called Heath-Jarrow-Morton, is also popular. I will discuss factor models first.

Throughout this section, I will use the principle of risk-neutral pricing. The dynamics of processes will be described relative to a fixed risk-neutral probability. To be specific, each Brownian motion is to be understood as a Brownian motion relative to the risk-neutral probability. I will also write E for expectation relative to the risk-neutral probability (rather than E^* as before).

Assume there is a finite number n of factors and label them as $X_1, \ldots, X_n$. Let X denote the column vector $(X_1, \ldots, X_n)$ consisting of all the factors.

Assume X satisfies the stochastic differential equation

$$dX(t) = \mu\big(X(t)\big)dt + \sigma\big(X(t)\big)dB(t), \qquad (21)$$

where μ $(X(t))$ is an n-dimensional vector, $\sigma(X(t))$ is an $n \times n$ matrix, and B is an $n \times 1$ vector of independent Brownian motions. The interpretation of (21) is that the expected change in X per unit time (the drift of X) is μ $(X(t))$, and the matrix of covariances per unit time (or volatility matrix) is $\sigma(X(t))\sigma(X(t))'$, where the "prime" denotes the matrix transpose. The process X is determined by (21) to be a Markov process.

Short Rate in a Factor Model

In view of (17), the yield curve is determined by the distribution of the short rate (under the risk-neutral probability). Assume

$$r(t) = R\big(X(t)\big)$$

for some function R. Then the dynamics of $r(t)$ and hence the expectations defining discount bond prices in (17) are fully specified by R, μ, and σ.

Fundamental Partial Differential Equation

In a factor model, discount bond prices should depend only on the factors. Therefore, there should be a function p such that at each time t and for each date of maturity $u > t$, the discount bond price is

$$P(t,u) = p\big(X(t), u-t\big).$$

Fixing the maturity u, and assuming p is sufficiently regular, we can compute the dynamics of the bond price from Itô's Formula. The result is

$$dP(t,u) = p_t dt + \sum_{i=1}^{n} p_i dX_i + \frac{1}{2} \sum_{i=1}^{n} \sum_{j=1}^{n} p_{ij} d\langle X_i, X_j \rangle, \qquad (22)$$

where the subscripts i and j on p denote first or second partial derivatives with respect to the corresponding elements of the vector X, and p_t is the time-derivative of p. This can be made more explicit by applying the rules given earlier for calculating differentials $d\langle X_i, X_j \rangle$ to the definition (21).

Since we are operating under the risk-neutral probability, the drift in (22) should equal the riskless return on the price $P(t,u)$; that is, the drift should equal $r(t)P(t,u) = r(t)p(X(t),u-t)$. Equating the drift to rp yields a partial differential equation (p.d.e.) in p, which is called the fundamental p.d.e.

Earlier papers in the literature deduce the fundamental p.d.e. from the arbitrage approach described earlier. Some then note that the expectation (17) is a solution of the fundamental p.d.e. The expectation is called the Feynman-Kac solution of the p.d.e. This indirect proof of (17) is replaced in more recent papers by the principle of risk-neutral pricing, which directly implies both the expectation formula and the fundamental p.d.e. Bond prices can be computed either by computing the expectation or by solving the p.d.e. One or the other may be easier, depending on the model. Both will be illustrated below.

Affine Factor Models

Most of the factor models considered in the literature fall under the heading of what Duffie and Kan (forthcoming) call *affine factor models*. A factor model is an affine factor model if R, μ, and $\sigma\sigma'$ are affine (linear plus a constant) functions of $X(t)$. An affine factor model has the property that yields are also affine functions of the vector $X(t)$ (see Duffie-Kan, Proposition 1). This means that deterministic functions of time exist, say a and b (where a is a scalar and b is an n-vector), such that for each t and $\tau > 0$,

$$r(t, t+\tau) = a(\tau) + b(\tau)' X(t). \qquad (23)$$

Duffie and Kan show how to calculate the functions a and b from (R, μ, σ).

The question arises as to what the factors should be. One approach is to fix times to maturity $\tau_1, \ldots \tau_n$, and define

$$Y_n(t) = r(t, t + \tau_n).$$

Applying (23) for each of the maturities $t + \tau_n$ allows us to write

$$Y(t) = A + BX(t), \tag{24}$$

where $Y(t)$ denotes the column vector $(Y_1(t), \ldots, Y_n(t))'$, A denotes the column vector $(a(\tau_1), \ldots a(\tau_n))'$ and B is the matrix of stacked row vectors $b(\tau_1)', \ldots b(\tau_n)'$. Assuming B is nonsingular, this shows that there is a one-to-one correspondence between the vectors $X(t)$ and $Y(t)$. Therefore, we can take yields at fixed times to maturities to be the factors.

Duffie and Kan caution that arbitrary definitions of R, μ, and σ are not feasible when using yields as factors, since one must guarantee that (24) holds when $X(t) = Y(t)$, i.e., $Y(t) = A + BY(t)$. Since A and B are calculated from (R, μ, σ), this requirement imposes some restrictions on (R, μ, σ).

One yield that is typically included among the state variables is the short rate.[15] In particular, the single-factor models of Vasicek and CIR use the short rate as the single factor. In an affine single-factor model, yields are given by

$$r(t, t + \tau) = a(\tau) + b(\tau)r(t) \tag{25}$$

for some deterministic functions a and b. The Vasicek and CIR models determine specific functions a and b, as we will see below.

In order for $\sigma\sigma'$ to be an affine function of a vector of factors $X(t)$ (which may or may not be a vector of yields), each row of σ must be a vector of constants scaled by the square root of an affine function of $X(t)$. This explains the popularity of constant-volatility and square-root-volatility models, which originated with the single-factor models of Vasicek and CIR.

Vasicek Model

Vasicek studies a single-factor model in which the short rate, the single factor, satisfies

---

15 This determines R. For example, taking the short rate to be the first yield $(X_1(t) = r(t))$ implies $R(X(t)) = X_1(t)$. Therefore, the model is specified by (μ, σ).

$$dr(t) = \kappa\{\theta - r(t)\}dt + \sigma dB(t) , \tag{26}$$

where κ, θ, and σ are positive constants, and B is a Brownian motion. The process r is an example of an Ornstein-Uhlenbeck process. The drift term always pushes the short rate towards θ, which is the long-run mean of the process. The parameter κ determines the rate at which the short rate is pushed towards its long-run mean.

One can verify by Itô's Formula that

$$r(u) = \theta + e^{-\kappa\{u-t\}}\{r(t) - \theta\} + \sigma\int_t^u e^{-\kappa\{u-a\}}dB(a)$$

for any time $u > t$. We can deduce from this that, conditioning on the information at time t, the integral

$$\int_t^{t+\tau} r(u)du$$

for each $\tau > 0$ is normally distributed with mean

$$m(r(t),\tau) = \theta\tau + \left(1 - e^{-\kappa\tau}\right)\frac{r(t) - \theta}{\kappa}$$

and variance

$$v(\tau) = \frac{\sigma^2}{2\kappa^3}\left(4e^{-\kappa\tau} - e^{-2\kappa\tau} + 2\kappa\tau - 3\right).$$

This result allows us to compute discount bond prices by computing the expectation (17).[16] The result is

$$P(t, t+\tau) = \exp\left\{-m(r(t),\tau) + \frac{v(\tau)}{2}\right\}.$$

From this formula, we can easily compute the functions a and b in (25).

This method of solving the Vasicek model is described by Dybvig (1988). Prices for discount bond options are given by Jamshidian (1989). The option-pricing formula has similarities to the Black-Scholes formula since discount bond prices are lognormally distributed in the Vasicek model, as is the asset in the Black-Scholes model. The Vasicek model has the advantage of simplicity, but it has the disadvantage that yields are normally distributed and hence can be negative.

---

16 The formula for the expectation of the exponential of a normally distributed random variable may be recognized in terms of the moment-generating function of the normal distribution.

Cox-Ingersoll-Ross Model

Cox, Ingersoll, and Ross (CIR) introduce a single-factor model[17] in which the short rate satisfies

$$dr(t) = \kappa\{\theta - r(t)\}dt + \sigma\sqrt{r(t)}dB(t), \tag{27}$$

where κ, θ, and σ are positive constants as before, and B is again a Brownian motion. Like the Vasicek model, this short-rate process has a long-run mean of θ. The difference here is that the volatility is proportional to the short rate rather than constant.

This model is more complicated than the Vasicek model. The properties of the short-rate process (27) are described by CIR, relying on work of Feller (1951). The advantage of the model is that the short rate can never be negative. Intuitively, the reason is that the volatility $\sigma^2 r(t)$ is very small if $r(t)$ is near zero, so the drift will dominate the change in $r(t)$ pushing it upwards towards θ.

The following transformation of r leads to a well-studied process.[18] Define

$$h(t) = \frac{\sigma^2}{4\kappa}\left(e^{\kappa t} - 1\right),$$

and let h^{-1} denote the inverse function.[19] Define

$$\hat{r}(u) = \exp\left\{\kappa h^{-1}(u)\right\}r\left(h^{-1}(u)\right).$$

We can show that

$$d\hat{r}(u) = \delta du + 2\sqrt{\hat{r}(u)}dZ(u), \tag{28}$$

for a Brownian motion Z, where δ is defined as $4\kappa\theta/\sigma^2$. The process r is a member of the class BESQ$^\delta$. The symbol BESQ stands for *Bessel squared*.[20] The parameter δ determines whether r can ever reach zero. If $\delta \geq 2$, then with probability one, r is always strictly positive; whereas, if $\delta < 2$, then with positive probability, r will sometimes hit zero (but will never go negative). In the particular (rare) case that δ is an integer, the squared length of a δ-dimensional vector of independent

---

17 CIR also discuss multifactor models, but the single-factor model is so well known that it is often simply called the CIR model.

18 I learned this transformation from unpublished lecture notes of Hans Buehlmann.

19 The purpose of this somewhat awkward construction is to facilitate later comparison with a model having time-varying coefficients. Here, of course, we can write down the inverse function explicitly as $h^{-1}(u) = \log(1 + 4\kappa u/\sigma^2)/\kappa$.

20 See, for example, Revuz and Yor (1991).

Brownian motions is a process satisfying (28). For this reason, Rogers (1995) calls the CIR interest rate process (27) a "squared Gaussian model."[21]

The functions a and b in (25) can be computed by substituting (25) into the fundamental p.d.e. With r as the single factor, it is convenient to let p_r and p_{rr} denote the first and second partial derivatives with respect to r of the discount bond price $p(r, u - t)$, where u denotes the fixed maturity. Applying Itô's Formula shows that the expected rate of change of the bond price is

$$\left\{ p_t + \kappa(\theta - r)p_r + \frac{1}{2}\sigma^2 rp_{rr} \right\} / p \, .$$

Equating this to the riskless rate of return r yields the fundamental p.d.e.

$$rp = p_t + \kappa(\theta - r)p_r + \frac{1}{2}\sigma^2 rp_{rr} \, .$$

Here, the time-derivative p_t is the negative of the derivative of p with respect to its second argument (time to maturity). Writing τ for the time to maturity $u - t$ yields an equivalent form of the p.d.e.

$$rp = -p_\tau + \kappa(\theta - r)p_r + \frac{1}{2}\sigma^2 rp_{rr} \, .$$

Define $\alpha(\tau) = \tau a(\tau)$ and $\beta(\tau) = \tau b(\tau)$. The affine formula (25) for yields implies

$$p(r, \tau) = \exp\left\{ -\alpha(\tau) - \beta(\tau)r \right\} \, . \tag{29}$$

We must have $\alpha(0) = \beta(0) = 0$ in order to ensure $p(r,0) = 1$. We can easily check that (29) satisfies the fundamental p.d.e. if and only if

$$\beta'(\tau) = 1 - \kappa\beta(\tau) - \frac{1}{2}\sigma^2\beta^2(\tau) \, , \tag{30}$$

and

$$\alpha'(\tau) = \kappa\theta\beta(\tau) \, , \tag{31}$$

where the "primes" denote derivatives. Equation (30) is an equation of the Riccati type with the solution

$$\beta(\tau) = \frac{2\left(e^{\gamma\tau} - 1\right)}{c(\tau)} \, , \tag{32}$$

---

21 For further discussion of this topic, see Maghsoodi (1996).

where

$$c(\tau) = (\kappa + \gamma)(e^{\gamma\tau} - 1) + 2\gamma,$$

and

$$\gamma = (\kappa^2 + 2\sigma^2)^{1/2}.$$

Integrating (31) then gives

$$\alpha(\tau) = \frac{-2\kappa\theta}{\sigma^2}\left[\frac{(\kappa + \gamma)\tau}{2} + \log\frac{2\gamma}{c(\tau)}\right]. \tag{33}$$

CIR also give a formula for the price of an option on a discount bond.

Combining Independent Factors

Cox, Ingersoll, and Ross (CIR) suggest constructing a multifactor model by adding independent factors. In the case of two factors, this means writing the short rate as

$$r(t) = R(X_1(t), X_2(t)) = X_1(t) + X_2(t).$$

where

$$dX_1(t) = \mu_1(X_1(t))dt + \sigma_1(X_1(t))dB_1(t), \tag{34a}$$

and

$$dX_2(t) = \mu_2(X_2(t))dt + \sigma_2(X_2(t))dB_2(t), \tag{34b}$$

for some functions μ_1, μ_2, σ_1, and σ_2 and independent Brownian motions B_1 and B_2. The independence of the factors X_1 and X_2 implies that we can write discount bond prices as

$$P(t,u) = E_t\left[\exp\left\{-\int_t^u X_1(s)ds\right\}\right] \cdot E_t\left[\exp\left\{-\int_t^u X_2(s)ds\right\}\right]$$

and yields as

$$r(t,u) = r_1(t,u) + r_2(t,u), \tag{35}$$

where $r_i(t,u)$ represents what the yield on a u–maturity bond would be at time t if the short rate process were X_i. Thus, if a solution for the yield curve is available when the short rate follows each of the processes (34), then a solution for the yield curve is available in the multifactor model.

The factor model with two independent square-root diffusions, which was introduced by CIR, was studied further by Longstaff and

Schwartz (1992), and Chen and Scott (1992).[22] Longstaff and Schwartz provide formulas for discount bond options, and Chen and Scott (1992) also give formulas for options on other interest-rate derivatives. Longstaff and Schwartz note that the volatility of the short rate is also a linear combination of the two factors, so we can take the short rate and its volatility as the two factors, in the same way that a vector of yields can be taken as the factors in any affine factor model. However, as Chen and Scott point out, for computational purposes it is simpler to work with independent factors than with the short rate and its volatility (which are correlated).

Matching the Current Yield Curve

In practice, we may want the model to match the actual yield curve, at maturities for which the yields are reliably known. As discussed earlier, this is a feature of so-called arbitrage-free models. A variety of methods can be used to modify factor models so as to match the yield curve.

One method proposed by CIR is to combine two independent factors as above, where one of the factors is a deterministic function of time. For convenience, I will focus on the single-factor CIR model, though the method is general. So, suppose the short rate is the sum of a square-root diffusion r as in (27) and a deterministic function. Letting t denote the date at which we want to match the yield curve, we can write the deterministic function as $X(t,u)$ and the short rate as $r(u) + X(t,u)$, for $u \geq t$. Set $X(t,t) = 0$, so that $r(t)$ denotes the short rate at time t. The formula (35) for yields specializes to

$$r(t,u) = a(\tau) + b(\tau)r(t) + \frac{1}{\tau}\int_t^u X(t,s)ds, \qquad (36)$$

where a and b are the same as in the single-factor CIR model and $\tau \equiv u - t$. For any values of the parameters κ, θ, and σ, we can choose X so that (36) matches the observed yield curve at time t. Dybvig (forthcoming) discusses the pricing of interest-rate derivatives in this framework.

An alternative approach that has been studied for the single-factor CIR model is to let the parameters κ, θ, and σ be time-varying. CIR suggests letting θ be time-varying, keeping κ and σ as constants. The advantage of this modification is that the function b does not

---

22 In this model, each of the processes X_i satisfies an equation of the form (27), with possibly different κ's, θ's, and σ's and with independent Brownian motions.

depend on θ—see (30). Thus, integrating (31) shows that the yield curve in the modified model is

$$r(t, t + \tau) = \hat{a}(\tau) + b(\tau)r(t),$$

where

$$\hat{a}(\tau) = \frac{\kappa}{\tau} \int_0^\tau \theta(t + s)\beta(t + s)ds,$$

and β(τ) = τb(τ) as before.

Jamshidian (1993) suggests another modification of the single-factor CIR model. He proposes selecting κ, θ, and σ so that

$$\frac{4\kappa(t)\theta(t)}{\sigma^2(t)} = \delta$$

for a constant δ. One feature of this modification is that it is a transformation of a $BSEQ^\delta$ process, just as is the original single-factor CIR model. Here, the $BESQ^\delta$ process is

$$\hat{r}(u) \equiv \exp\left\{ \int_0^{h^{-1}(u)} \kappa(s)ds \right\} r\left(h^{-1}(u)\right),$$

where

$$h(t) = \frac{1}{\delta} \int_0^t \kappa(u)\theta(u) \exp\left\{ \int_0^u \kappa(s)ds \right\} du.$$

HEATH-JARROW-MORTON APPROACH

The main motivation given by Heath, Jarrow, and Morton (1992)—hereafter, HJM—for their work is that, in a factor model, the drifts of factors under the risk-neutral probability are unknown.[23] It is possible to infer the drifts from prices; for example, in the CIR single-factor model, κ and θ could be chosen so that the yield curve generated by the model matches the actual yield curve as closely as possible.[24] If one desires a better match to the actual yield curve, a second deterministic factor can be included, as discussed above. However, HJM argue that this method of choosing the drifts can be computationally intensive.

---

23 Equivalently, the prices of risks are unknown. See the previous subsection, "Derivative Security Pricing."

24 Note that σ in the CIR single-factor model can be estimated from historical data on the short rate, since instantaneous variances are the same under the risk-neutral probability as under the actual probability.

We do know some things about drifts under the risk-neutral probability. In particular, the expected rate of change of a discount bond price under the risk-neutral probability is the short rate. This fact has implications for the drifts of variables defined from bond prices, for example, yields and forward rates. The main result of HJM is that the drifts of forward rates under the risk-neutral probability are entirely determined by their volatilities. Since the volatilities under the risk-neutral probability are the same as under the actual probability, they can in principle be estimated from historical data on forward rates.[25] The current forward-rate curve can be input as an initial condition, thereby guaranteeing that the model matches actual prices at the time it is initiated. The ease with which the yield curve can be matched is another motivation often given for the HJM approach, though, as was discussed above, it is also easy to do this with a factor model.

Forward Rates

The forward curve at date t is the function $f(t,u)$ for $u \geq t$ defined by

$$f(t,u) = \frac{-d\log P(t,u)}{du}. \tag{37}$$

This implies that discount bond prices are

$$P(t,u) = \exp\left\{-\int_t^u f(t,s)ds\right\}.$$

The short rate at time t is the forward rate for maturity t; i.e.,

$$r(t) = f(t,t).$$

Drifts of Forward Rates

We want to study how the forward rate $f(t,u)$ evolves, as the date t changes, keeping the maturity u fixed. Assume, for the sake of simplicity, that there is only a single source of uncertainty (i.e., a single Brownian motion) driving the yield curve. The generalization to multiple sources of uncertainty is straightforward.

---

25 However, since forward rates are rates of change of log bond prices—see (37)—they are quite sensitive to errors in bond prices and to the method of interpolation between maturities. Thus, there may be considerable noise in historical forward rates.

To make it clear that the maturity u is to be regarded as fixed, I will write the forward rate as $f^u(t)$ and the discount bond price as $P^u(t)$. We can assume the forward rate evolves as

$$df^u(t) = \mu^u(t)dt + \sigma^u(t)dB(t),$$

for some stochastic processes μ^u and σ^u.[26] Here, we are taking B to be a Brownian motion under a risk-neutral probability. The goal is to see what can be said about $\mu^u(t)$.

Write $Y^u(t) = \int_t^u f^s(t)ds$ so discount bond prices are

$$P^u(t) = \exp\left\{-Y^u(t)\right\}.$$

Applying Itô's Formula to $P^u(t)$, we have

$$\frac{dP^u(t)}{P^u(t)} = -dY^u(t) + \frac{1}{2}d\langle Y^u, Y^u\rangle(t). \tag{38}$$

Using Fubini's Theorem for stochastic integrals[27] and making the substitution $f^t(t) = r(t)$, we obtain

$$dY^u(t) = -r(t)dt + \left\{\int_t^u \mu^s(t)ds\right\}dt + \left\{\int_t^u \sigma^s(t)ds\right\}dB(t), \tag{39}$$

which implies

$$\frac{d\langle Y, Y\rangle(t)}{dt} = \left(\int_t^u \sigma^s(t)ds\right)^2$$

$$= 2\int_t^u \left\{\sigma^s(t)\int_t^s \sigma^a(t)da\right\}ds,$$

the last equality following from integration by parts.

The upshot is that the expected instantaneous rate of return of the discount bond is

$$r(t) - \int_t^u \mu^s(t)ds + \int_t^u \left\{\sigma^s(t)\int_t^s \sigma^a(t)da\right\}ds.$$

Equating this to the short rate $r(t)$ implies

$$\int_t^u \mu^s(t)ds = \int_t^u \left\{\sigma^s(t)\int_t^s \sigma^a(t)da\right\}ds.$$

---

26 For each t and $u \geq t$, $\mu^u(t)$, and $\sigma^u(t)$ can only depend on information available at time t, e.g., on the yield curve at times $s \leq t$.

27 See, for example, Protter (1990, Theorem IV.45).

This holds for all $u \geq t$ if and only if

$$\mu^u(t) = \sigma^u(t) \int_t^u \sigma^s(t) ds \qquad (40)$$

for all $u \geq t$. Equation (40) is the HJM formula for the drift of the forward rate in terms of the volatility of the forward rate and the volatilities of intermediate forward rates. By substituting (39) into (38), we see that

$$\int_t^u \sigma^s(t) ds$$

is the standard deviation of the maturity–u discount bond return. Therefore, (40) states that the drift of the forward rate is the product of the standard deviations of the forward rate and discount bond return.

Short Rate

The formula for $\mu^s(t)$ implies

$$f^u(t) = f^u(0) + \int_0^t df^u(s)$$

$$= f^u(0) + \int_0^t \sigma^u(s) \int_s^u \sigma^a(s) da \, ds + \int_0^t \sigma^u(s) dB(s).$$

Applying this with $u = t$ gives

$$r(t) = f^t(0) + \int_0^t \sigma^t(s) \int_s^t \sigma^a(s) da \, ds + \int_0^t \sigma^t(s) dB(s). \qquad (41)$$

Therefore, the distribution of the short rate is also determined by the forward rate volatilities.

Factor Models

The HJM *approach* to modeling the yield curve is to specify, at each date t at which interest-rate-sensitive securities are to be priced, a forward curve $f(t,u)$ and forward-rate volatility processes $\sigma(t,u)$.[28] I emphasize that this is an approach to modeling rather than a model, because it does not identify a specific model. In fact, any yield curve model in which there are no arbitrage opportunities is consistent with this approach, provided we are willing to recalibrate the parameters at each date t. In particular, factor models can be written in

---

28 I am now using the typographically more convenient notation $\sigma(t,u)$ instead of $\sigma^u(t)$.

the HJM form. To clarify this statement, I will explain how the single-factor CIR model is consistent with the HJM approach.

Consider the modification of the single-factor CIR model in which a deterministic function $\{X(t,u) \mid u \geq t\}$ is added to the short rate. This model was discussed in the subsection "Matching the Current Yield Curve." In this model, yields are given by (36). Setting $\alpha(\tau) = \tau a(\tau)$ and $\beta(\tau) = \tau b(\tau)$ as before, forward rates are

$$f(t,u) = \alpha'(\tau) + \beta'(\tau)r(t) + X(t,u)$$

where $\tau \equiv u - t$. Using the formulas (30) and (31) for α' and β', one can check that the standard deviation of the forward rate is

$$\sigma(t,u) = \sigma\beta'(\tau)\sqrt{r(t)}, \tag{42}$$

and the drift is

$$\mu(t,u) = \sigma^2\beta(\tau)\beta'(\tau)r(t), \tag{43}$$

where σ on the right-hand sides of the above equations is the constant σ in the definition (27) of the square-root diffusion. Equation (43) is consistent with the HJM equation (40), as we knew it would be, given that (40) holds for any model in which there are no arbitrage opportunities.

The preceding shows how the parameters, κ, θ, and σ and the function $X(t,u)$, given the short rate at time t, imply a specification of the forward curve and forward-rate volatility processes.[29] Similar reasoning applies to any factor model. For example, in the Vasicek model, the forward rate volatilities are

$$\sigma(t,u) = \sigma\exp\{-\kappa(u-t)\},$$

where the parameters σ and κ on the right-hand side are the coefficients in (26). The Vasicek model (and any other factor model) can be modified to fit the current yield curve by adding a deterministic function of time, as we have discussed in the context of the single-factor CIR model. The modified Vasicek model with $\kappa = 0$ (i.e., without mean reversion) is the continuous-time version of the Ho-Lee (1986) model.[30]

---

29 Actually, the parameter θ is redundant. It does not affect the forward rate volatilities, and its effect on the forward curve is overridden by choosing X to match the actual forward curve.

30 See Heath, Jarrow, and Morton (1992) or Dybvig (forthcoming). Because of the unreasonable variance assumption in the non-mean-reverting Vasicek model, Dybvig argues that the Ho-Lee model should not be relied upon for pricing long-term securities.

Ritchken and Sankarasubramanian (1995a) show that a model written in the HJM form is a two-factor model if and only if

$$\sigma(t,u) = \exp\left\{ -\int_t^u g(s)ds \right\} Y(t),$$

for some deterministic function g and stochastic process Y. They also show that the short rate can always be used as one of the factors. A particular class of examples proposed by Ritchken and Sankarasubramanian is

$$\sigma(t,u) = \sigma \exp\left\{ -\kappa(u-t) \right\} r(t)^\gamma,$$

for constants σ, κ, and γ. This nests the Vasicek model, though not the single-factor CIR model. See also Ritchken and Sankarasubramanian (1995b).

Path Dependence

The advantage of a factor model, relative to an arbitrary specification of forward-rate volatility processes, is that factor models are *path independent*—the yield curve depends only on the values of the factors and not on the entire history (path) of the random variables that affect the yield curve. When a model is path dependent, it is not possible to construct a recombining tree (lattice) version of the model to do pricing. This significantly limits the number of time steps that can be taken and hence practically limits one to valuing short-term instruments.[31] In contrast, for example, recombining binomial trees can be built for the single-factor Vasicek and CIR models.[32]

---

31 See Heath, Jarrow, Morton, and Spindel (1992) for a discussion of pricing in the HJM framework with a nonrecombining tree.
32 See Nelson and Ramaswamy (1990) for the CIR model.

REFERENCES

Arrow, K. J. "The Role of Securities in the Optimal Allocation of Risk-Bearing." *Review of Economic Studies* 31 (1964), pp. 91–6 (translation of "Le Rôle des Valeurs Boursieres pour la Repartition la Meillure des Risques," *Econometrie,* 1952).

Back, K., and S. R. Pliska. "On the Fundamental Theorem of Asset Pricing with an Infinite State Space." *Journal of Mathematical Economics* 20 (1991), pp. 1–18.

Black, F., and M. Scholes. "The Pricing of Options and Corporate Liabilities." *Journal of Political Economy* 81 (1973), pp. 637–54.

Brennan, M. J., and E. S. Schwartz. "A Continuous Time Approach to the Pricing of Bonds." *Journal of Banking and Finance* 3 (1979), pp. 133–55.

Chen, R.-R., and L. Scott. "Pricing Interest Rate Options in a Two-Factor Cox-Ingersoll-Ross Model of the Term Structure." *Review of Financial Studies* 5 (1992), pp. 613–36.

Cox, J. C., and S. A. Ross. "A Survey of Some New Results in Financial Option Pricing Theory." *Journal of Finance* 31 (1976), pp. 383–401.

Cox, J. C.; J. E. Ingersoll, Jr.; and S. A. Ross. "A Theory of the Term Structure of Interest Rates." *Econometrica* 53, (1985) pp. 385–407.

Dothan, L. U. "On the Term Structure of Interest Rates," *Journal of Financial Economics* 6 (1978), pp. 59–69.

Duffie, D., and R. Kan. "A Yield-Factor Model of Interest Rates." *Mathematical Finance* (forthcoming).

Dybvig, P. H. "Inefficient Dynamic Portfolio Strategies or How to Throw Away a Million Dollars in the Stock Market." *Review of Financial Studies* 1 (1988a), pp. 67–88.

Dybvig, P. H. "Bond and Bond Option Pricing Based on the Current Term Structure." in M. A. H. Dempster and S. R. Pliska, eds., *Mathematics of Derivative Securities,* Cambridge University Press, forthcoming.

Dybvig, P. H., and S. A. Ross. "Arbitrage," in *The New Palgrave: Finance* eds. J. Eatwell, M. Milgate, and P. Neuman. New York: W. W. Norton, 1989.

Feller, W. "Two Singular Diffusion Problems." *Annals of Mathematics* 54 (1951), pp. 173–82.

Harrison, J. M., and D. M. Kreps. "Martingales and Arbitrage in Multiperiod Securities Markets." *Journal of Economic Therapy* 20 (1979), pp. 381–408.

Harrison, J. M., and S. R. Pliska. "Martingales and Stochastic Integrals in the Theory of Continuous Trading." *Stochastic Processes and Their Applications* 11 (1981), pp. 215–60.

Heath, D.; R. Jarrow; and A. Morton. "Bond Pricing and the Term Structure of Interest Rates: A New Methodology for Contingent Claims Valuation." *Econometrica* 60 (1992), pp. 77–105.

Heath, D.; R. Jarrow; A. Morton; and M. Spindel. "Easier Done than Said," *Risk* 5 (1992), pp. 77–80.

Ho, T. S. Y., and S.-B. Lee. "Term Structure Movements and Pricing Interest Rate Contingent Claims." *Journal of Finance* 41 (1986), pp. 1011–29.

Hogan, M. "Problems in Certain Two-Factor Term Structure Models." *Annals of Applied Probability* 3 (1993), 576–81.

Jamshidian, F. "An Exact Bond Option Formula." *Journal of Finance* 44 (1989), pp. 205–9.

Jamshidian, F. "A Simple Class of Square-Root Interest Rate Models." Working paper, Fuji International Finance PLC, 1993.

Karatzas, I., and S. E. Shreve. *Brownian Motion and Stochastic Calculus.* New York: Springer-Verlag, 1987.

Longstaff, F. A., and E. S. Schwartz. "Interest Rate Volatility and the Term Structure: A Two-Factor General Equilibrium Model." *Journal of Finance* 47 (1992), pp. 1259–82.

Maghsoodi, Y. "Solution of the Extended CIR Term Structure and Bond Option Valuation." *Mathematical Finance* 6 (1996), pp. 89–109.

Nelson, D. B., and K. Ramaswamy. "Simple Binomial Processes as Diffusion Approximations in Financial Models," *Review of Financial Studies* 3 (1990) pp. 393–430.

Protter, P. *Stochastic Integration and Differential Equations.* Berlin: Springer-Verlag, 1990.

Revuz, D., and M. Yor. *Continuous Martingales and Brownian Motion.* Berlin: Springer-Verlag, 1991.

Richard, S. F. "An Arbitrage Model of the Term Structure of Interest Rates." *Journal of Financial Economics* 6 (1978), pp. 33–57.

Ritchken, P., and L. Sankarasubramanian. "Volatility Structures of Forward Rates and the Dynamics of the Term Structure." *Mathematical Finance* 5, (1995a), pp. 55–72.

Ritchken, P., and L. Sankarasubramanian. "Near Nirvana." *Risk* 8 (1995b), pp. 109–11.

Rogers, L. C. G. "Which Model for the Term Structure of Interest Rates Should One Use?" In *Mathematical Finance* eds. M. Davis, D. Duffie, W. Fleming, and S. Shreve. *IMA Volumes in Mathematics and its Applications,* Berlin: Springer-Verlag, (1995) pp. 93–115.

Schachermayer, W. "Martingale Measures for Discrete-Time Processes with Infinite Horizon." *Mathematical Finance* 4 (1994), pp. 25–55.

Tuckman, B. *Fixed Income Securities.* New York: Wiley, 1995.

Vasicek, O. "An Equilibrium Characterization of the Term Structure." *Journal of Financial Economics* 5 (1977), pp. 177–88.

2

⑥ COMPUTATIONAL ASPECTS OF TERM STRUCTURE MODELS AND PRICING INTEREST RATE DERIVATIVES

Les Clewlow,[*] Stewart Hodges, Kin Pang, and Chris Strickland[*]
Financial Options Research Centre
University of Warwick, United Kingdom

and

[*]*Centro de Finanzas*
Instituto de Estudios Superiores de Administración
Caracas, Venezuela

In this chapter we give an overview of some of the computational aspects involved in implementing interest rate models for pricing and hedging derivatives. One way of constructing a no-arbitrage model for interest rates is in terms of the process followed by the short rate, r. The process for the short rate in a risk-neutral world determines the current term structure and how it can evolve. The standard assumption of no-arbitrage tells us that discount bond prices are given by

$$P(t,s) = \hat{E}_t\left[\exp\left(-\int_t^s r(\tau)d\tau\right)\right] \tag{1}$$

where $\hat{E}_t$ denotes expectations (with the information set at time t) under the risk-neutral probabilities, with $r(\tau), \tau \in [t,s]$ denoting the path of the short rate from t to s. Time t interest rate derivative prices, $\varphi(t)$, are determined in an analogous way:

$$\varphi(t) = \hat{E}_t \left[\exp\left(-\int_t^T r(\tau) d\tau \right) \varphi(T) \right] \tag{2}$$

where $\varphi(T)$ is the payoff to the derivative at time T. A fundamental security is the Arrow-Debreu pure security or state price $Q(s)$ which pays one unit in one future state of the world (s) and zero in all other states. For example, in a discrete time and state world where time is indexed by i and states by j, equation (2) can be written

$$\varphi(t) = \sum_j Q(i,j) \varphi(i). \tag{3}$$

The outline of the chapter is as follows. We begin with an overview of the different approaches to modeling the term structures and their advantages and disadvantages. Next we describe the general procedure for building trees that are consistent with the observed yield curve or term structure of interest rates and yield volatilities or term structure of interest rate volatilities. We then describe how the range of standard interest rate derivatives—coupon bond options, caps, floors, collars, and swaptions—can be priced using a short-rate tree. Following from this discussion, we describe how path-dependent interest rate exotics can be priced using the example of an index amortising rate (IAR) swap. We next look at an approach that models the whole yield curve directly, represented by the papers of Heath, Jarrow, and Morton [1992] and Carverhill [1995]. Our concluding remarks make up the last section.

AN OVERVIEW OF THE MODELS

During the late 1970s and the early 1980s, most models for pricing interest rate derivatives were based on models originally developed to explain the term structure of interest rates. Two of the best known are the Vasicek (1977) and Cox, Ingersoll, and Ross (CIR) (1985) models, which can be characterized by their assumptions about the short-term interest rate, assumed to be the single source of uncertainty:

$$dr = \alpha(\gamma - r)dt + \sigma(r)dz(t) \tag{4}$$

where $r = r(t)$ is the level of the short rate, at time t, with dz an increment in a Wiener process. The instantaneous drift models the process as mean reverting back toward some long-term level γ, at a speed α. The Vasicek paper assumes the short rate follows the Ornstein-Uhlenbeck diffusion process with the volatility of the process set equal to a constant α. In the CIR paper the volatility of the short rate increases with the square root of the rate itself. In both of these models the term structure of interest rates and the volatilities associated with those rates are uniquely determined once the risk-adjusted parameters of (3) have been fixed. We are also able to obtain closed-form solutions for bond option prices.

In recognition of the fact that bond prices are not instantaneously perfectly correlated, a number of authors have put forward models that involve more than a single source of uncertainty. Two of the more recent of these come from Longstaff and Schwartz (1992) and Fong and Vasicek (1992) who propose stochastic volatility models of the term structure. Both of these models can be represented by processes of the form:

$$dr = \alpha_r(t)dt + \sqrt{v}\, dz_1(t) \tag{5}$$
$$dv = \alpha_v(t)dt + \sigma_v(t)dz_2(t)$$

where $\alpha_r(t)$ and $\alpha_v(t)$ are the risk-adjusted drift terms of the short rate and the variance of the short rate respectively. $\sigma_v(t)$ is the instantaneous variance of the short-rate variance v. Again, both the terms structures of rates and rate volatilities are determined once the parameters of the risk-adjusted process are determined.

This traditional approach to pricing interest rate derivatives has the important advantage that all interest rate derivatives are valued on a common basis, namely, with respect to the term structure implied by the model. However, it has the severe disadvantage that the resulting term structures can only come from a limited family in which all traded bonds are not necesarily priced correctly. By valuing interest rate derivatives with reference to a theoretical yield curve rather than the actually observed curve, the traditional models produce contingent claims prices that disregard key market information affecting the valuation of any interest rate derivative security. Many models currently appearing in the literature seek to overcome this shortcoming. They are formulated to be consistent with the observed yield curve and some with the observed yield volatilities as well. We call models of this type *term structure consistent* models.

The term structure consistent models can be further subdivided into those that fit the term structure of interest rates only and those that fit both the term structure of rates and the term structure of rate volatilities. For models that don't fit the market volatility structure, the volatility structure has a form endogenous to the model. Consistency with the observed yield curve(s) has been achieved in two ways. One is to specify a process for the short rate, as in the traditional approach, and then effectively increase the parameterization of the model by using time-dependent parameters until all the observed market data can be matched.[1] Models in this category include Black, Derman, and Toy (BDT) (1990) and Hull and White (HW) (1993, 1994a, 1994b). The second approach starts by taking the initial yield curve and the yield volatilities as given and then determining the drift structure that makes the model arbitrage free. This is the approach of Heath, Jarrow, and Morton (1992) and Carverhill (1995).

A number of the models that start from an initial short-rate specification are popular with practitioners due to their level of analytical tractability. For example, the models of Ho and Lee (1986) and Hull and White (1992) both achieve closed-form solutions for pricing European options on discount bonds. The stochastic differential equations for these models are

Ho-Lee $\qquad dr = \theta(t)dt + \sigma dz(t)$ $\qquad\qquad$ (6)

Hull-White $\qquad dr = [\theta(t) - \alpha r]dt + \sigma dz(t).$ $\qquad\qquad$ (7)

The single time-dependent function in the drift of both models is chosen to ensure consistency with the initial yield curve. The constant parameters explicitly determine the volatility structure of spot rates. More general specifications of the short-rate process and lognormal models offer no analytical solutions for the prices of European options on discount bonds.

A major problem with using deterministic time-dependent parameters of the short-rate process to fit the model to the observed yield volatilities is that the yield volatilities are then constrained to evolve deterministically into the future. In particular, if the initial yield

---

1 In much the same way that the Black-Scholes model for pricing options on stocks can be inverted to obtain the implied volatility of stock prices consistent with the option price, the same principle could be applied to pricing bonds.

volatility curve does not have a negative exponential form, then it will not keep the same shape. Starting from typical market yield volatilities, the volatility structure will be forced to evolve to be flat.

An alternative approach to directly modeling the short rate was introduced by Heath, Jarrow, and Morton (1992). Their idea was to take the whole forward-rate curve together with a set of forward rate volatility curves as given by the market and to specify the no-arbitrage evolution of the forward rate curve via a system of stochastic differential equations,

$$df(t,T) = \alpha(t,T)dt + \sum_{i=1}^{n} \sigma_i(t,T)dB_i(t) \qquad (8)$$

where $f(t,T)$ and $\sigma_i(t,T)$ are the instantaneous forward rate at date t for date T in the future and its volatilities, and the $dB_i(t)$ are independent Brownian motions.[2] The volatility functions in general can be functions of the entire history of the forward rate curve, but this generality is extremely difficult to handle computationally. We will concentrate on the case where the volatilities are functions of time and maturity only, generally called Gaussian HJM (Heath, Jarrow, and Morton). The drifts of the forward rates under the risk-neutral measure are determined by no-arbitrage to be

$$\alpha(t,T) = \sum_{i=1}^{n} \left\{ \sigma_i(t,T) \left[\int_t^T \sigma_i(t,u)du \right] \right\} \qquad (9)$$

so that the expected return on a pure discount bonds is the riskless rate. The HJM formulation is rather opaque, and the model can equivalently be formulated more succinctly in terms of pure discount bond prices

$$\frac{dP(t,T)}{P(t,T)} = \big(r(t)\big)dt + \sum_{i=1}^{n} v_i(t,T)dB_i(t) \qquad (10)$$

where

$$v_i(t,T) = -\int_t^T \sigma_i(t,s)ds. \qquad (11)$$

This formulation makes explicit the no-arbitrage condition for the risk-neutral measure: that the expected return on a discount

---

2 Carverhill (1995) provides an excellent exposition of this model and the technical conditions required.

bond must be the riskless rate. This condition is extremely important and any computational implementation must not violate it. We will see its implications for constructing HJM trees in the section "Non-Markovian Short-Rate Models."

The implied process for the short rate in the HJM model is

$$dr = \left[\frac{\partial f(0,t)}{\partial t} + \sum_{i=1}^{n} \left\{ \int_0^t v_i(u,t) \frac{\partial^2 v_i}{\partial t^2}(u,t) + \frac{\partial v_i}{\partial t}(u,t)^2 du + \int_0^t \frac{\partial^2 v_i}{\partial t^2}(u,t) dB_i(u) \right\} \right] dt \quad (12)$$

$$+ \sum_{i=1}^{n} \frac{\partial v_i}{\partial t}(u,t) \bigg|_{u=t} dB_i(t).$$

The drift of the short rate depends on integrals of the second derivatives of the pure discount bond volatilities over the Brownian paths. It is therefore non-Markovian in general and when we construct HJM trees they are nonrecombining or exploding, that is, an upward move followed by a downward move is not the same as a downward move followed by an upward move. Monte Carlo simulation provides a way of dealing with this problem, although the use of Monte Carlo simulation makes pricing American-style options more computationally difficult. We will describe how HJM trees and Monte Carlo simulation can be implemented efficiently by judicious choice of the formulation.

We now go on to describe a methodology for building trees for the short rate that are consistent with the observed yield and yield volatility curves.

BUILDING TREES CONSISTENT WITH THE OBSERVED YIELD AND YIELD VOLATILITY CURVES

The idea behind constructing short-rate trees is the same as tree construction for the underlying asset price in, say, the binomial framework of Cox, Ross, and Rubinstein (1979). However, the methodology is extended in a number of ways. First, the state prices for each node in the tree are calculated as the tree is grown outwards from the current date. The state prices allow us to compute the prices of pure discount bonds as given by the tree. The tree is then adjusted so that these prices match the observed market prices either by adjusting the distance between nodes or the probabilities of transitions between nodes. We will use as an example the model of Black, Derman, and Toy (BDT) (1990). BDT developed a single-factor Markov model to match observed term structure data, which practitioners suggest is currently popular. BDT developed the model algorithmically, describing the evolution of the entire term structure in a discrete-time binomial lattice framework. A binomial tree is constructed for the short rate in such a way that the tree automatically returns the observed yield function and the volatilities of different yields. In a short-rate tree the variable at each node is the Δt period interest rate, and the movements of the rate in the tree are chosen to match some process that becomes a continuous time process in the limit. For pricing derivatives, interest rate trees work similarly to stock price trees except that the discount rate used varies from node to node.

Although the algorithmic description in the original BDT paper meant that this model's assumptions about the evolution of the short rate were rather opaque, several authors have shown that the implied continuous time limit of the BDT model is given by the following stochastic differential equation:

$$d\ln r(t) = \left[\theta(t) - \frac{\sigma'(t)}{\sigma(t)}\ln r(t) \right]dt + \sigma(t)dz(t). \qquad (13)$$

This representation of the model allows us to better understand implicit assumptions. The model incorporates two independent functions of time: $\theta(t)$, chosen so that the model fits the term structure of spot interest rates, and $\sigma(t)$, so that it fits the term structure of spot rate volatilities. Once $\theta(t)$ and $\sigma(t)$ are chosen, the future short rate volatility is, by definition, entirely determined. An unfortunate consequence of the model is that for certain specifications of the volatility function, namely, if the future short rate volatility declines over time, the short rate can be mean-fleeing rather than mean-reverting. Changes in the short rate are lognormally distributed, with the resulting advantage that interest rates cannot become negative, but with the disadvantage that analytic solutions for the prices of bonds or the prices of bond options are no longer available. The model also has the advantage that the short-rate volatility is expressed as a percentage, conforming with the market convention.

If the model is fitted to the rate structure only, with future short-rate volatility held constant, then the convergent limit reduces to the following, which is a lognormal version of Ho-Lee:

$$d\ln r(t) = \theta(t)dt + \sigma dz(t). \qquad (14)$$

We now go on to describe how a binomial short-rate tree for the BDT model can be constructed using forward induction.[3] This model is chosen because the details of the implementation are reasonably straightforward, so the general principle will be clear. Jamshidian (1991) shows that the level of the short rate at time t in the BDT model is given by

$$r(t) = U(t)\exp\big(\sigma_H(t)z(t)\big) \tag{15}$$

where $U(t)$ is the median of the (lognormal) distribution for r at time t, $\sigma_H(t)$ is a measure of the standard deviation of the distribution of the short rate at horizon t, and $z(t)$ is the level of the Brownian motion. In order to fit the model simultaneously to market yield and volatility curves, we have to determine both $U(t)$ and $\sigma_H(t)$ at each time step. If the model is implemented to fit just the yield curve, we only need to determine $U(t)$.

We divide the life of the instrument underlying the interest rate derivative into, say, $i = 1, \ldots, N$ equal segments each of length Δt and define the following functions that describe the initial yield and volatility curves:

$P(i)$:   Price at time 0 of a pure discount bond maturing at time $i\Delta t$.

$R(i)$:   Yield at time 0 on a bond maturing at time $i\Delta t$.

$V(i)$:   Proportional volatility at time 0 of yield $R(i)$.

The risk-neutral transitional probabilities in the tree are assumed to be equal to one-half. We label the states as in Figure 2–1.

The value of r on the tree at time 0 is the initial short rate r_0 and is the yield on a discount bond maturing at Δt. At time $i = 0$ there is a single state $j = 0$. At time $i = 1$ there are two states $j = -1$ and $j = 1$. At time $i = n$ there are $(n + 1)$ states $j = -n, -n + 2, \ldots, n - 2, n$. Therefore j has a centralized binomial distribution with mean 0 and variance n. $j\sqrt{\Delta t}$ is therefore distributed with mean 0 and variance t, which is the same as the random walk, implying that as Δt approaches 0 the binomial process $j\sqrt{\Delta t}$ converges to the Wiener process $z(t)$. Therefore we can represent the level of the short rate in the tree as[4]

---

3 The original paper to apply forward induction for constructing yield curve models is that of Jamshidian (1991).
4 See equation (9).

FIGURE 2–1

Black-Derman-Toy Short Rate Tree

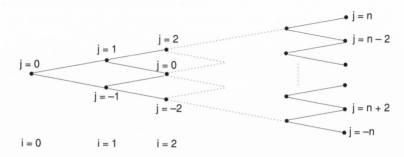

$$r(i,j) = U(i)\exp\left(\sigma_H(i)j\sqrt{\Delta t}\right). \tag{16}$$

In other words, we replace t by i and $z(t)$ by $j\sqrt{\Delta t}$. We denote the short rate at node (i,j) by $r(i,j)$. To build a tree for the short rate (i.e., determining $r(i,j)$ for all i and j), therefore, requires us to determine $U(i)$ and $\sigma_H(t)$. In order to determine these time-dependent functions we can use Arrow-Debreu pure security prices (or state prices). Define $Q(i, j)$ as the value, at time 0, of a security that pays \$1 if node (i,j) is reached and \$0 otherwise. As we saw above, the pure discount bond prices can be expressed as

$$P(i+1) = \sum_j Q(i,j)p(i,j) \tag{17}$$

where $p(i,j)$ denotes the price at time $i\Delta t$ and state j of the zero-coupon bond maturing at time $(i+1)\Delta t$ (the one-period discount factor), and where the summation takes place across all the nodes j at time i. For simple compounding we have

$$p(i,j) = \frac{1}{1 + r(i,j)\Delta t}. \tag{18}$$

Forward induction involves accumulating the state prices as we progress through the tree. Specifically, the pure security prices at time step $i+1$ are updated from the known values at time step i according to

$$Q(i+1,j) = \sum_{j^*} p(i,j^*)Q(i,j^*)q(j^*) \tag{19}$$

where the summation is over all nodes (i, j^*) that have branches to node $(i+1, j)$, and where $q(j^*)$ is the branch probability. Equation (19) is simply the discrete equivalent of the Kolmogorov forward equation. In the case of a binomial tree, this can be written explicitly as

$$Q(i+1, j) = \frac{1}{2}Q(i, j-1)p(i, j-1) + \frac{1}{2}Q(i, j+1)p(i, j+1) \tag{20}$$

$$= \frac{1}{2}Q(i, j-1)\frac{1}{1+r(i, j-1)\Delta t} + \frac{1}{2}Q(i, j+1)\frac{1}{1+r(i, j+1)\Delta t}.$$

In other words, for the two nodes that lead into node $(i+1, j)$ we sum the product of their state prices, one period discount factors, and transitional probabilities.[5]

First we look at fitting the lognormal model to the yield curve. Let $\sigma_H(t)$ be equal to a constant σ_H. Therefore equation (16) becomes

$$r(i, j) = U(i)\exp\left(\sigma_H j\sqrt{\Delta t}\right). \tag{21}$$

Using equations (17) and (21), the time step $i+1$ pure discount bond prices can be constructed as

$$P(i+1) = \sum_j Q(i, j)\frac{1}{1+r(i, j)\Delta t} \tag{22}$$

$$= \sum_j Q(i, j)\frac{1}{1+U(i)\exp\left(\sigma_H j\sqrt{\Delta t}\right)\Delta t}.$$

As the initial discount function is known, the only unknown in equation (22) is $U(i)$. Unfortunately, we cannot rearrange equation (22) to obtain $U(i)$ explicitly, and we need to use a fast numerical search technique such as Newton-Raphson. Once $U(i)$ has been determined, we can use equation (21) to determine all the rates in the tree for that time step. This process is repeated for each time step in the tree.

The extended methodology of fitting the model to both the rate and volatility structures has the same general form. In order to fit the term structure of volatilities, σ_H must now be made time dependent, so the level of the short rate at node (i, j) is given by equation (15). Let the up-node from the first time step (node (1,1)) be denoted by U and the down-node (node (1,-1)) be denoted by D. Also, let

---

5 For the extreme nodes $(i + 1, j + 1)$ and $(i + 1, -j - 1)$, there is a unique transitional path.

$P_U(i)$ and $P_D(i)$ (for $i \geq 1$) be the discount function as seen from nodes U and D, respectively, with $R_U(i)$ and $R_D(i)$ the corresponding bond yields. Specifying both the spot rate yield and volatility curves at the initial time $i = 0$ is equivalent to specifying, at period $i = 1$, the two discount functions $P_U(i)$ and $P_D(i)$. First, we need to determine $R_U(i)$ and $R_D(i)$ for all $i \geq 1$. These must be consistent with the known values of $R(i)$ and $V(i)$. Therefore we need to solve simultaneously

$$e^{-r_0 \Delta t}\left[0.5e^{-(i-1)R_U(i)\Delta t} + 0.5e^{-(i-1)R_D(i)\Delta t}\right] = e^{-iR(i)\Delta t} \tag{23}$$

$$V(i)\sqrt{\Delta t} = 0.5\log\frac{R_U(i)}{R_D(i)}. \tag{24}$$

Equation (23) simply equates the discounted expected pure discount bond prices over the first time step equal to their observed values, and equation (24) equates the yield volatilities over the first time step to their observed values. These equations can be solved as

$$R_D(i) = R_U(i)e^{-2V(i)\sqrt{\Delta t}} \tag{25}$$

where $R_U(i)$ is found as the solution to[6]

$$e^{-(i-1)R_U(i)\Delta t} + e^{-(i-1)R_U(i)\exp\left(-2V(i)\sqrt{\Delta t}\right)} = 2e^{(r_0 - i)R(i)\Delta t}. \tag{26}$$

The solutions for $R_U(i)$ and $R_D(i)$ are consistent with the observed yield and yield volatilities. For $i = 2$ equations (25) and (26) determine the short rate for the two nodes at time Δt:

$$r_u = r(1,1) = R_U(2), \quad r_D = r(1,1) = R_D(2).$$

The tree is constructed from time t onward using a procedure similar to that for fitting the yield curve only, described earlier. Now we have two equations similar to (17):

$$P_U(i+1) = \sum_j Q_U(i,j)p(i,j) \tag{27}$$

$$P_D(i+1) = \sum_j Q_D(i,j)p(i,j) \tag{28}$$

where $\quad p(i,j) = \dfrac{1}{1+r(i,j)\Delta t} = \dfrac{1}{1+U(i)\exp\left(\sigma_H(i)j\sqrt{\Delta t}\right)\Delta t}.$

$Q_U(i,j)$ and $Q_D(i,j)$ are defined as the values, as seen from nodes U and D respectively, of a security that pays off \$1 if node (i, j) is

---

6 This must be solved using a numerical search technique.

reached, and zero otherwise. Therefore (27) and (28) are two equations with two unknowns, $U(i)$ and $\sigma_H(i)$. These can be solved by a two-dimensional Newton-Raphson technique.

Hull and White use the same general procedure to build trinomial short-rate trees consistent with observed yield and yield volatilities. Trinomial trees generally have better stability and convergence properties than binomial trees. The extra branch from each node gives them more flexibility so that the changes in the short rate between the nodes can be kept fixed and only the probabilities changed to achieve the fitting. A further improvement can be obtained by arranging for the central path of the tree to follow the expected behavior of the short rate. This ensures that the tree most efficiently approximates the future distribution of the short rate.

PRICING INTEREST RATE DERIVATIVES USING TREES

Once the tree has been constructed, we know the short rate at every time and every state of the world consistent with our original assumptions about the process, and we can use it to price a wide range of interest rate derivatives in the usual manner via backward induction. Caps, floors, and collars are simply portfolios of options on discount bonds. Swaptions and coupon bond options are options on portfolios of discount bonds, which Jamshidian (1989) showed can be decomposed into portfolios of options on discount bonds in one-state variable models. We will therefore describe the pricing of an option on a discount bond as the basic building block. Let $C(i, j)$ represent the value of the contingent claim at node (i, j). Its value is related to the two connecting nodes at time step $i + 1$ by the usual discounted expectation:

$$C(i,j) = \tfrac{1}{2}p(i,j)\big[C(i+1,j+1) + C(i+1,j-1)\big] \qquad (29)$$

Assume that we are pricing a T-maturity option on an s-maturity discount bond ($T \leq s$) with a strike price of K. Let N_s and N_T represent the number of time steps to the maturity of the bond and option respectively (so $s = N_s\,\Delta t$ and $T = N_T\,\Delta t$. We assume that the short rate tree has been constructed out as far as N_s. Let $P(i,j)$ represent the value of the s-maturity bond at node (i,j).

First, set the maturity condition for the bond underlying the option, $P(Ns,j) = 1$ for all j, and then perform backward induction for the bond price, calculating the value of the *s*-maturity bond for every node in the tree.[7]

$$C(i,j) = \tfrac{1}{2} p(i,j) \big[P(i+1,j+1) + P(i+1,j-1) \big] \qquad (30)$$

Next, evaluate the maturity condition for the option.

$$C(N_T, j) = \max\{0, P(N_T, j) - K\} \quad \text{for all } j. \qquad (31)$$

For European options, the value is obtained by applying equation (30) back through to the origin of the tree. For American options, we need to allow for the possibility of early exercise in the normal way by taking the maximum of the discounted expectation and the intrinsic value of the option at each node.

$$C(i,j) = \max\big\{ P(i,j) - K, \tfrac{1}{2} p(i,j) \big[C(i+1,j+1) + C(i+1,j-1) \big] \big\}. \qquad (32)$$

A more efficient procedure for valuing European option prices utilizes the fact that the pure security prices are equivalent to discounted probabilities. The value of any European option can be calculated directly from the tree as the sum of the product of the maturity condition of the option and the pure security price, for each node at the maturity time, for example, for a call option:

$$\text{call value} = \sum_j Q(N_T, j) \max\{0, P(N_T, s) - K\}. \qquad (33)$$

PRICING INTEREST RATE EXOTICS USING SHORT-RATE TREES

So far we have concentrated on pricing interest rate derivatives where the payoff to the derivative only depends on the level of the short rate at each node and not on the path that the short rate took to achieve that level. If the payoff of the derivative at a node depends on the path the short rate took to reach that node, then in general the derivative can have a different value corresponding to each possible path to that node. Since the number of paths reaching a given node increases exponentially as we go out through the tree, it is not feasible to store all the possible values. The solution, first introduced by Hull and White (1993), is simply to store a small subset of the full set of possible values of the derivative. This technique can be used to price any

---

7 Note that we only have to go back as far as N_T for European options.

path-dependent interest rate derivative, for example, average rate caps, barrier caps, and barrier swaptions, using a short-rate tree. As an example of the technique, we describe the pricing of an index amortising rate (IAR) swap. IAR swaps are agreements to exchange fixed for floating rate payments on prespecified dates on a principal amount that may decline through time; the reduction in principal depends on the level of interest rates. A typical principal reduction schedule is illustrated in Table 2–1. The schedule determines how the principal underlying the swap will be reduced according to some index. Throughout this example we will use the three-month LIBOR as the index, but other popular choices include LIBOR of different tenors and constant maturity treasury (CMT) rates.

Consider a three-year IAR swap with a starting principal of $100 million, where the principal repayments are determined according to the above schedule. The base rate, X, is determined at the outset of the swap at, say, 10 percent. Payments are only made on the quarterly interest-payment dates, and the principal reduction may not exceed the outstanding principal. Suppose that the three-month LIBOR is currently 10 percent. The annual amortization rate is therefore 20 percent. A LIBOR level of 9.5 percent would lead to an amortisation rate of 30 percent.[8]

Like a plain-vanilla swap, the value of an index IAR swap is the difference between the value of the two bonds, which we denote by B_{fix} for the fixed side and B_{fl} for the floating side, underlying the

TABLE 2–1

Principal Reduction Schedule for an Index Amortizing Swap

Index Level Relative to Base Rate X	Principal Reduction
X – 300 bps or lower	100
X – 200	60
X – 100	40
X	20
X + 100	10
X + 200	5
X + 300 or higher	0

8 We are assuming that the terms of the deal specify that linear interpolation applies to the reduction schedule.

swap. The floating side equals the swap principal immediately after a reset date, while the fixed side must be calculated from the short rate tree. The value of the fixed-rate bond depends on the level of interest rates and the outstanding principal PR. PR satisfies the condition that its level at time $t + \Delta t$ can be calculated from the level at time t and the interest rate at time $t + \Delta t$, so we can apply the techniques in Hull and White (1993).

Depending on the path of the short rate through the tree, the number of alternative principal amounts that can be realized at any node grows quickly with the number of time steps. Instead of keeping track of all the possible alternatives, we compute the value of the fixed-rate bond at any node only for certain values of the principal. Specifically, we evaluate the maximum and minimum values of PR at each node and then approximate the set of all possible PRs with M (say four) equally spaced values at each node. Define PR_{ijk} $(k = 0,1, \ldots, M)$ for the outstanding principal at node (i,j) and $B_{i,j,k}$ for the value of B_{fix} at (i,j) when PR has this value. To calculate the outstanding principal, we apply forward induction.[9]

The principal amounts at node (i, j) depend on the relevant levels at the nodes that lead into (i, j) and the LIBOR rate at the node. We can determine the three-month LIBOR at node (i, j), which we denote by $L(i, j)$, according to the following:

$$L(i,j) = \frac{1}{0.25}\left[\frac{1}{P(i,j,0.25)} - 1 \right] \tag{34}$$

where $P(i,j, 0.25)$ is the price of a pure discount bond with three months to maturity, which can be determined from the short-rate tree. $L(i,j)$ is then used to determine the percentage principal reduction, pr, according to the scheme in Table 2–1. If we are moving from node $(i - 1, j + 1)$ to (i,j) and if the amortisation rate applies to the outstanding principal, then the amount the principal is reduced by is $pr\, PR_{i-1, j+1,k}$, which is used to determine the maximum and minimum principals at the (i, j)th node. If the rate applies to the original principal, PR_0, then to keep the principal from becoming negative the reduction is given by min $(pr\, PR_0, PR_{i-1, j+1,k})$. A similar procedure is performed for the other parent node $(i - 1, j - 1)$. This process continues until the end of the life of the swap.

---

9 As we perform forward induction, we only update $PR_{i,j,0}$ and $PR_{i,j,M}$, the maximum and minimum values of PR at node (i, j) respectively.

Once the forward induction step is completed, the value of the bond at maturity, $B_{n,j,k}$, can be calculated for all j and all k:

$$B_{n,j,k} = PR_{n,j,k} .$$

To calculate the value of B_{fix} at node (i, j) for $i < n$, we use backward induction. Suppose $PR_{i,j,k}$ leads to $PR_{i+1, j+1,k_u}$ when there is an up movement in the short rate and $PR_{i+1, j-1,k_d}$ when there is a down movement. For a European derivative this implies that

$$B_{i,j,k} = e^{-r(i,j)\Delta t} \left[\frac{1}{2} B_{i+1,j+1,k_u} + \frac{1}{2} B_{i+1,j-1,k_d} + c_{i,j} \right] \tag{35}$$

where $c_{i,j}$ is the cash flow (interest plus principal reduction) during the period $(i, i + \Delta t)$.

Due to the nature of the forward induction (we only hold M values of the principal at each node) $B_{i+1,j+1,k_u}$ and $B_{i+1,j-1,k_d}$ might not be known at time step $i + 1$, and so we interpolate from the set of known values. For example, we interpolate $B_{i+1,j+1,k_u}$ from $B_{i+1,j+1,k_1}$ and $B_{i+1,j+1,k_1}$ where k1 and k2 are the closest values of PR to $PR_{i+1, j+1,k_u}$ such that $PR_{i+1,j+1,k_1} \leq PR_{i+1,j+1,k_u} \leq PR_{i+1,j+1,k_2}$. This procedure is repeated for all k at node (i, j). We determine $B_{i+1, j-1,k_d}$ similarly. The value of the swap for the receiver of fixed payments is then the difference between $B_{fix} - PR$.

NON-MARKOVIAN SHORT-RATE MODELS

Our starting point for these models is the discount bond formulation

$$\frac{dP(t,T)}{P(t,T)} = r(t)dt + \sum_{i=1}^{n} v_i(t,T)dB_i(t) \tag{36}$$

where

$$v_i(t,T) = -\int_t^T \sigma_i(t,s)ds .$$

The discount bond price formulation of the model described by equation (36) has a number of advantages for pricing and hedging derivatives. Since the model is formulated in terms of prices, there is a natural measure under which prices are martingales. This change of measure removes the necessity of computing the short rate directly. All interest rate derivatives depend, either directly or indirectly, on the prices of pure discount bonds and most, for example, caps, floors, coupon bond options, and swaptions, depend directly on these prices. Therefore in pricing a derivative we must model only a relatively small number of discount bonds. In contrast, the forward rate formulation (equation (8)) requires integration over the forward rate curve to obtain discount bond prices. In practice this formulation requires modeling a very large number of points on the forward rate curve in order to obtain accurate prices.

So, in order to price derivatives, we first transform to the natural risk-neutral measure so that equation (36) becomes

$$\frac{dP(t,T)}{P(t,T)} = +\sum_{i=1}^{n} v_i(t,T)d\tilde{B}_i(t) \tag{37}$$

where $d\tilde{B}_i(t) = dB(t) + \dfrac{r(t)}{v_i(t,T)}dt$.

We first show how trees for the discount bond prices can be constructed. Consider a binomial process for the discount bond prices

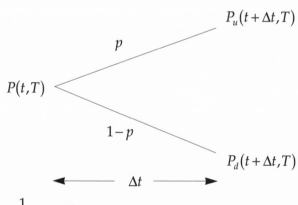

where $p = \dfrac{1}{2}$ and

$$P_u(t+\Delta t,T) = P(t,T)\exp\big(\alpha(t,T)\Delta t + v(t,T)\sqrt{\Delta t}\big)$$

$$P_u(t+\Delta t,T) = P(t,T)\exp\big(\alpha(t,T)\Delta t - v(t,T)\sqrt{\Delta t}\big).$$

Now the no-arbitrage condition is that the discount bond prices must be martingales, in other words,

$$E\left[\tilde{P}(t+\Delta t,T)\right] = \tilde{P}(t,T).$$

So we must choose the $\alpha(t,T)$ to satisfy this condition. This gives

$$P_u(t+\Delta t,T) = P(t,T)\frac{2}{1+\exp\left(-v(t,T)\sqrt{\Delta t}\right)} \tag{38}$$

$$P_d(t+\Delta t,T) = P(t,T)\frac{2}{1+\exp\left(+v(t,T)\sqrt{\Delta t}\right)}.$$

As we already noted, the tree is nonrecombining, that is, an upward move followed by a downward move does not lead to the same discount bond price as a downward move followed by an upward move. This is simply because of the time-varying volatility. The number of nodes in the tree therefore increases exponentially, and it is only possible to build trees with up to a maximum of roughly 20 time steps (corresponding to over 1 million nodes). Once the tree has been built, we can use the standard backward induction to price derivatives. However, because of the large number of nodes the procedure is much slower than with recombining trees. Monte Carlo simulation provides a way of dealing with this problem. Next we describe how Monte Carlo simulation can be implemented efficiently.

Consider pricing an option on a coupon bond with certain cash flows C_k at dates s_k, $k = 1, \ldots, m$.[10] The price of this call option is given by

$$Call_{CB}\left(t,K,T,\{s_k\}\right) = \tilde{E}_t\left[\max\left(0,\sum_{k=1}^{m}C_k P(T,s_k) - KP(T,T)\right)\right] \tag{39}$$

where

$$P(T,s) = \exp\left[\sum_{i=1}^{n}\left\{\int_t^T v_i(u,s)dB_i(u) - \frac{1}{2}\int_t^T v_i(u,s)^2 du\right\}\right]$$

(see Carverhill [1995]). This can be written as

$$Call_{CB}\left(t,K,T,\{s_k\}\right) = \tilde{E}_t\left[\max\left(0,\sum_{k=1}^{m}C_k P(t,s_k)Y(t,T,s_k) - KP(t,T)Y(t,T,T)\right)\right] \tag{40}$$

where

---

10 Caps, floors, collars, and swaptions can all be considered as options on coupon bonds (see
   Clewlow and Strickland [1996]).

$$Y(t,T,s) = \exp\left[\sum_{i=1}^{n}\left\{\int_{t}^{T} v_i(u,s)dB_i(u) - \frac{1}{2}\int_{t}^{T} v_i(u,s)^2 du\right\}\right]$$

and are exponential martingales. This formulation in terms of the $Y(t,T,s)$ is important because it allows us to efficiently implement Monte Carlo simulation using variance reduction.

Let M be the number of simulations, N be the number of time steps of size Δt, and ε be a standard normal random number, then the Monte Carlo estimate of the option value is given by

$$Call_{CB}(t,K,T,\{s_k\}) = \frac{1}{M}\sum_{j=1}^{M}\left[\max\left(0,\sum_{k=1}^{m}C_kP(t,s_k)Y_j(t,T,s_k) - KP(t,T)Y_j(t,T,T)\right)\right] \quad (41)$$

where

$$Y_j(t,T,s) = \exp\left[\sum_{l=1}^{n}\sum_{i=1}^{N} v_l(u_i,s)\varepsilon_l(u_i)\sqrt{\Delta t} - \frac{1}{2}v_l(u_i,s)^2\Delta t\right].$$

Carverhill and Pang (1995) show how the accuracy of this Monte Carlo estimate can be improved by using the exponential martingales $Y(t,T,s)$ as control variates. Consider taking the Monte Carlo estimate as

$$Call_{CB}(t,K,T,\{s_k\}) = \frac{1}{M}\sum_{j=1}^{M}\left[\begin{array}{l}\max\left(0,\sum_{k=1}^{m}C_kP(t,s_k)Y_j(t,T,s_k) - KP(t,T)Y_j(t,T,T)\right)\\ -\beta_1(Y_j(t,T,T)-1)-\sum_{k=1}^{m}\beta_{k+1}(Y_j(t,T,s_k)-1)\end{array}\right]. \quad (42)$$

Now we have $\tilde{E}_t\left[Y_j(t,T,s_k)-1\right]=0$ and so the expectation of the expression in the square brackets will be unaffected by the addition of the extra terms. But the $Y(t,T,s)$ are correlated with the payoff and so by taking short positions in them they act like a hedge, reducing the variance of the payoff and thus increasing the accuracy of the Monte Carlo estimate. The β's can be estimated by least-squares regression as follows: rewrite the Monte Carlo estimate with the payoff (y_j) and control variates (x_{jk}) for each path j. The estimate of the option value C is

$$C = \frac{1}{M}\sum_{j=1}^{M}\left(y_j - \sum_{k=1}^{m}\beta_k x_{j,k}\right). \quad (43)$$

A least-squares regression estimate of C and the β's is

$$\beta = \left(X'X\right)^{-1}X'Y \tag{44}$$

where $\beta = (C,\beta_1,\ldots,\beta_m)$, X is a matrix whose rows are $(1,x_{j,1},\ldots,x_{j,m})$, and Y is the vector of payoffs. The matrices $X'X$ and $X'Y$ can be accumulated as the simulation proceeds using

$$\left(X'X\right)_{k,l}^{j+1} = \left(X'X\right)_{k,l}^{j} + x_{j+1,k}x_{j+1,l} \tag{45}$$

$$\left(X'Y\right)_{k}^{j+1} = \left(X'Y\right)_{k}^{j} + x_{j+1,k}y_{j+1} \tag{46}$$

where $x_{j,0}=1$, and $x_{j,k}$ and y_j are the values returned by the jth simulation. The final estimate of the option value should be obtained via equation (42) after estimating the β's by the least-squares regression or the estimate will be biased. This is because, with a simultaneous estimation, the β's will be correlated with the $Y_j(t,T,s)$s and so the control variates will no longer have mean zero. Note that the β's remain constant along the path and so we can interpret the role of the control variates in equation (42) as a static hedge. Clewlow and Strickland (1996) show how the technique can be extended to use a dynamic hedge and achieve much greater variance reduction.

CONCLUSIONS

In this chapter, we have attempted to give an overview of the current state of interest-rate term structure modeling and derivative pricing. In particular we have tried to show how theory meets practice, and how the complexity of the real world can be dealt with using the combined tools of stochastic calculus and advanced numerical techniques.

REFERENCES

Black, F.; E. Derman; and W. Toy. "A One-Factor Model of Interest Rates and Its Application to Treasury Bond Options." *Financial Analysts Journal,* January–February 1990, pp. 33–9.

Carverhill, A. "A Simplified Exposition of the Heath, Jarrow and Morton Model." *Stochastics and Stochastics Reports* 53 (1995), pp. 227–40.

Carverhill, A., and K. Pang. "Efficient and Flexible Bond Option Valuation in the Heath, Jarrow, and Morton Framework." *Journal of Fixed Income* 5, no. 2 (1995), pp. 70–7.

Clewlow, L. and C. Strickland. "Monte Carlo Pricing of American Options in the Gaussian Heath, Jarrow, and Morton Model." Financial Options Research Centre Working Paper, Warwick University, 1996.

Cox, Ingersoll, and Ross. "A Theory of the Term Structure of Interest Rates." *Econometrica* (March, 1985).

Cox, Ross, and Rubinstein. "Option Pricing: A Simplified Approach." *Journal of Financial Economics* (September 1979), pp. 229–63.

Fong, H. G., and O. A. Vasicek. "Interest Rate Volatility as a Stochastic Factor." Gifford Fong Associates Working Paper, 1992.

Heath, D.; R. Jarrow; and A. Morton. "Bond Pricing and the Term Structure of Interest Rates: A New Methodology for Contingent Claim Valuation." *Econometrica* 60, no. 1 (1992), pp. 77–105.

Ho, T. S. Y., and S. -B. Lee. "Term Structure Movements and Pricing Interest Rate Contingent Claims." *Journal of Finance* 41, no. 5 (December 1986), pp. 1011–29.

Hull, J., and A. White "Pricing Interest Rate Derivative Securities." *The Review of Financial Studies* 3, no. 4 (1990).

Hull, J., and A. White. "Efficient Procedures for Valuing European and American Path-Dependent Options." *The Journal of Derivatives,* Fall 1993, pp. 21–31.

Hull, J., and A. White. "Numerical Procedures for Implementing Term Structure Models I: Single Factor Models." *The Journal of Derivatives,* Fall 1994, pp. 7–16.

Hull, J., and A. White "Numerical Procedures for Implementing Term Structure Models I: Single Factor Models." *The Journal of Derivatives,* Winter 1994, pp. 37–48.

Jamshidian, F. "An Exact Bond Option Formula." *Journal of Finance* XLIV, no. 1 (1989), pp. 205–9.

Jamshidian, F. "Forward Induction and Construction of Yield Curve Diffusion Models." *Journal of Fixed Income* 1, no. 1 (1991).

Longstaff, F. A., and E. S. Schwartz. "Interest Rate Volatility and the Term Structure: A Two-Factor General Equilibrium Model." *The Journal of Finance* XLVII, no. 4 (September, 1992), pp. 1259–82.

Vasicek, O. "An Equilibrium Characterisation of the Term Structure." *Journal of Financial Economics,* no. 5 (1977).

⑥ # A FUNDAMENTAL APPROACH FOR FORECASTING INTEREST RATES WITH AN APPLICATION TO THE DEUTSCHE MARK YIELD CURVE

Christian L. Dunis
Vice President
Quantitative Research and Trading Group
Chemical Bank, London

Macroeconomic policy coordination has often stumbled in recent years on divergent monetary policies between countries and, even more so, divergent interest rate trends. In August 1993, the Exchange Rate Mechanism (ERM) nearly collapsed as a result of massive pressures. These were mostly caused by market sentiment that interest rate increases needed in some countries to maintain ERM parities were incompatible with domestic economic requirements at a time of a sharp cyclical downturn. In those circumstances, the interactions between domestic and foreign determinants of interest rates were once again put into light.

In this chapter, we derive a forecasting methodology that discriminates between the impact of domestic and foreign factors on interest rates, while at the same time distinguishing between the long and the short end of the yield curve.

First, we present some theoretical considerations for the analysis of both short-term and long-term rates. Second, we discuss our empirical investigation and the econometric methodology we have chosen and, finally, we present our practical results for the deutsche mark (DEM) yield curve.

THEORETICAL CONSIDERATIONS

Short-Term Interest Rates[1]

As far as short-term interest rates are concerned, two major theories are competing: the Fisherian domestic model based on real interest rates and the Keynesian international arbitrage model of nominal interest rate parity. From experience we know that interest rate variations can be caused by modifications in domestic economic policies, exchange rate fluctuations, or both. The "true" model of interest rate determination therefore seems to be a mixture of the "domestic" model and the "international arbitrage" model. Before we review our own approach, we give a brief summary of these two models, which have been extensively studied in the literature.

The Domestic Model

The Fisherian model states that *the interest rate level is equal to a constant real rate of return plus the expected inflation rate* in the country considered (see Fisher [1930]).

Calling the nominal interest rate prevailing in time t, r_t the real rate of return, and p_t the inflation rate, the domestic model states that

$$i_{t-1} = r_{t-1} + E(p_t) \qquad (1)$$

where $E(x_t \mid I_{t-1})$ denotes the mathematical conditional expectation operator that is conditional on the information set available to market participants at time $t - 1$.

This domestic model can be easily extended to a two-country world. Using an asterisk (*) to denote the foreign country, if we further assume that the real rates of return are equal in the two countries, that is $r = r^*$, we can then concentrate on the nominal interest-rate differential by writing, after rearranging:

$$i_{t-1} - i^*_{t-1} = E(p_t) - E(p^*_t). \qquad (2)$$

---

1 This section draws heavily on Dunis (1993).

In other words, the assumption of equal real rates implies that the nominal interest rate differential is equal to the expected inflation differential between the two countries. We can thus rewrite equation (2) as

$$i'_{t-1} = E(p'_t) \tag{2'}$$

where the prime sign (') denotes the difference between the home and the foreign country.

At this point, it should be stressed that what is important *for empirical work* is *not* the strict assumption that real rates are equal, but only that their difference, if any, remains *constant over time*. Nevertheless, in a good review of the literature on the subject, MacDonald and Taylor (1992, p. 39) report a large number of studies whose results "indicate a resounding rejection of real interest parity."

The International Model

As shown by Dornbusch (1976), with rational expectations and efficient money markets, interest rates should reflect expected exchange rate movements instantaneously so as to avoid arbitrage opportunities. In other words, and following Keynes (1930), in a risk-neutral world (i.e., one where no risk premia exist), the nominal interest-rate differential should be equal to the expected exchange rate movement.

Taking our former notations and calling S_t the exchange rate prevailing at time t (i.e., the number of units of domestic currency per unit of the foreign currency), we can write, assuming rational expectations:

$$i'_{t-1} = E(dS_t) = 100\left[(F_{t-1} / S_{t-1}) - 1\right] \tag{3}$$

where F_{t-1} is the forward exchange rate for time t prevailing at time $t - 1$, and d is the first difference operator.

Unfortunately, as is widely recognised, the empirical evidence does not tend to support this view. In their review of the literature on the subject, MacDonald and Taylor (1992, p. 31) note that the most widely accepted reason for this is that "there is a nonzero, time-varying risk premium that drives a wedge between the forward rate and the future spot rate."

Some Further Theoretical Considerations

We can go one step further by combining equation (2') and equation (3). This yields

$$E(p'_t) = E(dS_t),\qquad(4)$$

which is the "efficient markets" version of purchasing power parity (PPP). In other words, the combination of the domestic model *and* the international arbitrage model is consistent with PPP theory, which states

$$dS_t = p'_t.\qquad(5)$$

In fact, all that is required by the combination of the domestic and the international approach to interest rate determination is that PPP should hold *ex ante,* even if there are *large ex post deviations.*

Long-Term Interest Rates

The economic literature on long-term interest rates and the yield curve is far less abundant than that on short-term rates. As with short-term rates, two major theories about long-term rates are in competition: the Feldstein-Eckstein "structural" approach, which is also sometimes referred to as "preferred habitat" analysis because it relies on fundamental macroeconomic factors and the assumption of a relatively segmented asset market; and the expectations theory of the term structure of interest rates, which states that the slope of the yield curve is determined by market expectations about future short-term interest rates.

The Market Segmentation Model

This approach derives mostly from the seminal work by Feldstein and Eckstein (1970) who relate the long-term rate to several macroeconomic variables including long-term price expectations, a measure of policy-controlled liquidity of the economy (i.e., the ratio of real per capita monetary base to real per capita GNP), and the stock of government debt. It has been refined further and included in several macroeconometric models, for instance the Data Resources, Inc. (DRI) model of the U.S. economy (see Eckstein [1983] for more details, particularly chapter 4, pp. 77–90).

Basically, in its simplest form, this approach postulates that investors and borrowers have different preferences concerning the term of their lending or borrowing (this is why it is also often called the *preferred habitat* theory). It therefore implies that *interest rates across the yield curve are determined by the relative demand and supply for fixed-interest debt at each maturity.*

A general and simple reduced-form equation for this approach, then, is

$$Y_t - i_t = \alpha + \beta \log K_t + \varepsilon_t \qquad (6)$$

where Y_t denotes the long-term interest rate for a given maturity and K_t the stock of fixed-interest debt for that same maturity, and where the coefficient is expected to be positive as an increase in K_t is associated with a lower bond price and thus a higher bond yield.

In a brief survey, Boughton (1988, p. 48) contends that several studies since the 1970s have shown only limited success for this approach and that "the best way to describe the determination of long-term interest rates remains an open question." Nevertheless, in a more recent study of empirical models of the yield curve for the United Kingdom, Taylor (1992, p. 536) concludes that he achieved "more encouraging results when a simple empirical formulation of the market segmentation approach was estimated."

The Expectations Theory Model
The Expectations Theory is not a new development in economic analysis, as it rests on the works of both Fisher (1930) and Keynes (1930). As mentioned above, its main contention is that the slope of the yield curve is determined by the market's expectations about the future course of short-term interest rates. This theory therefore implies the possibility of effective arbitrage among assets with different maturities as it postulates a high level of integration of the securities market of the given country.

In its simplest form, the expectations theory model can be represented by the following reduced-form equation:

$$Y_t = \alpha + \beta i_t + \sum_{t+1}^{t+n} \gamma_j \cdot i_j^{(E)} + \varepsilon_t. \qquad (7)$$

where $\gamma_j \cdot i_j^{(E)}$ is the weighted expected short-term interest rate at time j, with $j = (t + 1, \ldots, t + n)$.

In practice, expected short-term interest rates are generally expressed as a function of the past history of short-term interest rates according to an adaptive, regressive, or extrapolative expectations scheme.

Still, despite the intuitive appeal of this approach to market participants, Boughton (1988, p. 48) notes that if "many attempts have been made to estimate term-structure equations on the basis of the expectations theory, . . in general the results have not supported the theory." Recent empirical studies like those by Engle, Lilien, and Robins (1987) or even Taylor (1992) have also failed to give it any substantive support.

In the end, neither theoretical approach appears empirically warranted beyond any doubt, and most authors would probably agree with Boughton (1988, p. 49) that, from an empirical point of view, "the behavior of long-term rates is primarily autoregressive."

THE EMPIRICAL INVESTIGATION

As we have seen from the previous section, former empirical research on the determination of both short-term and long-term interest rates does not provide us with an unquestionable framework to work with. We are therefore obliged to derive our own approach by combining economic theory with the practical experience of interest rate markets.

Short-Term Interest Rates

As we have seen above, the key relationships for short-term interest rate determination are given by equations (2') and (3):

$$i'_{t-1} = E(p'_t) \tag{2'}$$

for the domestic model, and

$$i'_{t-1} = E(dS_t) = 100\left[(F_{t-1}/S_{t-1}) - 1\right] \tag{3}$$

for the international model.

The problem with empirical work is that exchange rate and inflation expectations are not readily available, contrary to interest rate differentials. Can't we instead use proxy variables? Is it in fact possible to test a relationship such as

$$i'_t = \alpha + \beta \sum_1^n p'_{t-j} + \gamma \sum_1^n dS_{t-j} + \varepsilon_t \tag{8}$$

despite obvious measurement errors on expectations? If the answer is negative, then we are left with testing the stochastic counterpart of equations (2') and (3):

$$p'_t = \alpha + \beta i_{t-1} + \varepsilon_t \tag{9}$$

and

$$dS_t = \alpha + \beta i'_{i-1} + \varepsilon_t \tag{10}$$

For equation (9), (i.e., the domestic model), former empirical research has shown that, for most countries, β is significantly different from unity, which is the value expected from the simple Fisherian model. Moreover, the adjusted coefficient of determination R^2 is generally very low, that is, the model only explains a marginal part of the variance of inflation differences between countries. As mentioned in the previous section, MacDonald and Taylor (1992) have surveyed a large number of such studies, and they conclude by unequivocally rejecting the real interest parity theory.

Despite this poor statistical relationship, it is worth noting that the Fisherian model still bears some intuitive appeal, as illustrated in Figure 3–1, which compares the three-month DEM nominal interest rate with the equilibrium rate (defined as the sum of the average real rate estimated over the long term, plus the inflation rate).[2]

Equation (10) is nothing more than the strong version of the efficient market hypothesis for the foreign exchange market whereby the forward premium is assumed to be an unbiased predictor of the future spot rate change. As mentioned before, this view does not seem to have drawn much support in recent empirical work.

In these circumstances, and since we know from experience that changes in short-term interest rates are caused in reality by modifications in domestic economic policies, exchange rate fluctuations, or both, we would suggest testing the basic idea that the interest rate level for a given currency depends essentially on two sets of factors: domestic factors (DF), for instance the expected call money rate (itself possibly the result of the combination of a real rate of return plus the expected inflation rate); and international factors, namely, the expected interest rate served on other relevant currencies (we can safely assume, for example, that French franc (FRF) short-term interest rates are determined to a large extent by corresponding deutsche mark

---

2 The *equilibrium rate* is defined as the theoretical level of the nominal interest rate that would prevail if the instantaneous real interest rate was standing at its mean long-term level. The equilibrium rate approach combines two aspects of economic theory: the Fisherian model of interest rate determination, which states that the nominal interest rate is equal to a constant real rate of return plus the expected inflation rate; and the Von Neuman model of economic equilibrium, which states that, in an economy growing steadily under constant returns to scale, the rate of growth should equal the real rate of interest.

F I G U R E   3–1

Fisherian Model

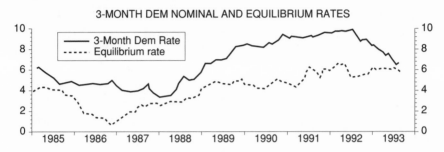

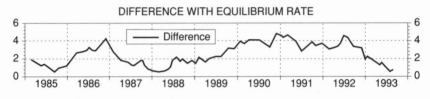

Source: Datastream

(DM) rates) weighted by the expected risk on these very currencies. For this purpose, we intend to use the *error correction methodology* proposed by Engle and Granger (1987), as it has the great advantage of imposing on the retained model *long-term constraints* that are consistent with economic theory while allowing the data to determine its *short-term dynamics.* This approach seems further warranted by the fact that a broad consensus has emerged in the recent literature that interest rates are best described as *nonstationary I(1) processes.*[3]

Using this two-stage procedure, we would look to estimate equations such as equation (11):

$$i_t = \alpha + \beta DF_t + \gamma i_t^* + \delta \sum_1^n dS_{t-j} + \varepsilon_t \qquad (11)$$

---

3 An $I(n)$ variable is a variable integrated of order n, that is, which must be differenced n times to become stationary. (A time series is said to be stationary when its mean and variance do not depend on the size of the chosen sample.) Here in equation (11), interest rate levels that are $I(1)$ series are combined with exchange rate changes, which are typically $I(0)$ series. This leads to the presence of both $I(0)$ and $I(-1)$ series in the error correction equation; still, contrary to the consequences of an underdifferencing, this overdifferencing does not invalidate our results.

where DF represents *the influence of domestic monetary policy* and the two other variables represent *the impact of potential currency substitution,* in other words, the international factor. The domestic factor DF could be the call money rate, as in Ettlin and Bernegger (1992); a futures implied interest rate or the equilibrium rate; i^*_t, a relevant foreign interest rate; and $\sum_1^n dS_{t-j}$, a proxy variable for the exchange rate risk.

With a similar type of approach, Ettlin and Bernegger (1992) have constructed a quarterly model over the period 1976 Q1 to 1990 Q4 that explains 90.4 percent of the variance in the quarterly change in the three-month EuroCHF interest rate. Moreover, their model does more than pass in-sample statistical tests successfully; it appears also to survive the acid test of out-of-sample forecasting. True, they use the current call money rate as a proxy for its expected value, namely, as the domestic factor, and we would argue that for simulation purposes the exercise becomes largely redundant: the knowledge of the future call money rate is clearly a decisive advantage if one has to forecast the corresponding three-month rate![4]

Still, their result is encouraging and it is certainly a good incentive for us to explore our own ideas along those lines. For the reason just mentioned, we shall concentrate on the equilibrium rate or, when the data is available for a long enough period, the futures implied interest rate.

Long-Term Interest Rates

As we have seen from our rapid survey on the determination of long-term interest rates, this issue remains an open one, and recent empirical work does not unequivocally favor the market segmentation model rather than the Expectations Theory model.

From a practical point of view, it is worth noting that the stock of fixed-interest debt, a key variable in the market segmentation model as evidenced in equation (6), is not always readily available. Even if it is, it may not be easy to forecast, although doing so is a prerequisite if equation (6) is to be used for forecasting purposes. In these circumstances, and bearing in mind such practicalities, we would suggest combining the expectations theory approach with the *theory of distributed lags.*

---

4 In a later paper on monthly EuroCHF interest rates, Ettlin and Bernegger (1994) replace the contemporaneous call money rate by its two- or three-month moving average, depending on the maturity studied.

According to the expectations theory, long-term rates are a weighted average of present and future short-term rates, such as those represented for instance by equation (7):

$$Y_t = \alpha + \beta i_t + \sum_{t+1}^{t+n} \gamma_j \cdot i_j^{(E)} + \varepsilon_t. \tag{7}$$

Expectations Theory can also be conveniently represented by the following reduced-form equation:

$$Y_t = \alpha + \beta \sum_0^n \gamma^j \cdot i_{t-j} + \varepsilon_t. \tag{7'}$$

Then, following Koyck (1954), under the assumption of adaptive expectations and the further assumption that the weighting coefficients γ^j decrease geometrically, we can use a *Koyck transformation* on equation (7') so that it is rewritten as:

$$Y_t = \gamma Y_{t-1} + \beta i_t + \lambda + \eta_t \tag{12}$$

with $\lambda = \alpha (1 - \gamma)$ and $\eta_t = \varepsilon_t - \gamma \varepsilon_{t-1}$. With equation (12), we have a simple autoregressive model for the long-term rate that only requires the short-term rate as an extra input for forecasting purposes.

We have seen that there is a wide consensus among recent authors to describe the behavior of long-term rates as autoregressive. Yet this formalism is *not* purely empirical because it rests on the theory of distributed lags and the assumptions mentioned above. Whether these assumptions are warranted is clearly an empirical question, which we will answer in our tests of equation (12). For this purpose, we intend to use the same error correction methodology as for the short-term interest rate.

From a practical point of view, we should certainly bear in mind the *econometric consequences of an autoregressive specification* of the model: an artificially high coefficient of determination R^2, a relative inertia and lagged reaction to reversals, and finally, the risk of an accumulation of forecasting errors in the simulation process. Thus, a cautious use of the model and out-of-sample validation are certainly necessary here more than ever.

Last, let us stress that our model does not make any direct reference to potential *international determinants* of long-term rates; in theory, these foreign factors should be captured *via their impact on short-term rates*, but, in practice, it may be necessary to reintroduce them more explicitly in equation (12).

AN APPLICATION TO THE
DEUTSCHE MARK YIELD CURVE

The Data

Our deutsche mark (DEM) interest rate models were estimated on *monthly data*, from September 1985 to September 1993 (i.e., over a 97-month period, our data bank covering the entire period from October 1981).

All the data for this research were taken from various daily and monthly Datastream data banks.

The short-term rate that we retained is the daily three-month EuroDEM rate, which was converted into monthly averages. We proceeded in the same way with the three-month eurodollar rate, which we included as a representative foreign interest rate in the estimation of equation (11). We also used Germany's 12-month inflation rate in order to construct the DEM equilibrium rate, which we used as the relevant domestic determinant of the German short-term interest rate.[5] We in fact computed it as the sum of the actual 12-month inflation rate, plus the average real interest rate over the 10-year period from January 1981 through December 1990. Finally, two measures of the exchange rate risk proved relevant to the determination of the three-month EuroDEM rate, namely past changes in both the USD/DEM and the DEM/FRF monthly exchange rates.[6]

It is, in fact, not surprising that both these exchange rates should play some part in the evolution of the DEM short-term rate: on one hand, a higher U.S. dollar (USD) can lift the cost of imported raw materials and thus lift inflationary expectations (all other things being equal), something the Bundesbank may wish to oppose; on the other hand, because of the importance of German bilateral trade with Europe and particularly France, a stronger DEM may be a good way to dampen inflationary expectations in Germany and, in any case, to reduce the cost of much of its imports.

Concerning the DEM long-term rate, we have taken Germany's 7- to 15-year public-sector bond yield on the secondary market, at the

---

5 It was unfortunately not possible to use futures-implied interest rates as the EuroDEM contract started to trade in June 1989 only.

6 In our estimation of equation (11), we used the two variables X3MAVG and DMPC3M, where X3MAVG is the three-year moving average of the DEM/FRF monthly percentage change and DMPC3M is the three-year cumulative change in the USD/DEM exchange rate.

end of each month. No other data were required for equation (12), which was estimated in its exact original form.

The Empirical Results

Our final most parsimonious equations are shown in Table 3–1 for the DEM short-term interest rate model and in Table 3–2 for the DEM long-term interest rate model.

Concerning the *short-term interest rate model*, the value of the Durbin-Watson statistic in the level equation confirms cointegration between the explanatory variables—the null hypothesis of a zero Durbin-Watson statistic is clearly rejected. Cointegration is further attested by the augmented Dickey-Fuller (ADF) test, a test between a variable and its first difference, which is successfully passed at the 1 percent significance level.[7]

All the estimated coefficients are statistically significant and have the expected signs. The impact of some exogenous variables is quite interesting: all other things being equal, a 100 basis points (b.p.) rise in the three-month EuroUSD rate tends to lift the equivalent EuroDEM rate by 26 b.p. in the long run; similarly a cumulative 10 percent rise in the USD/DEM exchange rate over the past three-year period lifts the EuroDEM level by only 13 b.p., whereas an average 0.1 percent monthly appreciation of the DEM/FRF rate over the previous three-year period tends to reduce the three-month EuroDEM rate by 31 b.p. (i.e., the equivalent of an 86 b.p. reduction for a cumulative 10 percent DEM/FRF appreciation over the previous three-year period).

Overall, the in-sample performance of our cointegration equation is quite satisfactory, as it accounts for over 98 percent of the monthly variance of the three-month EuroDEM level, with an average error of 30 b.p. This remains true even when dummy variables are not included.[8]

The results of our first difference equation are also quite good, as it explains over 79 percent of the *monthly change* in the three-month EuroDEM rate, with an average error of only 12 b.p.!

---

7 Critical values for the ADF statistic are -3.77 and -3.17, respectively, at the 1 and 5 percent significance level.

8 Without the dummies, the regression remains satisfactory, with all its coefficients significant and with the correct sign, an adjusted R^2 of .977, and a standard error of the estimate of .331.

TABLE   3–1

DEM Short-Term Interest Rate Model

Endogenous Variable		Cointegration Equation		Error Correction Equation	
		BDTR	(a)	DBDTR	(a)
Explanatory variables:					
Constant		.721	(1.94)	– .008	(– .64)
BDEQ10 (–3)	(a)	.287	(5.43)	.105	(2.98)
USTR (– 1)	(a)	.256	(7.14)	—	
BDTR (– 2)	(a)	.622	(10.59)	– .427	(– 5.06)
X3MAVG (– 12)	(a)	–3.124	(– 6.89)	—	
DMPC3M	(a)	.013	(4.02)	.008	(2.91)
DUM87	(b)	– .373	(– 3.26)	—	
DUM89	(c)	– .386	(– 2.99)	– .252	(– 2.66)
DUM91	(d)	.490	(4.87)	.145	(4.69)
DBDTR3	(a)	—		.517	(13.45)
RESIDUAL (*t* – 1)	(e)	—		– .334	(– 5.24)
Summary statistics:					
Adjusted R– squared		.980		.792	
Standard error of estimate		.302		.122	
Durbin-Watson statistic		.872		2.410	
Augmented Dickey-Fuller test		– 6.360		– 12.370	
Chow test		.897		.727	
F-statistic		597.330		52.12	

Notes:

Method of estimation: ordinary least squares.

Sample period: 1985:9 to 1993:9 for the cointegration equation; 1985:10 to 1993:9 for the error correction equation.

T-statistics are shown in parentheses and are adjusted for nonstandard distribution.

(a) BDTR is the three-month EuroDEM rate, BDEQ10 is the DEM equilibrium rate, USTR is the three-month euroUSD rate, X3MAVG is the three-year moving average of the DEM/FRF monthly percentage change, DMPC3M is the three-year change in the USD/DEM exchange rate, and DBDTR and DBDTR3 are respectively the first and the third difference of BDTR.

(b) DUM87: Dummy variable covering the period 1987:12 to 1988:4 and the impact of the stock market crash on the Bundesbank's policy.

(c) DUM89: Dummy variable covering the period 1989:3 to 1989:8 of sharp tightening of its monetary policy by the Bundesbank ahead of the fall of the Berlin Wall.

(d) DUM91: Dummy variable covering the period 1991:12 to 1992:8 following the July 1991 fiscal package and its impact on German inflation.

(e) Error correction term derived from the cointegration equation.

T A B L E 3–2

DEM Long-Term Interest Rate Model

Endogenous Variable		Cointegration Equation		Error Correction Equation	
		LRWG	(a)	DLRWG	(a)
Explanatory variables					
Constant		.639	(3.39)	.012	(.83)
LRWG (–1)	(a)	.855	(22.94)	—	
BDTR	(a)(b)	.065	(3.79)	–.246	(–5.44)
DLRWG3	(a)	—		.552	(9.77)
RESIDUAL (t–1)	(c)	—		–.610	(–5.88)
Summary statistics					
Adjusted R-squared		.961		.584	
Standard error of estimate		.199		.135	
Durbin-Watson statistic		1.380		1.770	
Augmented Dickey-Fuller test		–6.920		–5.280	
Chow test		.807		.137	
F-statistic		1169.540		45.470	

Notes:
Method of estimation: ordinary least squares.
Sample Period: 1985:9 to 1993:9 for the cointegration equation; 1985:10 to 1993:9 for the error correction equation.
T-statistics are shown in parentheses and are adjusted for nonstandard distribution.
(a) LRWG is the DEM Public Sector bond yield, BDTR is the three-month EuroDEM rate, and DLRWG and DLRWG3 are respectively the first and the third difference of LRWG.
(b) Because of multicollinearity, we had to lag DBDTR by one period in the error correction equation.
(c) Error correction term derived from the cointegration equation.

The short-term dynamics of the model are underlined by the inclusion in the error correction equation of the third difference of the EuroDEM rate—this in fact corresponds to the introduction of a time series analysis element in that equation.

As expected, the coefficient of the error correction term derived from the level equation is negative and strongly significant, thereby confirming cointegration between the explanatory variables. In fact, it appears that 33.4 percent of the gap between the actual and the long-term equilibrium values of the three-month EuroDEM rate are corrected within one month, all other things being equal.

As can be seen from Table 3–1, our model successfully passes a series of in-sample statistical tests, particularly stability tests. Still, for any model that is to be used in a dynamic forecasting exercise, the acid test is that of *out-of-sample validation*. For this purpose, we used the 12-month period from October 1992 to September 1993. After having reestimated our original model through September 1992, we sequentially reestimated it from October 1992, thus creating dynamic forecasts with the error correction equation through September 1993. As is standard in the economic literature, we then computed the *mean absolute error* (MAE) and the *root mean squared error* (RMSE) for our out-of-sample period. As a benchmark, we also computed the MAE and the RMSE for the naive random walk model, which states that the "best" prediction of the following month interest rate is its current level. The validation rule here was that our model should outperform the random walk. The results of these calculations are presented below:

Out-of-Sample Forecasting Accuracy		MAE	RMSE
Error correction model (ECM)	(1)	.057	.066
Random walk model	(2)	.126	.195
Augmented accuracy via ECM	(2)–(1)	.069	.129

They show, without any doubt, the superiority of our model over the random walk: Over the period from October 1992 to September 1993, our model manages to outperform the random walk forecast by an average monthly 7 b.p. or even 13 b.p., depending on which statistical measure is used for the comparison. It is also worth noting that there is a significant reduction of both the MAE and the RMSE when compared with the standard error of the estimate for the in-sample period.

Concerning the *long-term interest rate model*, as we see in Table 3–2, cointegration between the explanatory variables is attested by both the Durbin-Watson statistic, which is significantly different from zero, and by the value of the ADF test. Despite its rather simple specification, our level equation gives rather good results, as it accounts for roughly 96 percent of the monthly variance of the DEM long-term bond yield, with an average error of some 20 b.p.[9] This is also the case of our error correction equation, which explains over 58 percent of the variance in

---

9 The high value of the coefficient of determination R^2 partly reflects the presence of the lagged endogenous variable in equation (12).

the *monthly change* of the DEM bond yield, with an average error of less than 14 b.p. For the same reasons mentioned in the case of our short-term EuroDEM model, we have introduced a time series analysis element in our error correction equation with the third difference of the DEM bond yield. Here too, as expected, the lagged residual term from the level equation is both negative and strongly significant, correcting 61 percent of any difference between the actual and the long-term equilibrium values of the German bond yield within a month, all other things being equal.

Our DEM long-term interest rate model successfully passes a range of in-sample statistical tests. Still, as with the EuroDEM model, we checked whether it was able to forecast correctly out-of-sample. Accordingly, we followed the same procedure as that described above for the EuroDEM model: we used the same 12-month out-of-sample period from October 1992 to September 1993, reestimated our original model through September 1992, created dynamic forecasts with the error correction equation for the out-of-sample period, and finally, compared their MAE and RMSE with those derived from the naive random walk model. The results of these calculations are shown below:

Out-of-Sample Forecasting Accuracy		MAE	RMSE
Error Correction model (ECM)	(1)	.084	.100
Random walk model	(2)	.183	.135
Augmented accuracy via ECM	(2)–(1)	−.001	.035

At first sight, the results seem less satisfactory than those reached with our short-term EuroDEM model. If our DEM bond yield model outperforms the random walk model by some 3 b.p. according to the RMSE measure, it does not do any better according to the MAE computation.

Still, over the 12-month forecast period, from October 1992 to September 1993, the DEM bond yield moved down from 8.40 percent to 7.90 percent, in a quasi-linear fashion, in other words, at a mere 4 b.p. rate per month! Such an inertia certainly does not help our model; on the contrary, it strongly biases the calculation in favor of the random walk model, which, by definition, forecasts no interest rate change from month to month. Besides, the above results show a significant reduction of the model forecasting error, on both the MAE and the RMSE measures, when compared with the standard error of the estimate for the in-sample period.

That is why, in the end, we would argue that our DEM long-term interest rate model is more than acceptable, and it is able to complement advantageously our EuroDEM model to provide a framework for a prospective analysis of the DEM yield curve.

CONCLUSION

In this paper, we have seen that recent empirical research has failed to unequivocally confirm any of the dominant economic theories on interest rate determination, whether it be for short-term or long-term interest rates.

In light of this failure, we have presented a forecasting methodology that discriminates between the impact of domestic and foreign factors on interest rates, while at the same time distinguishing between the long and the short end of the yield curve. In particular, for short-term interest rates, we have seen that when futures implied rates are not available for a long enough period, the equilibrium rate could be used successfully in an attempt to model the domestic determinants of these rates. But foreign factors are important too: as we have seen, because of potential currency substitution, foreign interest rates and the perceived exchange rate risk also play an important part in determining the level of the short-term rate.

For long-term interest rates, we have shown that the combination of the traditional expectations theory with the theory of distributed lags could, under some not too restrictive assumptions, lead to the presentation of a rather simple autoregressive model.

Finally, we have presented an empirical application of our methodology to the DEM yield curve, adopting the two-stage error correction technique and estimating our model on monthly data from September 1985 to September 1993. Our practical results, both in- and out-of-sample, are more than satisfactory and they should go a long way toward vindicating our approach and extending its application to interest rates on other currencies.

REFERENCES

Boughton, J. M. "Exchange Rates and the Term Structure of Interest Rates." *IMF Staff Papers* 35 (March 1988), pp. 36–62.

Dornbusch, R. "Expectations and Exchange Rate Dynamics." *Journal of Political Economy* 84 (December 1976), pp. 1161–76.

Dunis, C. "An Empirical Investigation of the Determinants of Interest Rates: Some Preliminary Remarks for a Research Agenda." Working paper, Chemical Bank, London, January, 1993.

Eckstein, O. *The DRI Model of the U.S. Economy.* New York: McGraw-Hill, 1983.

Engle, R. F., and C. W. J. Granger. "Cointegration and Error Correction: Representation, Estimation and Testing." *Econometrica* 55 (March 1987), pp. 251–76.

Engle, R. F.; D. M. Lilien; and R. P. Robins. "Estimating Time Varying Premia in the Term Structure: The ARCH-M Model." *Econometrica* 55 (March 1987), pp. 391–407.

Ettlin, F., and M. Bernegger. "Interest Rate Determination in the Eurocurrency Market." in *Economic Policy Coordination in an Integrating Europe*, H. Motamen-Scobie and C. C. Starck eds. Helsinki: Bank of Finland, Helsinki, (1992) pp. 91–9.

Ettlin, F., and M. Bernegger. "The Domestic and International Determinants of Euro-Swiss Franc Interest Rates." Presentation to the "Forecasting Financial Markets" Conference organized by Chemical Bank and Imperial College, London, February 2–4, 1994.

Feldstein, M. S., and O. Eckstein. "The Fundamental Determinants of the Interest Rate." *Review of Economics and Statistics* 52 (November 1970), pp. 363–75.

Fisher, I. *Theory of Interest.* New York: Macmillan, 1930.

Keynes, J. M. *Treatise on Money.* New York: Macmillan, 1930.

Koyck, L. M. *Distributed Lags and Investment Analysis.* New York: North-Holland, 1954.

MacDonald, R., and M. P. Taylor. "Exchange Rate Economics: A Survey." *IMF Staff Papers* 39 (March 1992), pp. 1–57.

Taylor, M. P. "Modelling the Yield Curve." *The Economic Journal* 102, (May 1992), pp. 524–37.

MEASURES OF RISK

4

⑥ THE GRAVER RISK MEASURE

A New Multidimensional Methodology for Risk Measurement

Paul Graver
Managing Director
Financial Risk Strategy Practice, Inc., Chicago

Risk, relating to interest-rate-sensitive instruments, takes on many shapes and sizes. The three predominant risks associated with these instruments are price, credit, and liquidity risk. The Financial Risk Strategy Practice is the first firm to introduce and utilize a proprietary single risk measure that captures these multidimensional elements. This new development is called the Graver risk measure.

PRICE RISK

Price risk is measured by dividing convexity by duration. This methodology is used so that instruments with relatively low duration, yet very high convexity (i.e., inversely leveraged ISDA swap agreements), can be compared more directly with less complex instruments. The scale is set at 1 to 10 and the calculated number is rounded off to the nearest whole number. Price risks calculated to be greater than 10 are set to 10.

Mathematically, duration is the first-order derivative of the yield-to-maturity formula. Duration is the present value of cash flows denominated in years and is a good proxy for measuring interest rate sensitivity for small changes in interest rates. The duration of zero coupon bonds is simply the maturity itself; for all other bonds the duration is less than the maturity. In addition to this time dimension, duration can be modified or adjusted to mathematically quantify the price sensitivity of a bond. For example, if one bond has twice the duration of another bond, then its relative price change is twice as large for equal rate changes—all other things being equal. This is solely a mathematical property for equal yield changes. During actual trading, the observed daily volatility may not be two to one, thereby reflecting unequal or nonparallel yield shifts. Convexity measures the extent to which the price yield curve for a bond is nonlinear. Graphically, convexity measures the relative rate of ascent of a bond's price/yield curve while adjusted duration measures its relative slope.

Where an issue does not have a mathematical duration or convexity, (e.g. interest-only securities) the empirical duration or convexity is utilized.

For sake of simplicity and ease of calculation for large amounts of securities in a portfolio, it is more convenient to utilize the methodology providers use for portfolio sensitivity measures (see Table 4–1). This calculation shorthand methodology provides a good proxy for duration and convexity.

TABLE 4–1

Sample Calculation of Sensitivity Measures

Issue:	U.S. Treasury 7.25 5/16/16
Settlement:	4/6/94
Accrued interest:	2.84
Yield:	7.17% (Y)
Price:	100.869
Principal + accrued	103.714 (A)

Reflecting 1 Basis Point Shift in Yields

Yield	7.16	7.17	7.18
Price	100.981	100.870	100.759
Change in price		.110918 (B)	.110753 (C)

Duration = 10,000/A * (B + C)/2* (1 + Y/200) = 11.066
Convexity = 1,000,000/A * (B – C) = 1.764

CREDIT RISK

The credit risk is derived from one of the four predominant credit rating agencies (Standard & Poor's, Moody's, Fitch, or Duff & Phelps). Moody's and Standard & Poor's are the most common bond rating agencies. Each give letter grades as their rating instrument. In cases of multiple ratings, an average is used. The ratings are then adjusted by an equivalence based system on a scale of 1 to 10, 1 being the highest bond rating and 10 being the lowest. Split rated, pluses (+), or minuses (–) are rounded to the nearest whole number. If the instrument is a gilt-edged security like a Treasury bill, it will be rated 1, and if it is an issue in technical and legal default, it will be rated 10. Where no publicized rating exists, then either Best's or Dun & Bradstreet is utilized. Lacking any of the aforementioned, a restricted shadow rating is assigned. The debt rating is a current assessment of the creditworthiness of an obligor with respect to a specific obligation. This assessment may take into consideration obligors such as guarantors, insurers, or lessees. The ratings are based on current information furnished by the issuer or obtained from other sources considered reliable. Information may come from a formal audit or may rely, on occasion, on unaudited financial information. This shadow rating involves many considerations including, but not limited to (1) the likelihood of default capacity and willingness of the obligor in regard to the timely payment of interest and repayment of principal in accordance with the terms of the obligation; (2) the nature of and provision of the obligation; and (3) the protection afforded by, and relative position of, the obligation in the event of bankruptcy, reorganization, or other arrangement under the laws of bankruptcy and other laws affecting creditor's rights.

The equivalency ratings are as follows:

Credit Rating	S&P	Moody's	Fitch	D&P	Best's	D&B
(1)	AAA	Aaa	AAA	AAA	A++	5A1

Obligations rated (1) have the highest rating assignable. The capacity to pay interest and repay principal is extremely strong.

Credit Rating	S&P	Moody's	Fitch	D&P	Best's	D&B
(2)	AA	Aa	AA	AA	A	4A1

For debt rated (2) there is a very strong capacity to pay interest and repay principal. This type of debt differs from the higher traded issues to a negligible degree.

Credit Rating	S&P	Moody's	Fitch	D&P	Best's	D&B
(3)	A	A	A	A	B++	5A2

For issues rated (3) there is a strong capacity to pay interest and repay principal, although they are somewhat more susceptible to the adverse effect of changes in circumstances and economic conditions than debt in higher rated categories.

Credit Rating	S&P	Moody's	Fitch	D&P	Best's	D&B
(4)	BBB	Baa	BBB	BBB	B	4A2

Debt rated (4) is viewed as having an adequate capacity to pay interest and repay principal. Whereas it normally exhibits adequate protection parameters, unfavorable economic conditions or changing circumstances are more likely to lead to a lessened capability to pay timely principal and interest in this category than in higher rated categories.

Credit Rating	S&P	Moody's	Fitch	D&P	Best's	D&B
(5)	BB	Ba	BB	BB	C++	5A3

Issues rated (5) and lower are regarded as speculative with respect to the ability to pay interest and principal. Although many issues will likely have some quality and protective characteristics and covenants, these are outweighed by large uncertainties or major risk exposures to adverse economic conditions. Issues rated (5) and higher have less near-term vulnerability to default than other speculative issues. However, major uncertainties or exposure to adverse business, financial, or economic conditions exist that could lead to inadequate capacity to meet timely interest and principal payments.

Credit Rating	S&P	Moody's	Fitch	D&P	Best's	D&B
(6)	B	B	B	B+	C+	4A3

Obligations rated (6) have the capacity to meet interest payments and principal payments, but they are more vulnerable than better rated issues. Adverse business, financial, or economic conditions will likely impair the ability or willingness to pay interest and repay timely principal.

Credit Rating	S&P	Moody's	Fitch	D&P	Best's	D&B
(7)	CCC	Caa	CCC	B	C	5A4

Issues in this category have immediate vulnerability to default and depend upon favorable business, financial, and economic conditions to meet timely payment of interest and principal. In the event of adverse business, financial, or economic conditions, it is not likely that interest will be paid and principal repaid.

Credit Rating	S&P	Moody's	Fitch	D&P	Best's	D&B
(8)	CC	Ca	CC	B–	D	4A4

Generally this rating category is reserved for debt subordinated to senior debt that is assigned a rating of (7).

Credit Rating	S&P	Moody's	Fitch	D&P	Best's	D&B
(9)	C	C	C	CCC	E	3A

This rating is reserved for issues that are current of debt service payments but where a bankruptcy petition has been filed. These issues are in technical, yet not legal, default (the payments are within the grace period).

Credit Rating	S&P	Moody's	Fitch	D&P	Best's	D&B
(10)	D	D	D	DD	F	—

Debt rated (10) is in legal and technical default. The (10) rating is also issued when a bankruptcy petition is filed.

LIQUIDITY RISK

Liquidity risk, on a set scale from 1 to 10, is assigned by the Financial Risk Strategy Practice's proprietary liquidity risk model, which incorporates many considerations. Those considerations include, but are not limited to, depth and breadth of market, issue size, frequency of trading, number of market makers, and so on. A rating of 1 is assigned to the most liquid securities such as Treasury Bills, and a rating of 10 to the least liquid securities. It is important to note that the relative liquidity of most instruments will change over time as the market environment changes. This is because early generations of securities that are popular today may not necessarily be popular tomorrow as later generations achieve the same investment objective with more efficient security types. For instance, a five-year-average-life collateralized mortgage obligation targeted amortization class currently has a liquidity risk rating of 6, whereas two years ago, when this type of tranch was enjoying greater popularity, its liquidity risk rating was 5. Hence a liquidity risk measure is dynamic and subject to change.

The Financial Risk Strategy Practice's liquidity risk measure has currently categorized over 500 types of obligations based on liquidity. Table 4–2 is a partial listing that can be used as a guide in establishing the liquidity risk measure.

TABLE   4-2

Partial Listing of Liquidity Risk Rankings

Liquidity Risk Rank	Sample Securities
1	U.S. Treasury bills, Fed Funds, Overnight LIBOR, London Eurodollars
2	Overnight Repurchase, U.S. Treasury notes and bonds, N.Y. Stock Exchange listed stocks, major listed futures exchange contracts (i.e., S&P contract, bond contract), OTC currency—industrialized countries (e.g., yen, pound, franc)
3	Government agency notes, top-grade corporate notes, commercial paper, certificate of deposit, bankers acceptances, high-grade money markets, current-coupon mortgages, stable CMO PAC classes, asset-backed auto/credit card, American Stock Exchange listed stocks, NASDAQ national market issues, listed equity options, index options trading, industrialized foreign equity markets, Canadian equity markets, futures options, OTC currency options, OTC currencies—nonindustrialized countries (e.g., Irish pound, Egyptian dollar), lesser listed futures exchange contracts (e.g., peso contract, winter wheat contract)
4	High-grade corporate obligations, medium Investment grade money markets, stable CMO TAC classes, short plain-vanilla CMO classes, stable CMO floaters, asset-backed home equity/health care, NASDAQ small-cap listed stocks, LEAPS—long-term options, Philadelphia currency options
5	Medium Investment grade corporate obligations, New York Stock Exchange bonds, lower grade money markets, news tax-exempts, broken CMO PAC classes, stable CMO short PO, NASDAQ small-cap issues, simple agency issued structured notes, OTC nonlisted equity options
6	Lower Investment Grade Corporate Obligations, AMEX listed bonds, NASDAQ convertible debentures, type II CMO PACs, CMO TAC classes, nonindustrialized foreign equity markets, ISDA conforming swap agreements with AAA credits
7	High-yield corporate notes, privately placed equities, unstable CMO floaters, low-leverage CMO classes, stable CMO IO classes, highly leveraged CMO PO classes, complex agency issued structured notes, seasoned tax-exempts
8	High-yield corporate bonds, high-leverage CMO classes, unstable CMO IO classes, ISDA conforming swaps with less than investment grade credits, privately placed equity options
9	High yield—privately placed, high-yield—technical default, CMO residual, non-ISDA conforming swap agreements with less than investment grade credits
10	High-yield in technical and legal default

GRAVER RISK MEASURE

After plotting the three points of each instrument on a three-dimensional risk map, the linear distance from the point plot to the apex point is the Graver risk measure. The greater the distance from the point plot to the apex point, the greater the risk associated with that particular instrument. A sample hypothetical portfolio of three securities is diagrammed in Table 4–3.

T A B L E   4–3

Sample Portfolio

Security	Description	Price Risk	Credit Risk	Liquidity Risk
1	U.S. Treasury bill	1	1	1
2	Stable five-year PAC	3	1	3
3	ISDA negative leverage swap (counterparty: developing country)	8	10	10

After a portfolio of securities is plotted, the relative Graver risk measures can be connected to form the specific portfolio's risk map. The investor can then analyze the relative risk trade-offs among various securities.

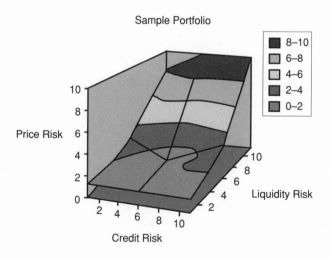

Sample Portfolio

A portfolio's single Graver risk measure (Table 4–4) will be the dollar-weighted amount of each instrument. For a portfolio the Graver risk measure is calculated as follows:

GRMI1 Graver risk measure of first issue

$V!$ Current value of first issue (price X quantity)

GRMI2 Graver risk measure of second issue

V2   Current value of second issue (Price X Quantity)

GRMI.. Graver risk measure of subsequent issue

$V..$ Current value of subsequent issue (Price X Quantity)

Sum[(GRMI1*$V$1)+(GRMI2*$V$2)+(GRMI..* V..]/Sum($V$1+$V$2+V..)

TABLE   4–4

Sample Portfolio

Security	Description	Price Risk	Credit Risk	Liquidity Risk	Graver Risk Measure	Value	Promised Return
1	U.S. Treasury bill	1	1	1	1.43	1mm	5%
2	Stable five-yr PAC	3	1	3	3.33	5mm	5.75%
3	ISDA negative leverage swap Counterparty— developing country	8	10	10	13.34	250m	8%
	Sum[(GRMI1*$V$1)+(GRMI2*$V$2)+(GRMI..* V.]/Sum($V$1+$V$2+V.)						

Hence the dollar-weighted single Graver risk measure for the portfolio is 3.42.

NEW EFFICIENT FRONTIER

Historically, the efficient frontier has been drawn by plotting the risk, as measured by standard deviation of return, versus promised return. By substituting the Graver risk measure and plotting against historical rates of return or against promised rates of return, we can gain a more thorough understanding of risk return. We suggest using a lognormal historical weighting in plotting the historical rate of return. This method assigns greater return weighting to the most recent past and lower return weighting to the older data because newer return market data are arguably more pertinent to future return data.)

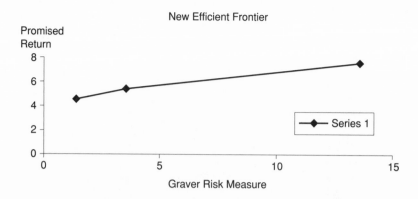

Using this methodology creates a new, more comprehensive efficient frontier. The Graver risk/return profile can identify optimal asset mixes. Investors can then directly compare portfolios against one another using the weighting methodology described above.

Using the Graver risk measure versus promised return basis, the incrementally optimal asset to own in the sample portfolio outlined in the previous section is Security 2, the stable five-year PAC.

While the Graver Risk Measure is by no means the final answer in single risk measurement, it certainly offers a more thorough understanding through quantification of the various elements associated with risk.

CHAPTER

5

⑥ MARKET VERSUS ACCOUNTING-BASED MEASURES OF DEFAULT RISK*

J. A. McQuown
Kealhofer, McQuown, Vasicek, San Francisco

Default occurs when a firm fails to service its debt obligations. When defaults occur, lenders typically suffer losses. Accordingly, borrowers pay lenders a spread over the default-free rate of interest proportional to their default probability.

Before the fact, there is no method to discriminate unambiguously between borrowers who will default and those who will not. Ex ante, that is, we can only make probability assessments of the prospects of default.

The typical borrowing firm has a default probability of 2 percent, over the ensuing year. Thus, the firm has a 98 percent complementary probability of not defaulting. Default is a deceptively rare event.

A naive lending approach would seem to be, simply, to assume firms will not default. After all, 98 percent of the time they don't. However, the consequent losses would bankrupt such a naive lender in short order.

The successful lender must discriminate between small default probabilities. For example, the odds of a AAA firm defaulting are only about 2 in 10,000 per year. A single-A firm has a probability of default that is five times higher. A CCC, the bottom of the agency scale, has 200 times the odds of default of a AAA, which is still only about 4 percent.

The strictly subjective judgments of old are no longer an adequate basis for discriminating among firms' default prospects. The measurement of default probabilities is rapidly evolving into a science. Two ingredients are critical to competitive default probability measurement: data and models. Models are the means by which data are transformed into default probabilities.

Data pertinent to estimating default probability arise from two sources: financial statements and market prices of firms' debt and equity. Presently, far more use is made of financial statements than prices in estimating firm-default probability. Statements are, inherently, reflections of what happened in the past. Prices, by contrast, are forward looking. Prices are formed by capital providers as they anticipate the future prospects of the firm. Prices contain, thereby, ex ante information. The most accurate default measurement derives from models employing both sources. There is a limit, of course, to the information that can be extracted from statements or prices.

The most functional models are grounded in theory that works. Unfortunately, there is not much theory in economics, macro or micro, that works. Most models are ad hoc, that is, they lack structure that reflects the causative linkage among the included variables. Even so, ad hoc models have considerable predictive power. But, alas, we cannot determine why they work. Ad hoc models are destined to remain undecipherable "black boxes," even to their designers.

The conclusion advanced here is simple. When available, we want to use market prices in default prediction, for they add substantial predictive power. Moreover, we want an integrating model whose conceptual structure is readily understandable and appealing to experienced intuition. And finally, the model's conformity to actual default experience must be rigorously tested.

Models using market prices are no more expensive to deploy than those using only financial statements. Moreover, market prices can be economically refreshed as often as you like, for example, daily, whereas models employing only financial statement data have an irreducible quarterly lag.

However, when estimating the default probability on private firms, we only have statement data. We must do the best we can with statement data. The model needs to deal with firms whose capital structure is at variance with the norm. For example, when examining the possible impact of a recapitalization, we will want to obtain an accurate estimate of the new default probability. These requirements lead us to a model based on causation rather than correlation.

Therefore, with private firms, we prefer a model whose conceptual structure is the same as that for public firms. Indeed, the conceptual model developed by KMV is the primary focus of this discussion. From it we can comprehend the value added by equity prices to the predictive power of statements alone. Moreover, its robustness in coherently appraising firms whose financial ratios deviate from the norm can be assessed. The conceptual model, accordingly, places private and public borrower-default assessment on common ground in bank credit portfolio management.

THE PROBLEM

Lending requires resolution of two fundamental questions: (1) what is the likelihood of default; and (2) what will be lost if default occurs? The probability of default derives from the dynamic fortunes of the borrower corporation. Default occurs when the borrower's resources are depleted to such an extent that a promise to pay cannot be met.

The loss given default depends, primarily, upon security and seniority. More generally, the facility agreement bears significantly on the prospects of loss, should default occur. The loss given default expectation is, then, highly facility dependent. Although, loss given default is an important source of uncertainty in lending, the dominant source of uncertainty, and thereby risk, is the default probability itself. This chapter will focus on measurement of the probability of default.

The anticipation of default by KMV's models is expressed as a probability distribution. The distribution has expected and unexpected parameters (or mean and standard deviation, in the parlance of conventional statistics). The role of loss given default is to transform the default distribution into a loss distribution, or "loss function."

The principal challenge of lenders is to characterize, ex ante, the default distribution of each borrower and then to follow the dynamic evolution of the default distribution—to monitor for quality degradation. Three primary sources have input to this process: (1) subjective appraisals; (2) financial statement data; (3) market prices of the borrower's debt and equity.

In the old days, subjective appraisals dominated the means of discrimination among borrowers. Serious financial statement analysis had to await the development of auditing, computers, and models, all quite recent developments. Market prices, as inputs to the process, are only now entering the practice of default measurement. So, the question of the incremental benefit from market prices requires demonstration.

Market prices do not fit readily into ad hoc models of default prediction that have been trained on financial statement data. One reason is that financial accounting has not evolved into a coherent conceptual picture of the economics of a firm, especially when distress threatens default. Indeed, uncertainty is not even definable in the prevailing financial accounting paradigm.

Market prices are formed by investors in anticipation of a firm's future cash flows. The present value of cash flows, the price, is obtained by discounting for the uncertainty of the cash flows. Thus, market prices have a measure of uncertainty embedded in them. (By contrast, financial statements are an agglomeration of past transactions; they contain no embedded discount rate). But, the discount rate embedded in an issuer's stock price is not directly applicable to the same issuer's bonds. Debt is a prior claim, relative to equity, on the cash flows generated by the firm's assets. Accordingly, the appropriate discount rate is systematically lower for debt.

In sum, the most accurate measurement of default probabilities requires the use of prices, equity prices most particularly. KMV has evolved a conceptually appealing model that uses equity prices when available, and otherwise just financial statements. This covers all the bases: publicly traded firms and privates as well.

A MARKET-BASED MEASURE OF DEFAULT RISK

Expected default frequency, EDF, from KMV's Credit Monitor system, is a measure of the probability that default could occur over the ensuing year (or other time horizon, out to five years, specified by the user). Default is the event of a borrower missing any scheduled payment.

EDF is different from expected loss. The expected loss is the EDF times the loss given default. Default is a characteristic of the borrower. Loss given default is a characteristic of the borrowing facility.

EDF contains information extracted from market prices, plus financial statement data. That is, EDF depends upon the behavior of the price of the borrower's common stock.

KMV's conceptual model advances an explicit causative condition of default. It says, in effect, that *borrowers default when their available resources have been depleted below a critical level.* The task is to find the causative links between measures of *resources, depleted,* and *when.* As evolved, EDF requires four critical variables:

1. Market value of assets.
2. Volatility of future asset values.
3. "Shape" of the distribution of future asset values.
4. Face value of obligations requiring servicing.

Figure 5–1 depicts the relationships among the model's variables (there are actually six of them, but the asset growth rate, variable 5, holds little discriminating power; and the time horizon, vari-

F I G U R E   5–1

Relationships among the Model's Variables

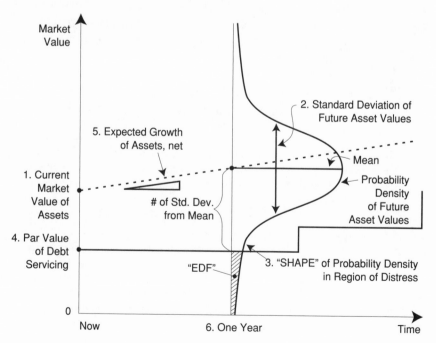

able 6, can be specified by the analyst). The variables have a causative relationship with each other, shown in the graph. The trade-off among all variables can be readily estimated, unlike ad hoc models that lack causative specification.

We obtain an estimate of the market value of assets, *variable 1*, by adding up the estimated market value of all liabilities, including equity. For publicly traded firms, we observe the equity's market value. Unfortunately, few firms with publicly traded equity have traded debt. For those that do, timely quotes are difficult to obtain. Instead, an alternative approach is adopted:

> The riskiness of equity results, necessarily, from the firm's underlying assets and its leverage. By the application of derivative asset pricing theory (a generalization of the options pricing theory of Black, Scholes, and Merton), empirically observed equity riskiness can be decomposed into its constituent asset risk and leverage components. That is, when we estimate the riskiness of debt and know its par value, we can deduce its market value. The riskier the equity, the lower the market value of the debt in relation to its par value.

From this methodology, an estimate of asset risk falls out. It is widely known that stock prices reflect the riskiness of the issuer's equity. The options approach to interpreting stock prices, by carving away the effect of leverage, makes it possible to measure the issuer's underlying asset riskiness, *variable 2*.

Variable 3, the shape of the distribution of future asset values is difficult to measure. Moreover, it cannot be assumed. For default measurement, the likelihood of large negative events is critical.

> We obtain the "shape" of distribution of asset returns in the region of distress from data on historical default and bankruptcy frequencies. Our measurements, from over 1,200 incidents of default or bankruptcy, reveal that distress is considerably more likely than from an assumption of normal density (i.e., that a "log normal" process is generating the cash flows). With historical data, we are able to estimate the probability density in the region of distress quite accurately. See Figure 5–2 for the default incidence we have discovered, shown quarterly, since 1973.

Unlike agency ratings, the time horizon used by EDF is explicit. It needs to be specified by the user. For use in early warning, we set the time horizon to one year, across all firms. Indeed, Credit

F I G U R E   5–2

Bankruptcies and Defaults (quarterly, 1973 to 1992)

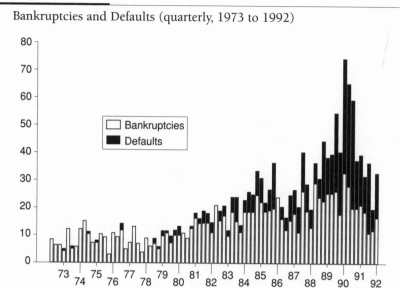

Source: KMV Default Database

Monitor displays one-year EDFs. In pricing a particular exposure, the requisite EDF should correspond to the exposure's tenor.

The face value of debt requiring servicing, *variable 4*, also depends on the choice of horizon. At one year, the requisite quantity is, by accounting definition, the observable level of current liabilities. At a longer horizon, we cumulate the debt servicing requirement to that horizon. For example, as the date a balloon payment on a term loan approaches, the EDF rises. If successfully refinanced with another term loan, the EDF falls. Thus, over a series of years going forward, the EDFs display a pattern that reflects the timetable of debt coming due (as well as asset riskiness and leverage.)

The model's parameters are combined by arithmetic, not regression. The probability of default, EDF, is the shaded area in Figure 5–1. Thus, unlike an ad hoc model, there is a causative structure underlying EDF. And, it is simple. The implementation problem lies in accurate determination of the model's four key parameters. The quality of the implementation is reflected in the model's default prediction "power," namely, the ability ex ante to discriminate between good and bad loans.

OBTAINING DISCRIMINATING "NUMBERS"

Assessment of Predictive Power

What do we mean by predictive power? Here, as usual, we have both a theoretical problem and an empirical one.

Consider a policy of never lending to firms below a rating of, for instance, B–. There is opportunity cost, however, in not lending to firms excluded by that policy that do not default. Thus, the ratio of defaults avoided to opportunity cost incurred is one theoretical approach to measuring default predictive power of these models.

KMV has collected an extensive library on defaulted companies. We have analyzed over 1,200 companies that have defaulted or entered bankruptcy. These defaults occurred in a population of some 60,000 company-years with data in Compustat. About 200 of the defaulting firms were rated, or nearly 2 percent of the subpopulation of 10,000 rated company-years. With this data we can test the predictive power of various models.

Figure 5–3 displays five years of monthly EDFs prior to the dates of default for over 1,200 companies, nonrated and rated.

FIGURE 5–3

EDF Prior to Default (rated and unrated)

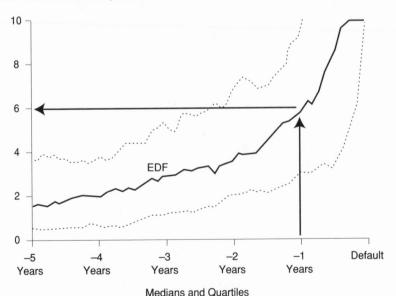

Medians and Quartiles

Default dates are aligned at the right. The number on the vertical scale, on the left, is the probability of default, EDF.

The level of EDFs is sloping upward, toward progressively higher default likelihood, as the date of default draws closer. The steepness of the slope sharpens as the date of default approaches. The median company's EDF one year prior to default, from Figure 5–3, is nearly 6 percent. This contrasts with the lowest S&P rated companies, CCC–, whose median EDF is about 4 percent. Concurrently, the median company in the whole population of defaulters and nondefaulters, taken together, has an EDF around 1.5 percent.

The subset of defaulting companies from Figure 5–3 that had agency ratings is plotted in Figure 5–4. Only about 15 percent of the entire nonfinancial U.S. population has ratings. This group has several striking features:

- The median EDF for defaulting firms that were rated reached 2 percent nearly three years before default occurred. The median rating only reached that level of probability (BB–/CCC+) a couple of months prior to default. This sug-

F I G U R E   5–4

Rating Prior to Default (rated companies only)

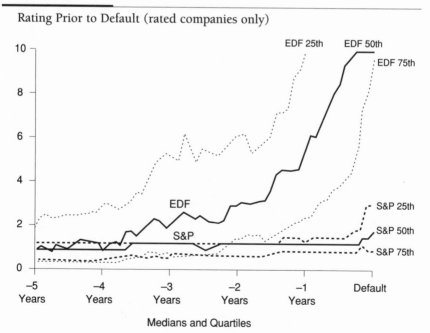

Medians and Quartiles

gests a median lead time of EDFs over S&P ratings approach-
ing three years.

- Median values show a *fivefold* difference in default probability between EDFs and S&P's ratings one year prior to default.
- By two years prior to default, the 75th percentile EDF (the
  highest quality quartile of defaulting firms) crossed over the
  25th percentile S&P rating (the lowest quality quartile of the
  defaulting firms). Thus, two years prior to default, the distribution of EDFs only overlaps with S&P ratings by 25 percent.

EDF has considerable sensitivity below 0.2 percent, as well. That
is, the preceding may, incorrectly, suggest that because EDF is sensitive at the high-distress end of the scale, it may not perform as well
among the highest quality firms. Figure 5–5, generated by Credit
Monitor, provides the IBM anecdote, and this picture is not atypical.

FIGURE   5–5

International Business Machines

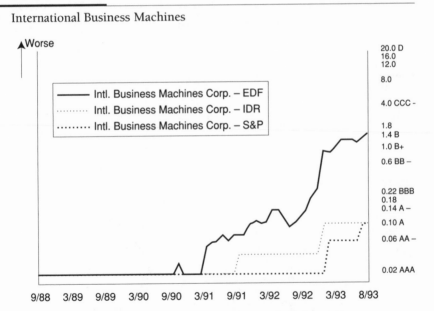

9/88   3/89   9/89   3/90   9/90   3/91   9/91   3/92   9/92   3/93   8/93

Key: The darkest and most volatile line is EDF. The intermediate line
       is KMV's rating analogue regression model, IDR. The lowest line,
       dashes, is S&P's rating

As of August 31, 1993, KMV's EDF had IBM at 158 bp, (single B).
This compares to Compaq at 35 bp, up from 28 bp on 12/31/92
and Apple at 153 bp, up from 16 on 12/31/92.

EDF "kicked up" to a probability level not reached by S&P until nearly two years later. Interestingly, IBM's quality has rapidly declined to
the point where it is riskier than the median, the 50th percentile company in the entire U.S. population. In February 1991, IBM was at the
99.99th percentile; no companies were higher in quality.

Default expectations vary considerably through time. Figure
5–6, generated by Credit Monitor, displays this variation. The median company, at the peak of the credit cycle (January 1991) had an
EDF of 2.3 percent. At the prior cycle trough (August 1989), the median low was 1.2 percent, 110 basis points lower in default probability.
By May 1993, the median company's EDF had returned, coinciden-
tally, to 1.2 percent.

It should be apparent that default estimates that are mid–credit-
cycle averages are of limited value. Pricing and portfolio management
models require default estimates that are credit-cycle sensitive.
Otherwise, originators would be overcharging at credit-cycle lows and
undercharging at cycle highs. Restated, an originator will be at a significant disadvantage to a competitor with a cycle-sensitive pricing model.

FIGURE 5–6

U.S. Population—Median

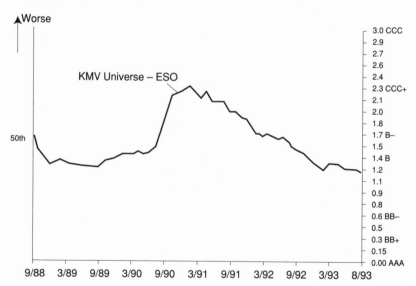

Note: Horizontal axis 60 months to 8/93; vertical axis 0–3, linear scale.

In sum, EDF can be effectively employed as a lending policy threshold, in early warning, in pricing, and in portfolio management models. It is consistently better than S&P ratings in discrimination and lead time. And the difficult task of adjusting ordinal default ranks to the period of the credit cycle is not left entirely to the intuition of the user.

Next, we address the opportunity cost. What is the frequency distribution of firms that did not default when their measured EDFs reached a given level?

We form the ratio of defaults avoided at each policy cut-off (discussed earlier in this section) to its corresponding opportunity cost. Dubbed "power curves," the ratio is plotted from the lowest quality end of the spectrum to the highest. This contrasts EDFs to ratings in both relevant dimensions. EDF remains the winner, as we see in Figure 5–7.

A simple measure of superiority of EDF cannot be easily summarized in a single metric. First, defaults avoided and opportunity cost are not of equal importance. Second, it is easier to act on a declining quality AA than a single-B: AAs can be refinanced far more readily than single-Bs.

F I G U R E   5–7

Default Predictive Power—EDF and S&P Rating (S&P Rated Universe)

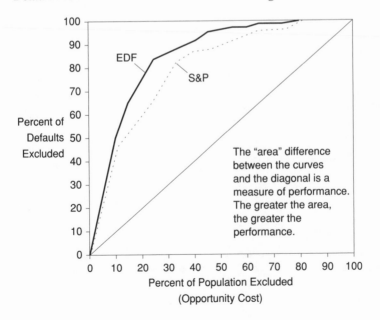

Ordinal versus Cardinal

Most conventional credit analysis sorts companies into an ordinal default rank. For both valuation and portfolio analysis, however, we require cardinal numbers, that is, real numbers, not letters without inherent numerical meaning. We need to know more than that a company is, for example, a BBB+. We need to know that its default probability is, say, 28 basis points at the one-year horizon. The first step in obtaining this linkage from ordinal to cardinal, derives from KMV's empirical analysis of historical default frequencies. Still, empirical analysis alone will not suffice. That is, setting the price for an exposure based on the average value during the credit cycle is not adequate.

Figure 5–8 displays the rise and fall of S&P's BBBs over the past five years, as measured by Credit Monitor. The three broken lines are, from top to bottom, the 25th, 50th, and 75th percentiles in the cross-section of companies rated BBB by S&P. The vertical scale is the default probability, linearly scaled. As of August 1993, 205 companies had BBB ratings, including both the pluses and minuses. The 50th percentile, the median, has varied from 43 to 13 basis points

F I G U R E   5–8

S&P BBB Rating

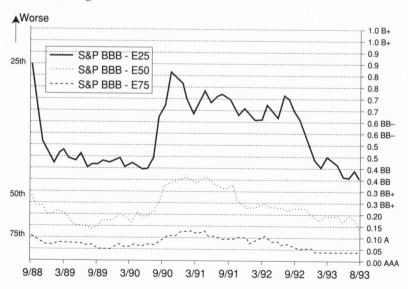

Note: Horizontal axis 60 months to 8/93; vertical axis 0–1, linear scale.

over the last five years. This implies that the compensatory spread for the median BBB should have nearly tripled from trough to peak of the credit cycle.

In other words, not only do pricing and portfolio models require cardinal numbers, they also need to be cycle adjusted. The importance of adapting pricing to the credit cycle is difficult to overemphasize.

The overall credit cycle in the United States (or anywhere) is not easily measured. Credit Monitor, however, obtains an excellent "picture" of it by aggregation of all publicly traded firms in the population. That is, without imposing any macrostructure, Figure 5–9 displays the waxing and waning of the cycle in the United States, as a whole. Contrast this picture with that of Sweden in Figure 5–10, which is, these days, immersed in a very serious credit crunch. (Note the differences in horizontal scales.)

FIGURE   5–9

U.S. Population

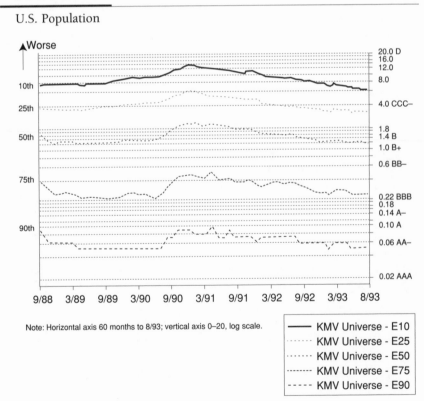

Note: Horizontal axis 60 months to 8/93; vertical axis 0–20, log scale.

———— KMV Universe - E10
······ KMV Universe - E25
······ KMV Universe - E50
------- KMV Universe - E75
- - - - KMV Universe - E90

FIGURE 5–10

Population—Sweden

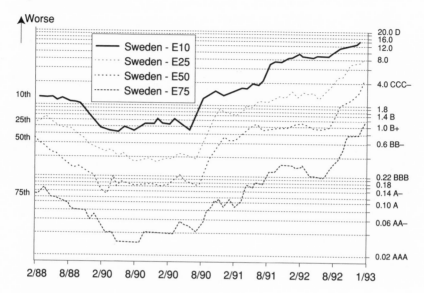

Note: Horizontal axis 60 months to 1/93; vertical axis 0–20, log scale.

To emphasize the point, Figure 5–11 displays only the 10th percentile, toward the worst end of the spectrum in the United States, on a linear scale (versus the natural log in Figures 5–9 and 5–10). From the peak of 1,350 basis points of default probability, the recent level of 600 basis points represents a whopping decline! Thus, from the perspective of EDF, the credit dimension of the economy has been improving since early in 1991.

Credit Monitor's EDFs are cardinal. KMV makes use of this feature to rescale the private-firm model quarterly. Credit Monitor, also, inherently takes the credit cycle into account. Accordingly, the output from KMV's default models, both public and private, can be used directly in valuation and portfolio analyses.

Figure 5–8 also reveals another important message about BBBs. The 25th percentile (the top line in the figure) EDF reached a high of 87 basis points during the last five years. The low of the 75th percentile (lowest line) EDF during the five years was six basis points. In other words, there is enormous variation in EDFs among BBBs.

FIGURE 5-11

U.S. Population—10th Percentile

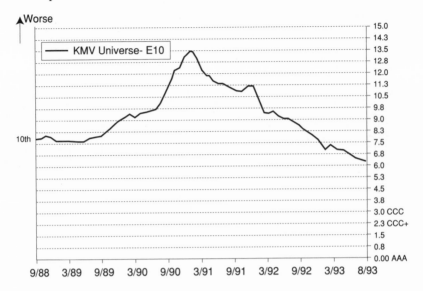

Note: Horizontal axis 60 months to 8/93; vertical axis 0–15, linear scale.

The horizontal lines in Figure 5–12 (under the broken lines connecting squares) span the 5th to the 95th percentiles for BBBs as of July 1992. From the perspective of EDF, BBBs are highly variegated.

From the perspective of EDF, the AAAs of Figure 5–12 are clearly separated from BBBs. The small triangle of dots at the far left does not overlap BBBs. Similarly, CCCs, the very flat triangle to the far right, are almost distinct from BBBs. All other rating classes are overlapped. That is, a single-A is about as likely to be a BBB or a AA as it is a single-A. AAAs, BBBs, and CCCs are nearly unambiguous. The in-between classes are "fuzzy."

S&P offers 19 different gradations, including the pluses and minuses. S&P's precision could be, therefore, no greater than 1 in 19. As suggested above, there appears to be evidence for only three unambiguous clusters. We suspect that the resolution of EDFs may be nearer 1 in 100. Banks, typically, use fewer than 10 gradations, of which 3 may be nonperforming. Most important, both S&P and EDF are considerably more discriminating than most bank-grading systems.

FIGURE 5–12

Frequency Distribution of EDFs by Debt Rating Category

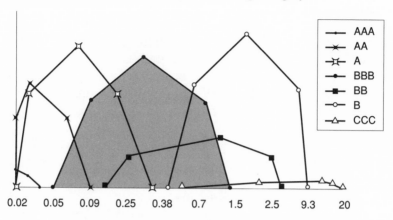

—•—	AAA
—✕—	AA
—✕—	A
—•—	BBB
—■—	BB
—○—	B
—△—	CCC

0.02   0.05   0.09   0.25   0.38   0.7   1.5   2.5   9.3   20

The "Freshness" of Default Estimates

From the perspective of predictive power, EDF is a technological advance. When the economics of acquiring EDFs is considered, the margin of value added increases further. Very important, EDFs can be reestimated frequently and inexpensively. Indeed, EDF technology makes explicit debt portfolio management feasible. Previously, it could require a calendar quarter to revise all default estimates in a bank's portfolio. With EDFs, it is feasible to reform the input requirements for a portfolio management model every day. Default estimation is required for valuation—establishing the economic price of the credit.

The frequency with which default estimates can be revised for either use depends upon (1) the frequency with which data is refreshed, (2) the feasibility of obtaining data, and (3) the time and cost required to produce the estimates.

Statement data on publicly traded firms are refreshed quarterly in the United States. In some cases, private-firm statements can be refreshed monthly. However, for private firms, no market prices can be observed. Information from statements is the only source for estimating the conceptual model's variables.

By contrast, share prices are refreshed with every recorded trade and are observable a few seconds later. Since prices are inherently ex ante, they require no pro forma adjustments. Thus, prices can be entered into Credit Monitor, and a few milliseconds later, a refreshed EDF emerges. EDFs on all publicly traded firms can be reestimated every few minutes, if need be. There are more than 12,000 publicly traded firms in the major Western trading nations (all of which KMV will soon be covering). These firms may account for three-quarters of all corporate productivity in these nations, and a considerably larger fraction of corporate borrowings.

Compared with pro formas of human origin, EDFs are inexpensive to obtain. It is expensive to recast pro formas for every portfolio exposure even quarterly, setting aside the issue of discriminating power. If portfolio analysis is to be conducted frequently enough to be of value, perhaps weekly, then the principal estimation burden must rest with models, not humans.

Thus, estimators of default based on market price are valuable for three reasons: discriminating power, freshness, and cost. This conclusion stops short, however, of the desired result. How can companies without traded equity be analyzed? The preceding analysis suggests our direction: We bring these companies into the same conceptual context as the public companies.

PRIVATE BORROWERS

Credit management in banks entails dealing with both privates and publics. Private firms default for the same reasons as public firms. Their default risk can be understood in precisely the same conceptual context as public companies. In other words, the problem in analyzing a private company is how to determine the variables described previously (asset market value, asset risk, level of obligations) without stock prices.

The problem can be viewed from an alternative perspective. Any method for measuring default risk can be distilled down to information about these three variables. If a method works, it is because it tells us something about asset risk, asset value, or the level of obligations.

Pursuing this line of research has led to the *private firm model*. The model estimates the firm's equity value and risk, from statement data, and then transforms them into asset value and risk. Obligations are determined in the usual way directly from financial statement items, starting with current liabilities in the instance of the one-year horizon.

Most important, the model's predictive power is already impressive. Figure 5–13 compares the default predictive power of a private-firm model with that of the public-company model in Credit Monitor. It displays admirable discriminating power, despite the lack of market data.

KMV has developed a number of models for rating private companies, including ad hoc fitted models similar to popular existing approaches. These have been used as "race horses" to provide competition for the private-firm model during the development process.

The extra default prediction power of the public-company model comes from having the actual equity valuation. Alas, there is no good substitute for knowing equity prices. Fortunately for the evaluation of private companies, equity risk, which plays a central role in the analysis, can be estimated quite well from statement data alone.

Whereas the shape of the asset value distribution (variable 3 in Figure 5–1) can be measured for public companies, no such data exist for privates. The model uses for privates the same function derived from public company experience. This is one illustration of the benefit of treating private companies commensurately with publics. Another is that Credit Monitor can be used to periodically recalibrate the private-firm model's ordinal ranks into cardinal numbers.

Another benefit is that the estimated private company model provides a point of departure for analyzing the effect of capital

FIGURE   5–13

Default Predictive Power—EDF, Private versus Public
(total universe 1979–1992)

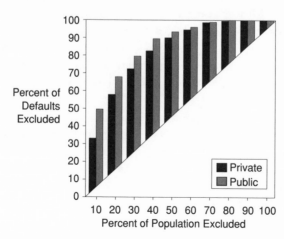

structure changes. Because the basic framework is causal, rather than fitted, it can be used credibly to assess the result of divestitures, recapitalizations, and so forth.

In sum, the private-firm model represents an analytically coherent model of default risk with substantial default prediction power, even by comparison with the public-company model. It is a means for integrating the risk assessment of private and public companies within a debt portfolio.

A POSTSCRIPT

The point of departure for this chapter is that market-based, timely, and powerful default-risk assessment is critical to economic lending. The chapter, then, describes KMV's conceptual approach to measuring default probabilities and its implementation in practice to both public and private companies. It emphasizes the need for cardinal versus ordinal risk-measures. It also discusses the need for a fast, efficient, and broad-scale measure in order to be applicable to *monitoring and managing loan portfolios.*

Why should we be concerned about the application of a measurement tool to loan portfolios? There is increasing awareness that the real issue in front of lenders, both bank and nonbank, is portfolio management. Valuation is important. Diversification is important. However, the only context in which they become actionable is that of a specific portfolio: how much to hold, how much to sell, how much to buy . . . while getting the price right.

The requirements for portfolio analysis go beyond default risk estimation alone. The relationship between default risks must also be measured—we must provide loss correlations. The technology that has been discussed here is ultimately of little use if it does not lend itself to the determination of correlations as well. In fact, this technology provides a means, perhaps the only feasible means, for determining loss correlations.

The riskiness of bank portfolios has never been appreciated more than it is today. The way to manage that risk lies in maximizing diversification relative to return opportunities. The default risk measurement techniques developed at KMV provide a path towards that objective.

THE INSTRUMENTS

⑥ CALCULATING AVERAGE LIFE FOR BONDS WITH EMBEDDED OPTIONS

Gunnar Klinkhammer
Vice President, Quantitative Research
Capital Management Sciences, Los Angeles

Robert Navin[1]
Quantitative Research
SBC Warburg Inc., Chicago

Barry Ryan[2]
Asset Trading Group
Nomura International PLC, London

Many securities have embedded options that allow the option holder to choose when to exercise the option. The valuation of such securities is well understood. Assuming the model contains all the economic variables that affect the option holder's exercise decision, the security's fair price must be based on an optimal exercise policy. An exercise policy states the time of exercise for each possible path the underlying economic variables may take between the valuation date and the expiration of the option. An exercise policy is called optimal if it maximizes the present value of the option.

Efficient algorithms exist to compute the fair price based on an optimal exercise policy. For example, in the case of a bond with an embedded American call, a modified partial differential equation

---

1 Robert Navin was consultant to Capital Management Sciences, Los Angeles, when the research described in this chapter was conducted.
2 Barry Ryan was vice president, quantitative research, at Capital Management Sciences when the research described in this chapter was conducted.

(PDE) approach can be invoked if a stochastic interest-rate process has been specified. Oddly, the implementation of these algorithms does not require the explicit calculation of the *expected time of exercise*—the time at which, on average, we expect the option to be exercised. Neither do we have to compute an explicit measure of the uncertainty of the time of exercise—the amount by which it may vary depending on the development of the underlying economic variables.[3] Nevertheless, knowledge of the expected time of exercise and its variance can be useful for structuring, trading, and investing in securities with embedded options. In this chapter, therefore, we show that the PDE-based algorithm for the fair price of a bond with an imbedded American call can be easily modified to compute the expected time of exercise (and its variance), and thus the average life of the bond. The algorithm we discuss is applicable to a wide variety of bonds with embedded options. In particular, it allows the computation of the average life of a step-up note, which is a bond whose coupon rate will increase on each of a sequence of dates unless the issuer calls the bond on that date.

In the first section we review the PDE-based formalism that allows the computation of the fair price of a bond with embedded options. As a concrete example, we show the resulting algorithm for a bond with an embedded American call, assuming a one-factor interest rate model. In the second section we introduce the adapted formalism for the computation of the expected time of exercise and its variance. We emphasize that while the computation of the fair price can be based on a risk-neutral approach, the estimation of the time at which an option will be exercised in the real world must incorporate the risk premium investors require when they invest in longer-dated cash flows. We illustrate this point with a one-factor interest rate model. In the third section, we demonstrate that our formalism can be modified to calculate expected values (and variances) of other quantities that are of interest in the analysis of derivative securities. We use the example of the number of caplets in a cap that are expected to be in the money. The third section also suggests a numerical study of the average life of step-up notes.

---

3 One of the authors (G. Klinkhammer) thanks D. Davis (formerly at Prudential Securities, Los Angeles) for emphasizing the importance of computing the variance of the time of exercise.

REVIEW OF THE VALUATION OF BONDS WITH EMBEDDED OPTIONS

The Partial Differential Equation for Bond Prices

The valuation of any security is based on the economic variables that determine the return offered by the security. In the case of a bond, the price movements of default-free, liquidly traded bonds (i.e., Treasury bonds) obviously affect the return from holding the bond. We can standardize quotation of these prices by converting them to a zero-coupon basis, in other words, by introducing the family of zero-coupon bond prices $P_T(t)$, where t denotes the pricing date and T denotes the time at which \$1 is to be received without default. The zero-coupon bond prices can be modeled to follow a stochastic process, possibly driven by several Brownian motions z_i (which we may assume to be uncorrelated with each other):

$$dP_T(t) = P_T(t)\left(\mu_T dt + \sigma_T^{(1)} dz_1 + \ldots + \sigma_T^{(n)} dz_n\right). \tag{1}$$

Specifying how the drift rates μ_T and the diffusion rates $\sigma_T^{(i)}$ depend on the time t and the price family $P_T(t)$ amounts to specifying an n-factor interest model.

If the returns from a given bond are indeed driven by the zero-coupon bond prices $P_T(t)$ only, then the bond is effectively a derivative of Treasury bonds, and the fair price P of the bond depends on the $P_T(t)$ in a way that must satisfy a partial differential equation quite like the *Black-Scholes equation* that governs how the price of an equity derivative depends on the price of the underlying stock. For the purpose of deriving this partial differential equation, it is convenient to transform the price process (1) into an interest rate process by writing

$$P_T(t) = \exp\left[-\int_t^T r_s(t) ds\right],$$

where $r_s(t)$ is the forward instantaneous rate implied at time t for time s.[4] We obtain a resulting interest rate process

---

4 For a review of the relation between zero-coupon bond price processes and interest rate processes, see the appendix to O. Cheyette, "Term Structure Dynamics and Mortgage Valuation," *Journal of Fixed Income*, March 1992, pp. 28–41.

$$dr_T(t) = v_T dt + \rho_T^{(1)} dz_1 + \ldots + \rho_T^{(n)} dz_n. \tag{2}$$

Although it appears that we have to keep track of the forward rates for all maturities T, our approach implies that there are really only n underlying economic variables. For a simple one-factor model ($n = 1$), we can identify this one factor with the short rate $r(t) \equiv r_t(t)$ and obtain a short-rate process:

$$dr = v dt + \rho dz. \tag{3}$$

Investors will require a higher expected return when they hold longer-maturity bonds because of the greater price risk they incur. It is natural, therefore, to model the drift rate of the zero-coupon-bond price process (1) to exceed the risk-free short rate

$$\mu_T = r + \lambda_1 \sigma_T^{(1)} + \ldots + \lambda_n \sigma_T^{(n)}, \tag{4}$$

where a risk premium λ_i is associated with each of the n factors. It is obvious that the risk premiums will also be reflected in the drift rate v_T of the interest rate process (2). For simplicity, we shall assume that the risk premium for the short-rate process (3) is a constant, λ, and write v_λ for v to show the dependence of the drift rate on the risk premium.

We are now in a position to write down the partial differential equation that governs the price P of a bond with cash-flow-rate C:

$$\left(\partial_t + v_{\lambda=0} \partial_r + \frac{\rho^2}{2} \partial_r^2 \right) P + C = rP, \tag{5}$$

where $v_{\lambda=0}$ is the risk-neutral drift of the short rate, corresponding to a world in which investors require no risk premium for holding longer-maturity bonds, that is, where $\mu_T = r(t)$ for all T. As Black and Scholes argued, a derivative can be priced correctly if the expected return of the underlying asset is assumed to be the risk-free short rate and the returns from the derivative are discounted at risk-free rates. In fact, based on the idea of risk-neutral valuation, we can interpret the PDE (5) in a very intuitive way. The first three terms of the left-hand side describe the price return from [in the same order as in (5)] the explicit time dependence of the bond price, the dependence on the short rate, which in turn is expected to drift at its risk-neutral rate, and the additional drift caused by the volatility of the short rate in conjunction with the nonlinearity ("convexity") of the relation between the bond price and the short rate. With the cash-flow rate added, the left-hand side represents the expected total return from holding the bond. This is then equated to the risk-free short rate times the price of the bond, as is appropriate in a risk-neutral world.

Although we have motivated equation (5) through its analogy with the Black-Scholes equation for equity derivatives, we shall interpret it now on the basis of the *transition probabilities* associated with the risk-neutral version of the short-rate process (3). This will greatly help our intuition when deriving a partial differential equation for the expected time of exercise for embedded options. The process (3) assigns probabilities to paths of the short-rate. In particular, it determines the conditional probability that the short rate will be r' at time t' if it was r at an earlier time t. This probability is called the Green function of the short rate process and denoted by $G(r, t; r', t')$. It turns out that the process (3) forces the Green function to satisfy a partial differential equation, the "backward Kolmogoroff equation"

$$\left(\partial_t + v_\lambda \partial_r + \frac{\rho^2}{2} \partial_r^2 \right) G(r,t;r',t') = 0, \tag{6}$$

subject to the initial condition $G(r, t; r', t) = \delta(r - r')$.

Comparison of the backward Kolmogoroff equation with (5) shows that the bond-price evolution is driven by the risk-neutral transition probabilities of the short rate. To make this more concrete, let us imagine that we know the bond price $P(r, t)$ at some time t for all levels of the short-rate r. (If t happens to be the maturity of the bond, the price equals the face amount and is in fact independent of r.) We would like to use this information as a boundary condition in solving (5) to find the price at an earlier time $t - \Delta t$. If Δt is small enough, we can approximate

$$P(r, t - \Delta t) \approx \frac{1}{1 + r \Delta t} \int G_{\lambda=0}(r, t - \Delta t; r', t) P(r', t) dr', \tag{7}$$

where $G_{\lambda=0}$ solves (6) for $\lambda = 0$. (We have assumed that no cash flows occur on or between the points $t - \Delta t$ and t.) This demonstrates that the price at $t - \Delta t$ is equal to the discounted expected price at t. Here, the expected price at t is obtained by summing the transition probability-weighted price at t over all possible levels of the short rate.

An example of a one-factor interest rate model is the Hull & White model with constant mean reversion.[5] It can be derived from the zero-coupon bond price process

---

5 J. Hull and A. White, "Pricing Interest Rate Derivative Securities," *Review of Financial Studies* 3, no. 4 (1990), pp. 573–92.

$$dP_T(t) = P_T(t)\left\{[r(t) + \lambda\sigma_T(t)]dt + \sigma_T(t)dz\right\}, \tag{8}$$

where $\sigma_T(t) = \sigma\tau(1 - e^{-(T-t)/\tau})$. The meaning of the constants σ and τ becomes clear when we consider the corresponding short-rate process

$$d[r(t) - r_t(0)] = \left\{-\frac{1}{\tau}[r(t) - r_t(0)] + w^2(t) - \lambda\sigma\right\}dt + \sigma dz, \tag{9}$$

where $w^2(t) = (\sigma^2\tau/2)(1 - e^{-2t/\tau})$. The process (9) shows that σ is the diffusion rate of the short rate, and τ is the mean reversion time scale that indicates how quickly the short rate reverts to the forward curve $r_t(0)$ implied by today's zero-coupon bond prices $P_T(0)$. Setting $r_t'(0) \equiv dr_t(0)/dt$ and $\lambda = 0$, we obtain the partial differential equation for bond prices

$$\left(\partial_t + \left\{r_t'(0) + w^2(t) - \frac{1}{\tau}[r(t) - r_t(0)]\right\}\partial_r + \frac{\sigma^2}{2}\partial_r^2\right)P + C = rP. \tag{10}$$

Bonds with Embedded Options

When a bond contains an embedded option, the bond's fair price must be based on the assumption that the holder of the option will follow an optimal exercise policy. If the holder has a choice as to when to exercise the option, an optimal policy states, loosely speaking, that exercise will occur when for the first time the expected return from holding the option fails to be commensurate with the risk incurred in holding the option. It may at first sight appear difficult to incorporate this prescription into the valuation formalism above. We will use the example of a bond that is continuously callable at a (possibly time-dependent) call price K to illustrate that the PDE-based formalism introduced above can be easily modified to accommodate an optimal exercise policy. Indeed, the fair price P of such a bond must satisfy the conditions

$$\left(\partial_t + v_{\lambda=0}\partial_r + \frac{\rho^2}{2}\partial_r^2\right)P + C \geq rP; \tag{11}$$

$$K \geq P; \tag{12}$$

$$(K - P)\left[\left(\partial_t + v_{\lambda=0}\partial_r + \frac{\rho^2}{2}\partial_r^2 - r\right)P + C\right] = 0.\qquad(13)$$

Condition (12) states that the price of the bond cannot exceed the call price since the issuer of the bond would otherwise exercise the call, reaping an immediate arbitrage profit. Condition (11) is the familiar partial differential equation (5) as long as equality holds. When it becomes an inequality, the expected return from owning the bond (in the risk-neutral world) exceeds the short rate. In that case, condition (13) demands that the bond price equal the call price because the issuer is expected to call the bond immediately.

Implementation of these conditions into an algorithm is straightforward. We start with the known bond price at the time of maturity T. Then we solve the partial differential equation (5), ignoring the possibility of a call, to obtain a "preliminary" price at time $T - \Delta t$, where Δt is a small time step. Now we compare this preliminary price with the call price that is in effect at time $T - \Delta t$. For those levels of the short rate where the preliminary price exceeds the call price, we must replace the preliminary price by the call price. For all other short-rate levels, we leave the preliminary price unchanged. Thus, we have obtained the "price curve" $P(r, T - \Delta t)$ for all levels of the short rate r. This price curve serves as a boundary condition as we go back to, say, $T - 2\Delta t$, repeating the same steps. Going back enough time steps in this manner, we eventually obtain the price curve for the desired valuation date.

It is obvious that similar algorithms can be constructed for bonds with more than one embedded option. Furthermore, the cash-flow-rate C need not be based on a constant coupon rate. The coupon rate may change according to a deterministic schedule, as in a step-up note. The coupon may even reset based on interest rates as of each coupon date, possibly constrained by a lifetime cap and a floor. Only if the coupon rate is path-dependent, due to a reset cap or to resets that are less frequent than the coupon dates, do we have to extend the formalism by introducing the coupon rate as a second dynamic variable, next to the short rate. Finally, in addition to being time-dependent, the call price can also be allowed to depend on interest rates as of each call date. This is the case in so-called yield maintenance bonds.

CALCULATION OF THE EXPECTED TIME
OF OPTION EXERCISE

A First Approach

Although the algorithm for pricing option-embedded bonds described in the previous section hinges on the concept of an optimal exercise policy, it does not explicitly calculate the expected time of exercise as of the pricing date. By this we mean the following. As of the pricing date, the interest rate model, fitted to the current yield curve and suitable volatility assumptions, assigns a probability to every possible path interest rates may take between the pricing date and the bond's maturity. For some of the paths, there will be a time before maturity when it is optimal for the option holder to exercise, because holding the option longer would result in an inadequate expected return. For other paths, it will never be optimal to exercise the option. For these paths, we may consider that the option is exercised at maturity, albeit without any benefit. (We have in mind a call price schedule that converges to par value at maturity.) Weighting the optimal exercise time for each interest rate path by the path's probability and summing over all interest rate paths, we obtain the expected time of exercise. In the case of a callable bond, the expected time of exercise determines the expected life of the bond.

We proceed by discussing an obvious way to compute the expected time of exercise for a continuously callable bond. As we proceed with the algorithm described in the previous section, we find at each time-step t a critical level for the short-rate $\bar{r}(t)$ such that the bond price $P(r, t)$ is modeled to equal the call price $K(t)$ for all levels of the short rate below $\bar{r}(t)$ and to be less than $K(t)$ for all levels above $\bar{r}(t)$. Thus, we trace out the boundary that separates the region where it is optimal to exercise the call from the one where it is optimal to hold the call. This boundary is often called the *optimal exercise boundary*, and the two regions in the space formed by interest rates and time are often called the *exercise region* and the *continuation region*, respectively. In keeping with our definition of the expected time of exercise, we consider any point beyond maturity to be part of the exercise region. The task at hand, then, is to compute the average time when an interest path first intersects the exercise boundary (the *first passage time*), given that interest rates start from their known values at time 0, or, today (see Figure 6–1).

F I G U R E   6–1

Along path 1, optimal exercise occurs at time t_1. Along path 2, the option is never exercised.

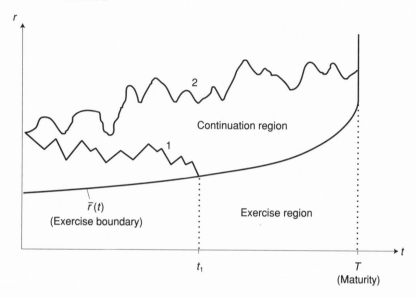

If we can compute the probability $p(t)$ that the path of the short rate does not intersect the exercise boundary between time 0 and time t then the expected time of exercise Θ is given by

$$\Theta = \int_0^T p(t)dt \,. \tag{14}$$

But $p(t)$ follows from the conditional probability $\overline{G}(r,t;r',t')$ that the short rate will be r' at time t' if it was r at an earlier time t and did not intersect the exercise boundary between t and t':

$$p(t) = \int_{\bar{r}(t)} \overline{G}(r(0),0;r,t)dr. \tag{15}$$

The special Green function $\overline{G}$ satisfies the backward Kolmogoroff equation, but is subject to the boundary condition $\overline{G}(r,t;r',t') = 0$ whenever $r' \leq \bar{r}(t')$; in other words, it must be zero whenever the short rate ends up on or below the exercise boundary. One could numerically solve the backward Kolmogoroff equation with this boundary condition and the initial condition $\overline{G}(r,t;r',t) = \delta(r - r')$

whenever $r > \bar{r}(t)$, after having numerically determined the exercise boundary, and then proceed to compute $p(t)$ and, finally, Θ. However, we shall present a PDE-based algorithm for Θ that is more intuitive and elegant and promises greater computational efficiency. Before we present the algorithm, we explain the role that risk premiums play in the computation of Θ.

The Role of Risk Premiums

We have seen that the expected time of exercise for a continuous call can be thought of as the average time when the path taken by interest rates first intersects the exercise boundary. This time will obviously depend on the drift of interest rates. For the purpose of calculating the price of a bond, the interest rate drift can be taken to correspond to a zero-risk premium if the returns from holding the bond are discounted at risk-free rates. As we have discussed, the partial differential equation (5) follows this prescription. The expected time of exercise, however, is intended to be an estimate of when, on average, an option will be exercised in the real world. It is not a quantity that is subject to discounting. Therefore, we must include risk premiums when calculating the expected time of option exercise.

To see immediately why the inclusion of a risk premium affects the average time of option exercise, we only need to consider the average time when a risky asset will first reach a certain price level P_0 (see Figure 6–2). If the asset offers a positive risk premium, it is expected to reach the level P_0 sooner than we would predict for a zero-risk premium. Likewise, the expected time of exercise for an option embedded in a bond is affected by the presence of risk premiums. It might be suspected that this argument is spurious because the computed exercise boundary, traced out with the help of a risk-neutral pricing algorithm, might itself appear to be a risk-neutral construct. This is not true, however, because the pricing algorithm computes at each time step a "preliminary" price that is a model of the price real investors would pay for the bond if the current call could be ignored. The comparison of this preliminary price with the (equally real) current call price then determines the location of the exercise boundary. Therefore, while the location of the computed exercise boundary is not affected by the risk-neutral pricing approach, the drift with which interest rates are modeled to

The price P of a risky asset reaches a certain level P_0 sooner in the real world than in the risk-neutral world.

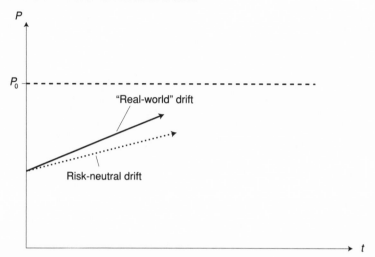

move towards or away from this boundary is different in a risk-neutral approach than in a "real-world approach" (see Figure 6–3).

Equations (8) and (9) form an example of a zero-coupon-bond price process and its associated interest rate process where a risk premium is included. The positive risk premium λ has to be estimated from empirical data. It causes the drift of the short rate to be less than is indicated by the forward curve, thus providing an expected return in excess of the risk-free rate to the holder of longer-maturity bonds. It is this "real-world" interest rate drift that enters the backward Kolmogoroff equation satisfied by the special Green function $\bar{G}$ in (15) as we calculate the expected time of exercise for an embedded call.

A Partial Differential Equation for the Expected Time of Exercise

To formulate a PDE-based algorithm for the expected time of option exercise, let $\Theta(r, t)$ denote the time of exercise that is expected at time t if the short rate at that time is r and the option has not yet been exercised. To be specific, Θ is an *absolute* time (a "calendar date"). Alternatively, we

FIGURE   6-3

The calculation of the expected time of option exercise must be based on
the "real world" drift of interest rates, not the risk-neutral drift.

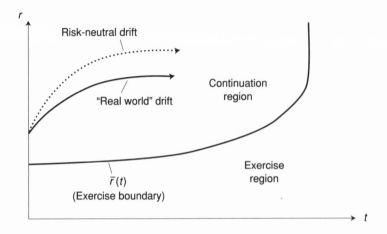

could compute the *remaining* time to exercise $\Theta - t$. Since we consider
that a bond that survives until its maturity T is called at maturity, we
immediately have the boundary condition $\Theta(r, T) = T$. We can now
approximate Θ at a slightly earlier time $T - \Delta t$ by writing

$$\Theta(r, T - \Delta t) \approx \int G(r, T - \Delta t; r', T)\Theta(r', T)dr' \text{ if } r > \bar{r}(T - \Delta t), \quad (16)$$

and

$$\Theta(r, T - \Delta t) = T - \Delta t \text{ if } r \leq \bar{r}(T - \Delta t), \quad (17)$$

Equation (16) involves the Green function G that solves the backward Kolmogoroff equation for the "real-world" interest rate
process with nonzero risk premium, subject to the initial condition
$G(r, t; r', t) = \delta(r - r')$. It states that as long as the short rate is in the
continuation region, the expected exercise time is obtained by summing up the transition probability-weighted expected exercise
times that will apply at the possible short-rate levels one time-step
later. Unlike for the bond price, there is of course no discounting

involved in this procedure. Equation (17) reflects the fact that exercise is expected to occur immediately if the short rate is on or below the exercise boundary.

Using the expected exercise time $\Theta(r, T - \Delta t)$ as a boundary condition, we can now repeat the procedure summarized in equations (16) and (17) to obtain, say, $\Theta(r, T - 2\Delta t)$. After a sufficient number of iterations, we obtain Θ as of the desired valuation date. It is clear that as the step size Δt goes to zero, this algorithm produces a solution to the following problem:

$$\left(\partial_t + v_\lambda \partial_r + \frac{\rho^2}{2} \partial_r^2 \right) \Theta = 0 \text{ if } r > \bar{r}(t), \tag{18}$$

and

$$\Theta = t \text{ if } r \leq \bar{r}(t), \tag{19}$$

subject to the boundary condition $\Theta(r, T) = T$. The advantage of calculating Θ in this manner is that we need not perform the integrations (14) and (15). Furthermore, we could solve the problem (18–19) simultaneously with the problem (11–13). We may, however, want to employ two different coordinate transformations to simplify (11) and (18), respectively, thus diminishing the benefits from a simultaneous solution of both problems.

The intuitive nature of the approach (18–19) allows us to find modified algorithms to compute the expectation values of other quantities of interest in the study of derivative securities, as we shall demonstrate in the last section. At this point, we show that our approach easily lends itself to the computation of the *variance* of the expected time of exercise. Θ, after all, is defined as a statistical average, and we may ask how widely actual observations of the exercise time may vary, given the same initial conditions. The variance of Θ is given by

$$\text{var}_\Theta(r, t) \equiv \Theta^2(r, t) - \left[\Theta(r, t) \right]^2 \tag{20}$$

where $\Theta^2(r, t)$ denotes the expectation value of the square of the time of exercise. Since we already have an algorithm for $\Theta(r, t)$, we only need to find one for $\Theta^2(r, t)$ in order to compute $\text{var}_\Theta(r, t)$. But from our derivation of equations (18) and (19), it is clear that Θ^2 must satisfy

$$\left(\partial_t + v_\lambda \partial_r + \frac{\rho^2}{2} \partial_r^2 \right) \Theta^2 = 0 \text{ if } r > \bar{r}(t) \tag{21}$$

and

$$\Theta^2 = t^2 \text{ if } r \le \bar{r}(t) \tag{22}$$

subject to the boundary condition $\Theta^2(r, T) = T^2$.

The partial differential equation satisfied by a first passage time is known in mathematics as *Dynkin's equation*. However, little, if any, work has been published on PDE-based algorithms for the computation of the expected time of option exercise and of similar quantities arising in the analysis of financial derivatives.[6]

OUTLOOK

It may be an interesting application to numerically solve the problem (18–19) for a selection of typical step-up notes. It would be particularly instructive to compare the computed average life of the step-up notes to their option-adjusted durations—their price sensitivities.

We conclude this chapter by demonstrating that PDE-based algorithms can be invoked for the computation of expected values and variances of other quantities of interest in the analysis of derivative securities. As an example, consider an interest rate cap that consists of M caplets for the short rate, with a strike rate R and caplet periods starting at times $0, t_1, t_2, \ldots, t_{M-1}$. Given an initial yield curve and term structure of volatility, one may wish to compute the number of caplets that are expected to be in the money. We shall assume a short-rate process $dr = v_\lambda dt + \rho dz$ as before.

Let us introduce $N(r, t)$, the number of the outstanding caplets that at time t are expected to be in-the-money if the short-rate level at time t is r. The boundary condition just before the last caplet period is readily seen to be $N(r, t_{M-1}^-) = 1$ if $r \ge R$ and $N(r, t_{M-1}^-) = 0$ otherwise. From the previous two sections, it is clear that N must satisfy the partial differential equation

$$\left(\partial_t + v_\lambda \partial_r + \frac{\rho^2}{2} \partial_r^2 \right) N = 0 \tag{23}$$

---

6 For a closed-form expression of the expected time of exercise under specialized assumptions, see R. Yaksick, "Expected Optimal Exercise Time of a Perpetual American Option: A Closed-Form Solution," *Journal of Financial Engineering*, March 1995, pp. 55–73. This article also contains numerous references to related work.

between any two of the caplet start dates t_i. On a caplet start date, N jumps by 1 if the caplet is in-the-money

$$N\left(r,t_i^-\right)-N\left(r,t_i^+\right)=1 \text{ if } r \ge R, =0 \text{ otherwise,} \qquad (24)$$

where $t_i^{\mp}$ are times right before and after the caplet start date t_i (see Figure 6–4).

As with the expected time of exercise for an option, we obtain the variance of N, $\text{var}_N(r,t) \equiv N^2(r,t)-[N(r,t)]^2$, if we can compute the expected squared number of caplets in the money $N^2(r,t)$. But N^2 satisfies

$$\left(\partial_t + v_\lambda \partial_r + \frac{\rho^2}{2}\partial_r^2\right)N^2 = 0, \qquad (25)$$

subject to the boundary condition $N^2\left(r,t_{M-1}^-\right)=N\left(r,t_{M-1}^-\right)$ and the jump condition

$$N^2\left(r,t_i^-\right)-N^2\left(r,t_i^+\right)=2N\left(r,t_i^+\right)+1 \text{ if } r \ge R, =0 \text{ otherwise.} \qquad (26)$$

F I G U R E   6–4

Above the strike rate, N jumps by 1 across each caplet start date t_i. Below the strike rate, N is continuous.

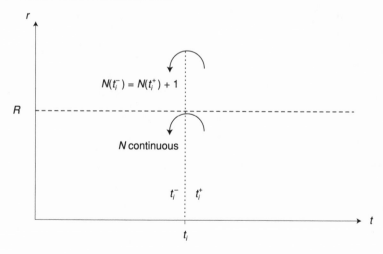

7

⑥ BLACK-SCHOLES APPROXIMATION OF COMPLEX OPTION VALUES: THE CASES OF EUROPEAN COMPOUND CALL OPTIONS AND EQUITY WARRANTS*

Alain Bensoussan
Universite´ Paris Dauphine and INRIA, France

Michel Crouhy
Canadian Imperial Bank of Commerce

Dan Galai
Jerusalem School of Business and SIGMA PCM

Many types of financial claims issued by the corporation have option features attached to them. Their value is usually contingent on the value of the firm's assets and its stochastic nature, as well as the firm's liability structure. The capital structure of the firm sets the priority rules for distributing the income of the corporation and its residual value; the sharing rules determine the contingency nature of the claims.

In a firm that is financed by debt and equity, equity can be considered as a call option on the firm's assets (see Galai and Masulis

* This research was partially supported by the HEC Foundation while M. Crouhy was at the HEC School of Management, France, and by the Krueger Center for Finance at the Jerusalem School of Business. We would like to acknowledge excellent research assistance from Veronique Lesourd.

[1976] and Merton [1974]). Debt issued by the corporation is also a contingent claim, similar to owning all the assets of the firm and writing a put against them. Equity volatility in a levered firm is non-stationary due to the so-called leverage effect.

While debt causes the risk of equity to increase relative to the volatility of the firm, the issuance of diluting securities, like warrants and convertible bonds, has the opposite effects. (See for example, Galai and Schneller [1978], and Crouhy and Galai [1994]). Equity call-warrants (thereafter named *warrants*) are rights issued by a firm to buy a certain number of new shares issued by the firm during a specific period (the exercise period) at a specific price (the exercise price).[1] Often, warrants are issued attached to a bond. Then, the investor initially buys a package, the bond with the attached warrant(s). Usually, the next day after the issuance of the warrant-bond package, the warrants are detached from the bond, and both the bonds and the warrants start to trade independently as two distinct securities. In the case of a warrant-bond package, the warrant premium is not paid upfront, but rather in the form of a reduced coupon rate with respect to the normal market conditions. When the warrants are exercised new shares are issued by the firm, and the exercise price of the warrants must be paid in cash.[2] Since the share price (post-exercise) is above the strike price when the warrants are exercised, old shareholders are diluted. However, the optimal decision to exercise the warrants is fully anticipated by market participants; thus, the current share price should reflect the dilution impact of the warrants. Warrants can be viewed as issuing additional shares with a built-in loan from the corporation that will be paid back only if the share price increases sufficiently and is, at maturity, above the predetermined exercise price. This *negative leverage effect* introduces nonstationarity in the volatility of the stock.

---

1 Equity warrants should not be confused with recent innovation like "covered warrants". Covered warrants are call options written either on existing shares of a company, or on a basket of existing shares of several firms. The issuer of covered warrants is usually a bank and not the company of the underlying stock. Some covered call warrants are traded on an exchange, whereas most of them are over-the-counter instruments. As with a traditional call option, no dilution is associated with the issuance of covered warrants.

2 Because of the deferred cash flow associated with the exercise of the warrants, the current market value of the warrant depends on the anticipated use by the firm of this cash payment, whether it is paid out as a dividend or it is reinvested in a scale project, or in a project with a different business risk. (See Crouhy and Galai [1994].)

Convertible debt is another claim issued by a corporation that simultaneously contains a bond plus a warrant. It usually has a positive leverage effect due to the dominance of the bond feature. However, its leverage effect is reduced by the dilution effect in the convertibility feature. The difference between a convertible bond and a warant-bond package is separability. Once the warrant-bond package has been issued, the warrant and the bond are detached and each trades independently. For a convertible bond the call option and the bond cannot be dissociated. The exercise price is not paid in cash for a fixed amount, but instead by redeeming the bond, provided it is profitable to exercise the conversion right. Therefore, pricing models and hedging strategies will differ for both warrants and convertible bonds.

The Black-Scholes (1973) model (BSM) has been so well accepted by practitioners that they are often tempted to use BSM to price any complex derivative securities other than standard European call or put options for which the model theoretically applies. BSM is very often applied to contingent claims issued by the corporation. The problem, however, is that while the theoretical models assume that the value of the firm's assets is known, such a value is usually unobservable and difficult to estimate. What is observable is the stock price, and its stochastic features can be estimated from the time series of prices. Therefore, the preference among practitioners is to value corporate claims and traded options based on stock prices rather than on the firm's value. But stock prices in a firm having a complex capital structure do not follow a stationary geometric Brownian motion anymore.

However, BSM for European options is derived under a number of strong restrictive assumptions: financial markets are perfect; trading securities takes place continuously; there are no transaction costs; the short-term interest rate is constant; the stock pays no dividends; and the stock price follows a *stationary* geometric Brownian motion with a constant variance rate. Although these assumptions have been further relaxed in more complicated models (see, for example, Cox and Rubinstein [1985, chapter 7] or Jarrow and Rudd [1983, chapters 9–12]), the key issue addressed in this paper is whether the Black-Scholes formula is robust—whether we can still use it, with or without some adjustments, under alternative sets of assumptions more relevant for nonstandard derivative securities like compound options, equity warrants, and others.

In the first part of the chapter, we derive general conditions under which the Black-Scholes formula can still be used to approximate prices of derivative securities. This section implies both a modification in the underlying instrument and an adjustment in the volatility parameter, which becomes a function that varies with time and the underlying price. Since stock volatility is not a constant any longer, BSM is then no longer correct. It can only be a convenient numerical approximation to the exact derivative security price. The approximation is quite accurate when the average volatility over the life of the option is not too different from the instantaneous volatility computed at the current time when pricing the derivative security. This is shown to be precisely the case for at-the-money and in-the-money options for the securities we have investigated.

The pricing biases related to the use of BSM for pricing options have been investigated in different contexts. Some authors have analyzed the accuracy of the Black-Scholes approximation when the underlying security price follows an arbitrary distribution different from the stationary geometric Brownian motion assumed in BSM (see, for example, Merton [1976], Jarrow and Rudd [1982], and Jarrow and Wiggins ([1989]). Jarrow and Rudd (1982) and Jarrow and Wiggins (1989) propose an adjustment technique based on BSM that adjusts the volatility parameter for the specific stochastic process that is supposed to hold and that differs from the lognormal process. Others have studied the pricing error caused by a stochastic volatility (see, for example, Hull and White [1988] and Heston [1993]).

In the second part of this chapter, we apply the previous results to the pricing of European compound call-options and equity warrants. For each case, we assess the accuracy of the BSM approximation using exact models already proposed in the literature and assuming that the reference asset, which in both cases is the total value of the firm, is observable.

PRELIMINARY TECHNICAL PROPERTIES

In the following V denotes the value of a financial asset. Its return follows a diffusion described by the stochastic differential equation:

$$\frac{dV(t)}{V(t)} = rdt + \sigma dZ(t) \tag{1}$$

where

r = the continuously compounded risk-free rate of interest, which is assumed to be a constant.

σ^2 = the instantaneous variance of the return on the asset, assumed to be a constant.

t = current time.

Z = a standard Brownian motion with respect to the equivalent uniform martingale measure Q under which the discounted asset price is a martingale.[3]

Consider a function $C(V, t)$ that satisfies the standard Black-Scholes partial differential equation (PDE):[4]

$$-C_t - \frac{1}{2}\sigma^2 V^2 C_{vv} - rVC_v + rC = 0. \qquad (2)$$

Consider also a function $\varphi(C, t)$, solution of the PDE:

$$-\varphi_t - \frac{1}{2}\sigma(C)^2 C^2 \varphi_{cc} - rC\varphi_c + r\varphi = 0 \qquad (3)$$

where C plays the role of the underlying asset for $\varphi, \sigma(C)$ denotes a volatility function that is not a constant, and that we shall make precise later. Now define the function

$$\psi(V,t) = \varphi\big(C(V,t),t\big).$$

The following property holds.

Theorem 1

If the function $\varphi(c, t)$ is the solution of (3), and $C(V, t)$ is the solution of (2), then the function $\psi(V, t)$ is the solution of the standard Black-Scholes PDE (2), that is:

$$-\psi_t - \frac{1}{2}\sigma^2 V^2 \psi_{vv} - rV\psi_v + r\psi = 0 \qquad (4)$$

iff

$$\sigma(C) = \sigma\frac{V}{C(V,t)}C_v.$$

---

3 It follows that the initial market value at time t of any redundant security claiming a random payoff X at time T is $E[e^{-r(T-t)}X]$, where E denotes the expectation operator under the "risk neutral" probability Q (see, for example, Duffie [1988]).

4 The usual subscript notation applies for partial derivatives.

The proof of Theorem 1 is in Appendix 1.

Next we refer to a consequence of the classical maximum principle for a PDE (see A. Friedman [1964]).

Theorem 2

For any function F(V, t) *that satisfies the Black-Scholes PDE (2), namely,*

$$-F_t - \frac{1}{2}\sigma^2 V^2 F_{vv} - rV F_v + rF = 0$$

if for any arbitrary time instant T

(i) $F(V,T) = \varphi[C(V,T),T]$, then $F(V,t) = \varphi[C(V,t),t] \forall t \leq T$

or,

(ii) $F(V,T) \leq \varphi[C(V,T),T]$, then $F(V,t) \leq \varphi[C(V,t),t] \forall t \leq T$.

The proof of Theorem 2 is in Appendix 2.

APPLICATIONS TO THE PRICING OF EUROPEAN COMPOUND CALL OPTIONS AND EQUITY WARRANTS

The Case of a European Compound Call Option

A compound option is an option on an option. The underlying instrument of the compound option is assumed to be a European call option, $C(S, t)$, which matures at time T, where S is the underlying exogenous asset whose return is the solution of the stochastic differential equation (1). $C(S, t)$ is the solution of the Black-Scholes PDE (2), that is:

$$-\varphi_t - \frac{1}{2}\sigma(C)^2 C^2 \varphi_{cc} - rC\varphi_c + r\varphi = 0 \tag{5}$$

subject to the boundary condition:

$$C(S,T) = (S - K)^+$$

where K is the strike price of the underlying option.

The European compound call option $C^*(S, t)$ with maturity $T_1, T_1 < T$ and strike price K_1 is the solution of the Black-Scholes PDE:

$$-C_t^* - \frac{1}{2}\sigma^2 S^2 C_{ss}^* - rSC_s^* + rC^* = 0 \text{ for } t < T_1 \tag{6}$$

subject to the boundary condition:

$$C^*(S,T_1) = \left[C(S,T_1) - K_1\right]^+.$$

A closed-form solution to (6) in terms of the underlying asset S has been derived by Geske (1979). The expression depends on the bivariate cumulative normal distribution.

As an alternative to Geske's formula, by application of Theorems 1 and 2, we can derive a much simpler Black-Scholes numerical approximation where the underlying instrument is the ordinary European call option $C(S, t)$.

Indeed, consider the function $\varphi[C(S, t),t]$ where φ is the solution of (3), and

$$\sigma(C) = \sigma\frac{S}{C(S,t)}C_s.\qquad(7)$$

In other words, φ is the solution of the PDE:

$$-\varphi_t - \frac{1}{2}\sigma(C)^2 C^2 \varphi_{cc} - rC\varphi_c + r\varphi = 0 \quad \text{for } t < T_1 \qquad(8)$$

subject to the boundary condition:

$$\varphi(C,T_1) = (C - K_1)^+,$$

then by Theorem 1, the function $\psi(S, t) = \varphi[C(S, t),t]$ is the solution of PDE (6) where C^* is replaced by ψ.

We further note that at the maturity date T_1 of the compound option:

$$C^*(S,T_1) = \varphi\left[C(S,T_1),T_1\right] = \left[C(S,T_1) - K_1\right]^+.$$

Therefore, by application of Theorem 2, it follows that

$$C^*(S,t) = \varphi\left[C(S,t),t\right] \text{ for all } t < T_1.$$

If $\sigma(C)$ in (8) were a constant over the life of the compound option, then the exact closed-form solution to the compound option value would be the Black-Scholes formula (BS). Since it varies, as S changes with time, the following Black-Scholes formula can only be a numerical approximation:

$$C^*(S,t) \cong BS\left[C(S,t),K_1,\overline{\sigma}(C),r,T_1 - t\right]\qquad(9)$$

$$= CN(d_1) - K_1 e^{-r(T_1-t)}N(d_2)$$

where

$$C = C(S,t) = BS(S,K,\sigma,r,T).$$

$$d_1 = \ln\left(C / K_1 e^{-r(T_1-t)}\right)\!\Big/\overline{\sigma}(C)\sqrt{T_1-t} + \frac{1}{2}\overline{\sigma}(C)\sqrt{T_1-t}.$$

$$d_2 = d_1 - \overline{\sigma}(C)\sqrt{T_1-t}.$$

$N(.)$ = the cumulative standard normal distribution.

$\overline{\sigma}(C)$ = the instantaneous volatility of C as defined in (7) and computed at current time t.

In order to test the accuracy of the Black-Scholes approximation (9), we have compared (9) to the true value of the European compound call option using Geske's (1979) formula.[5] The results are presented in Table 7–1 and Figures 7–1 and 7–2. The relative pricing error is less than 2.5 percent for in-the-money compound options. It is almost negligible (less than 1/10 of a percent) for near, at-the-money compound options. It increases substantially for out-of-money compound options, although it becomes irrelevant since the option premium becomes less than the usual bid/ask spread for such options.

As Bensoussan, Crouhy, and Galai (1995) showed, the quality of the approximation is good when the current value

$$\overline{\sigma}(C) = \sigma\big(C(S,t)\big) = \sigma\frac{S}{C(S,t)}C_s(S,t)$$

is a good approximation of the average volatility over the remaining life of the option. This is precisely the case for the simulations we carried out, except for deep out-of-the money options.

The Case of Equity Warrants

In this section, we consider the pricing of equity warrants first in an all-equity firm, and then in the more complex situation of a levered firm.

Pricing Equity Warrants in an All-Equity Firm
Bensoussan, Crouhy, and Galai (1995) (BCG) have investigated the Black-Scholes approximation for an equity warrant in the case of an all-equity firm.

---

5 Note that Geske's (1979) formula requires numerical approximations of several terms, in particular the bivariate cumulative normal distribution and the critical value for determining the exercise condition of the compound option in terms of asset S.

TABLE 7-1

Accuracy of the Black-Scholes approximation for the European compound call option

s	$T_1 = 1.0$				$T_1 = 0.5$				$T_1 = 0.2$			
	C	C*	BS	(BS–C*)/C*	C	C*	BS	(BS–C*)/C*	C	C*	BS	(BS–C*)/C*
60	7.8072	2.0838	2.4075	0.1553	5.4674	0.5868	0.7862	0.3398	4.0461	0.0490	0.0973	0.9853
61	8.3084	2.3446	2.6513	0.1308	5.8930	0.7060	0.9076	0.2855	4.4138	0.0699	0.1262	0.8050
62	8.8249	2.6243	1.9116	0.1094	6.3361	0.8418	1.0429	0.2389	4.8005	0.0978	0.1622	0.6579
63	9.3566	2.9233	3.1886	0.0907	6.7966	0.9952	1.1931	0.1980	5.2061	0.1343	0.2064	0.5370
64	9.9032	3.2417	3.4828	0.0744	7.2744	1.1672	1.3591	0.1643	5.6306	0.1811	0.2603	0.4371
65	10.4643	3.5795	3.7946	0.0600	7.7690	1.3589	1.5417	0.1345	6.0737	0.2403	0.3255	0.3542
66	11.0396	3.9368	4.1241	0.0475	8.2804	1.5709	1.4720	0.1088	6.5354	0.3140	0.4035	0.2852
67	11.6290	4.3136	4.4716	0.0366	8.8082	1.8042	1.9607	0.0867	7.0154	0.4042	0.4963	0.2277
68	12.2319	4.7098	4.8375	0.0271	9.3522	2.0594	2.1986	0.0676	7.5136	1.3524	0.6055	0.1797
69	12.8481	5.1253	5.2217	0.0188	9.9119	2.3369	2.4566	0.0512	8.0296	0.6432	0.7331	0.1396
70	13.4773	5.5599	5.6245	0.0116	10.4872	2.6373	2.7353	0.0371	8.5631	0.7963	0.8810	0.1063
71	14.1192	6.0134	6.0459	0.0054	11.0777	2.9609	3.0354	0.0251	9.1139	0.9745	1.0521	0.0787
72	14.7734	6.4856	6.4860	0.0000	11.6830	3.3079	3.3574	0.0149	9.6816	1.1796	1.2455	0.0559
73	15.4395	6.9762	6.9447	–0.0045	12.3027	3.6785	3.7019	0.0063	10.2658	1.4132	1.4658	0.0371
74	16.1174	7.4848	7.4220	–0.0083	12.9366	4.0726	4.0692	–0.0008	10.8662	1.6768	1.7137	0.0219
75	16.8065	8.0111	7.9177	–0.0116	13.5842	4.4903	4.4596	–0.0068	11.4824	1.9714	1.9907	0.0097
76	17.5067	8.5548	8.4318	–0.0143	14.2452	4.9312	4.8734	–0.0117	12.1141	2.2979	2.2981	0.0001
77	18.2176	9.1155	8.9640	–0.0166	14.9192	5.3953	5.3107	–0.0156	12.7607	2.6568	2.6772	–0.0073
78	18.9389	9.6928	9.5141	–0.0184	15.6059	5.8821	5.7715	–0.0188	13.4218	3.0483	3.0085	–0.0130
79	19.6702	10.2863	10.0819	–0.0198	16.3048	6.3913	6.2558	–0.0212	14.0972	3.4724	3.4129	–0.0171
80	20.4112	10.8956	10.6671	–0.0209	17.0156	6.9225	6.7634	–0.0229	14.7862	3.9288	3.8505	–0.0199

(continued)

TABLE 7-1 (concluded)

	$T_1 = 1.0$				$T_1 = 0.5$				$T_1 = 0.2$			
s	C	C*	BS	(BS–C*)/C*	C	C*	BS	(BS–C*)/C*	C	C*	BS	(BS–C*)/C*
81	21.1617	11.5201	11.2693	–0.0217	17.7379	7.4750	7.2941	–0.0242	15.4886	4.4169	4.3212	–0.0216
82	21.9214	12.1596	11.8882	–0.0223	18.4714	8.0484	7.8475	–0.0249	16.2039	4.9360	4.8248	–0.0225
83	22.6899	12.8135	12.5234	–0.0226	19.2156	8.6421	8.4232	–0.0255	16.9316	5.4852	5.3608	–0.0226
84	23.4669	13.4814	13.1745	–0.0227	19.9703	9.2555	9.0208	–0.0253	17.6713	6.0632	5.9281	–0.0222
85	24.2523	14.1628	13.8411	–0.0227	20.7351	9.8878	9.6397	–0.0251	18.4227	6.6689	6.5258	–0.0214
86	25.0456	14.8574	14.5228	–0.0225	21.5096	10.5385	10.2792	–0.0246	19.1853	7.3009	7.1526	–0.0203
87	25.8467	15.5646	15.2190	–0.0222	22.2934	11.2069	10.9387	–0.0239	19.9587	7.9579	7.8070	–0.0189
88	26.6553	16.2841	15.9293	–0.0217	23.0864	11.8922	11.6175	–0.0231	20.7424	8.6384	8.4875	–0.0174
89	27.4711	17.0153	16.6533	–0.0212	23.8881	12.5938	12.3148	–0.0221	21.5362	9.3410	9.1923	–0.0159
90	28.2938	17.7580	17.3904	–0.0207	24.6981	13.3110	13.0298	–0.0211	22.3396	10.0643	9.9199	–0.0143
91	29.1233	18.5115	18.1401	–0.0200	25.5163	14.0431	13.7617	–0.0200	23.1522	10.8068	10.6684	–0.0128
92	29.9592	19.2756	18.9021	–0.0193	26.3423	14.7894	14.5098	–0.0189	23.9736	11.5672	11.4362	–0.0113
93	30.8014	20.0499	19.6756	–0.0186	27.1757	15.5493	15.2732	–0.0177	24.8036	12.3443	12.2217	–0.0099
94	31.6497	20.8339	20.4604	–0.0179	28.0164	16.3221	16.0510	–0.0166	25.6417	13.1367	13.0233	–0.0086
95	32.5037	21.6272	21.2553	–0.0171	28.8639	17.1071	16.8425	–0.0154	26.4877	13.9433	13.8395	–0.0074
96	33.3634	22.4296	22.0616	–0.0164	29.7182	17.9039	17.6469	–0.0143	27.3411	14.7630	14.6690	–0.0063
97	34.2285	23.2406	22.8770	–0.0156	30.5788	18.7117	18.4634	–0.0132	28.2016	15.5949	15.5104	–0.0054
98	35.0988	24.0598	23.7018	–0.0148	31.4456	19.5300	19.2911	–0.0122	29.0691	16.4379	16.3627	–0.0045
99	35.9740	24.8870	24.5354	–0.0141	32.3182	20.3882	20.1295	–0.0112	29.9430	17.2911	17.2248	–0.0038
100	36.8541	25.7218	25.3774	–0.0133	33.1965	21.1959	20.9778	–0.0102	30.8232	18.1539	18.0958	–0.0032

The computations are carried out with the following parameter values: the maturity of the compound option is $T_1 = 1$, 0.5 and 0.2 year, the maturity of the underlying European call option is $T_1 + 1$ year, the volatility of the underlying asset is $\sigma = 30$ percent, the continuously compounded interest rate is $r = 10$ percent, the strike price of the underlying option is $K = 80$ and the strike price of the compound option is $K_1 = 13$. The simulation results around at-the-money for the compound option are located between horizontal lines. S is the current asset value at time $t = 0$, $C = C(S,0)$ is the current value of the underlying European call option given S, $C^* = C^*(S,0)$ is the current value of the European compound option given S computed using Geske's (1979) formula. BS is the Black-Scholes approximation (9), and $(BS – C^*)/C^*$ denotes the relative pricing error when using (9) instead of Geske's formula.

Accuracy of the Black-Scholes Approximation for the European
Compound Call Option

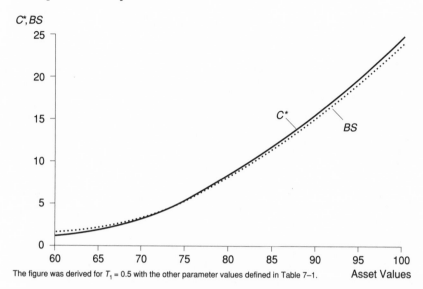

The figure was derived for T_1 = 0.5 with the other parameter values defined in Table 7–1.

Galai and Schneller (1978) derived a closed-form valuation formula for such a warrant, where the underlying instrument is the
value of the firm's assets:

$$w = w(V,t) = BS(V,K,\sigma,r,T-t)/(1+n) \qquad (10)$$

where

BS = Black-Scholes model.

K = strike price of the warrant.

T = expiration date of the warrant.

t = current time.

n = dilution factor = proportion of new shares issued by the
firm if the warrants are exercised at maturity, to all shares
outstanding at maturity, (for simplicity it is assumed that
the initial number of shares is equal to one).

V = the value of the firm's assets, which is assumed to be lognormally distributed and to follow a diffusion identical to (1).

w = the value of a warrant.

s = the price per share.

FIGURE 7–2

Relative Pricing Error When Using the Black-Scholes Approximation Instead of the Geske's (1979) Formula for the European Compound Call Option

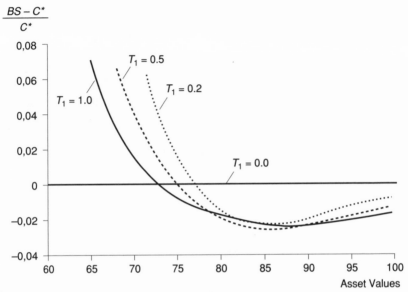

Parameter values and notations as in Table 7–1 also apply here.

The other variables have already been defined.

From these definitions, it follows that, for all $t, t < T$

$$V = s + nw, \tag{11}$$

which, using (10) can also be written as

$$s = s(V,t) = V - \frac{nBS(V,K,\sigma,r,T-t)}{1+n}. \tag{12}$$

However, V is not directly observable which makes (10) difficult to implement by practitioners. As an alternative to (10), BCG derived the Black-Scholes approximation (13) where the argument is the share price s, instead of V:

$$w \cong BS(s,K,\overline{\sigma}(s),r,T-t) \tag{13}$$

where

$$\sigma(s) = \sigma \frac{V}{s} s_v$$

and $\overline{\sigma}(s)$ is the value of $\sigma(s)$ computed at current time t.

This result is a direct application of Theorems 1 and 2. First, the warrant price $w(V, t)$ is the solution of the PDE (2) with the boundary condition

$$w(V,T) = (V - K)^+ / (1 + n).$$

Consider the function $\phi(s,t)$, solution of (3), with s replacing C, that is:

$$-\phi_t - \frac{1}{2}\sigma(s)^2 s^2 \phi_{ss} - rs\phi_s + r\phi = 0 \tag{14}$$

with

$$\sigma(s) = \sigma \frac{V}{s} s_v$$

and the boundary condition

$$\phi(s,T) = (s - K)^+.$$

By Theorem 1, $\psi(V, t) = \phi[\sigma(V, t), t]$ is solution of PDE (4) or equivalently PDE (2) where C is replaced by ψ.

Consider now $s(V, t)$ defined by (12), which is the solution of

$$-s_t - \frac{1}{2}\sigma^2 V^2 s_{vv} - rVs_v + rC = 0$$

$$s(V,T) = V - \frac{n}{1+n}(V - K)^+.$$

It is easy to show that

$$\phi(s(V,T),T) = w(V,T).$$

Then, from Theorem 2, it follows that

$$\phi(s(V,t),t) = w(V,t), \text{ for } t < T.$$

Since $\sigma(s)$ is not a constant, it follows that (13) is only an approximation.

As for the compound option case, BCG show that this approximation is quite accurate for at-the-money and in-the-money warrants. Figure 7–3 shows the relative approximation error for different times to maturity.

Pricing of Equity Warrants in a Levered Firm

The firm's assets $V(t)$ are assumed to be financed through equity, debt, and warrants. The debt is a zero-coupon bond that matures at time T

F I G U R E   7–3

Relative Approximation Error for the Pricing of a European Equity Warrant in an All-Equity Firm

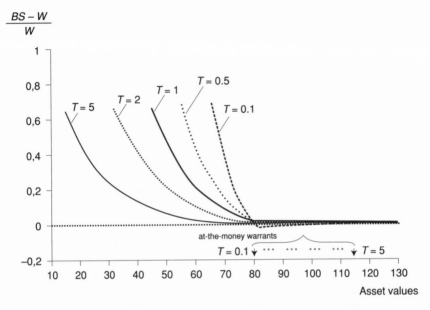

All the computations are derived for a dilution factor $n = 1$, an interest rate $r = 10$ percent, a strike price $K = 80$, and a volatility of assets' return $s = 30$ percent. V denotes the firm's asset value, w is the true value of the warrant, and BS is the Black-Scholes approximation.

with a face value F, and with a market value $B(t)$ at time t. There are n European warrants and m shares selling at a price $w(V, t)$ and $s(V, t)$, respectively, where V represents the underlying instrument, which is the value of the firm's assets. The warrants have a maturity date T_1, $T_1 < T$ and a strike price K. The value of the firm can then be written as

$$V = ms(V,t) + B(V,t) + nw(V,t) \ \forall t < T_1 \tag{15}$$

and is assumed to be lognormally distributed, and to follow a diffusion identical to (1). Let us define $ms(V , t) + nw(V , t)$ as the total equity of the firm. In what follows, we show the valuation model for w based on the current value of V, and also two approximations for w, one based on the value of the shares $ms(V , t)$ and the second being based on the value of total equity of the firm. We derive the PDE for all three approaches.

If the warrants are exercised at time T_1, the proceeds, nK, are assumed to be reinvested in a scale project so that the size of assets at time T_1 becomes

$$V(T_1)^* = V(T_1) + nK. \tag{16}$$

At time T_1 the conditional value of a share is

$$s(V,T_1) = \frac{BS(V+nK,F,\sigma,r,T-T_1)}{m+n}1_{V \geq \overline{V}_1} \tag{17}$$

$$+ \frac{BS(V,F,\sigma,r,T-T_1)}{m}1_{V < \overline{V}_1}$$

where:

- $\overline{V}_1$ is the critical asset value at which the warrant holder is indifferent between exercising or not exercising the warrants; $\overline{V}_1$ is thus defined as the value of V at time T_1 such that

$$\frac{BS(\overline{V}_1 + nK,F,\sigma,r,T-T_1)}{m+n} = K.$$

- $BS(V,F,\sigma,r,T-t)$ denotes the Black-Scholes formula for a European call option on the assets of the firm V, with a strike price F equal to the face value of the debt, and maturity $T-t$ where t is the current time and T is the maturity date of the option.

- $1_{[condition]}$ is an indicator function that is equal to 1 when the condition is satisfied, and 0 otherwise.

The value of a warrant at the maturity date is

$$w(V,T_1) = \left[\frac{BS(V+nK,F,\sigma,r,T-T_1)}{m+n} - K\right]1_{V \geq \overline{V}_1} \tag{18}$$

$$= \left[\frac{BS(V+nK,F,\sigma,r,T-T_1)}{m+n} - K\right]^+$$

and the conditional value of debt is

$$B(V,T_1) = \left[V + nK - BS(V+nK,F,\sigma,r,T-T_1)\right]1_{V \geq \overline{V}_1} \tag{19}$$

$$+ \left[V - BS(V,F,\sigma,r,T-T_1)\right]1_{V < \overline{V}_1}.$$

It can be easily verified that

$$ms(V,T_1)+nw(V,T_1)+B(V,T_1)=V.$$

At any time $t, t < T_1$, $s(V,t)$, $w(V,t)$ are the solution of the following PDE's:

$$-s_t - \frac{1}{2}\sigma^2 V^2 s_{vv} - rVs_v + rs = 0 \qquad (20)$$

with the boundary condition (17), and

$$-w_t - \frac{1}{2}\sigma^2 V^2 w_{vv} - rw_v + rw = 0 \qquad (21)$$

with the boundary condition (18).

Crouhy and Galai (1994) have derived a pseudo-analytic solution to the simultaneous equilibrium pricing of $s(V,t)$, $w(V,t)$, and $B(V,t), t < T_1$, when the underlying asset price is V. In the following we propose an alternative BS approximation for $w(V,t)$ in terms of $s(V,t)$, which is assumed to be observable at any date t.

First, $w(V,t)$ is the solution of the Black-Scholes PDE (21) with boundary condition (18). Second $s(V,T)$ is the solution of the PDE (20) with boundary condition (17). Consider the function $\varphi(s(V,t),t) = \psi(V,t)$ where φ is solution of the PDE (22):

$$-\varphi_t - \frac{1}{2}\sigma(s)^2 s^2 \varphi_{ss} - rs\varphi_s + r\varphi = 0 \qquad (22)$$

with

$$\sigma(s) = \sigma \frac{V}{s} s_v \qquad (23)$$

and φ satisfies the boundary condition (24):

$$(V,T_1) = \left[s(V,T_1) - K \right]^+. \qquad (24)$$

By Theorem 1, it follows that $\psi(V,t)$ is the solution of PDE (21) where w is replaced by ψ.

Before we can apply Theorem 2, we need to compare the boundary conditions (18) and (24). This will be done in two steps.

Lemma 1

$$BS(V + nK, F, \sigma, r, T - t) - nK \le BS(V, F, \sigma, r, T - t).$$

The proof of Lemma 1 is in Appendix 3.

Lemma 2

No arbitrage condition:

$$w(V,T_1) \le \left[s(V,T_1) - K \right]^+.$$

The proof of Lemma 2 is in Appendix 4.

Theorem 3

$$w(V,t) \le \varphi\big(s(V,t),t\big) \quad \forall t < T_1.$$

This result is a direct application of Theorem 2, since $w(V,t)$ and $\varphi(s,t)$ are solutions of the PDE's (21) and (22), respectively, and the boundary conditions satisfy Lemma 2.

However, the volatility parameter in (22) is not a constant so that BSM is not the exact solution of (22) – (24). We chose as an approximation

$$BS\big(s,K,\overline{\sigma}(s),r,T_1-t\big) \tag{25}$$

where $\overline{\sigma}(s)$ is the value of (23) computed at current time t.

Contrary to the previous derivative securities we analyzed, namely, the European compound call option and the equity warrant in an all-equity firm, $\varphi(s(V,t),t)$ is not exactly equal to the option price. It is now a theoretical upper bound that is numerically approximated by (25).

Nevertheless, we can try to improve the upper bound of the warrant value by changing the underlying asset in the Black-Scholes formula. As a substitute for $s(V,t)$, let us take the total value of equity, which is defined as the sum of the share and warrant values:

$$E(V,t) = ms(V,t) + nw(V,t). \tag{26}$$

Since $s(V,t)$ and $w(V,t)$ satisfy the Black-Scholes PDE's (20) and (21) then $E(V,t)$ is solution of

$$-E_t - \frac{1}{2}\sigma^2 V^2 E_{vv} - rVE_v + rE = 0 \tag{27}$$

with the boundary condition:

$$E(V,T_1) = \left[BS(V,F,\sigma,r,T-T_1) \right] 1_{V < \overline{V}_1} \tag{28}$$
$$+ \left[BS(V+nK,F,\sigma,r,T-T_1) - nK \right] 1_{V \ge \overline{V}_1}.$$

Lemma 3

$$w(V,T_1) \le \frac{\left(E(V,T_1) - mK\right)^+}{m+n}.$$

The proof of Lemma 3 is in Appendix 5.

Theorem 4

$$w(V,t) \le \frac{\varphi\left(E(V,t),t\right)}{m+n}$$

where

$$-\varphi_t - \frac{1}{2}\sigma(E)^2 E^2 \varphi_{ee} - rE\varphi_e + r\varphi = 0$$

$$\varphi(E,T) = (E - mK)^+$$

with

$$\sigma(E) = \sigma \frac{V}{E(V,t)} E_v.$$

Theorem 4 follows directly from application of Theorems 1 and 2.

When the stock price $s(V,t)$ or the total equity value $E(V,t)$ are the arguments of the BS model, both the BSM approximations are upper bounds to the warrant value. But $\varphi(E(V,t),t)$ provides a tighter bound to $w(V,t)$ than $\varphi(s(V,t),t)$. This follows from the property described in the next lemma.

Lemma 4

$$\frac{\left[E(V,T_1) - mK\right]^+}{m+n} \le \left[s(V,T_1) - K\right]^+.$$

The proof of Lemma 4 is in Appendix 6.

Table 7–2 and Figure 7–4 illustrate the accuracy of the BS numerical approximations to the warrant price in a levered firm.

CONCLUSION

Valuation of complex contingent claims is often done through numerical methods. In many of those models an implicit critical value for exercising the contingent claim must be found by trial and error. Moreover, these models require the knowledge of the current

TABLE 7-2

Accuracy of the Black-Scholes Approximation for a European Equity Warrant in a Levered Firm

n = 1   T_i = 1

V	S	w	BSS	BSE	(BSS−w)/w	(BSE−w)/w
80.00	16.15158	3.95646	4.23175	3.77882	0.06958	−0.04490
81.00	16.64344	4.20728	4.45959	3.97368	0.05997	−0.05552
82.00	17.13670	4.46624	4.69564	4.17786	0.05136	−0.06457
83.00	17.63119	4.73320	4.93995	4.39158	0.04368	−0.07218
84.00	18.12678	5.00806	5.19256	4.61504	0.03684	−0.07848
85.00	18.62331	5.29068	5.45349	4.84841	0.03077	−0.08359
86.00	19.12067	5.58090	5.72274	5.09184	0.02542	−0.08763
87.00	19.61874	5.87860	6.00028	5.34546	0.02020	−0.09069
88.00	20.11742	6.18360	6.28607	5.60935	0.01657	−0.09069
89.00	20.61662	6.49575	6.58007	5.88355	0.01298	−0.09425
90.00	21.11625	6.81489	6.88220	6.16811	0.00988	−0.09491
91.00	21.61623	7.14084	7.19233	6.46298	0.00721	−0.09493
92.00	22.11650	7.47343	7.51060	6.76812	0.00497	−0.09438
93.00	22.61702	7.81248	7.83619	7.08344	0.00303	−0.09332
94.00	23.11768	8.15785	8.16987	7.40879	0.00147	−0.09182
95.00	23.61848	8.50932	8.51092	7.74402	0.00019	−0.08994
96.00	24.11937	8.86673	8.85932	8.08891	−0.00084	−0.08772
97.00	24.62032	9.22990	9.21489	8.44323	−0.00163	−0.08523
98.00	25.12128	9.59865	9.57743	8.80670	−0.00221	−0.08251
99.00	25.62223	9.97282	9.94676	9.17901	−0.00261	−0.07960
100.00	26.12315	10.35221	10.32267	9.55983	−0.00285	−0.07654

n = 1   T_i = 0.2

V	S	w	BSS	BSE	(BSS−w)/w	(BSE−w)/w
80.00	13.97074	0.56354	1.04365	0.82141	0.85195	0.45759
81.00	14.53450	0.66952	1.15711	0.91266	0.72827	0.36316
82.00	15.09609	0.78915	1.28022	1.01456	0.62228	0.28564
83.00	15.65471	0.92312	1.41383	1.10806	0.53158	0.22201
84.00	16.20970	1.07205	1.55886	1.25412	0.45409	0.16983
85.00	16.76053	1.23645	1.71626	1.39365	0.38805	0.12714
86.00	17.30678	1.41673	1.88700	1.54750	0.33194	0.09230
87.00	17.84818	1.61317	2.07198	1.71649	0.28442	0.06405
88.00	18.38457	1.82593	2.27207	1.90130	0.24434	0.04128
89.00	18.91591	2.05506	2.48800	2.10256	0.21067	0.02311
90.00	19.44224	2.30049	2.72039	2.32073	0.18253	0.00880
91.00	19.96370	2.56204	2.96986	2.55617	0.15910	−0.00229
92.00	20.48050	2.83944	3.23606	2.80909	0.13968	−0.01069
93.00	20.99291	3.13230	3.51963	3.07955	0.12366	−0.01684
94.00	21.50123	3.44018	3.82019	3.36747	0.11046	−0.02114
95.00	22.00582	3.76255	4.13737	3.67262	0.09962	−0.02390
96.00	22.50703	4.09881	4.47061	3.99462	0.09071	−0.02542
97.00	23.00525	4.44833	4.81921	4.33296	0.08338	−0.02594
98.00	23.50086	4.81043	5.18231	4.68698	0.07731	−0.02566
99.00	23.99422	5.18442	5.55900	5.05591	0.07225	−0.02479
100.00	24.48569	5.56958	5.94830	5.43890	0.06800	−0.02346

The computations are carried out with the following parameters: there is initially one share outstanding ($m = 1$) and the firm has issued one warrant (the dilution factor is $n = 1$). The maturity of the warrant is $T_i = 0, 2$ year and $T_i = 1$ year, the maturity of the zero-coupon debt is $T = T_i + 1$ year and its face value is $F = 80$; the volatility of the assets of the firm is $\sigma = 30$ percent; the continuously compounded interest rate is $r = 10$ percent; and the strike price of the European equity warrant is $K = 20$. For these parameters the critical value $\bar{V}_i^* = 91.81$ such that if at the maturity of the warrant $V < \bar{V}_i^*$, the warrant expires worthless, and if $V \geq \bar{V}_i^*$, it is exercised. BSS denotes the Black-Scholes formula $BS(s, K, \bar{\sigma}, r, T_i)$, and BSE denotes the adjusted Black-Scholes formula $\frac{1}{m+n} BS(E = ms + nw, mK, \sigma(E), r, T_i)$. The relative pricing errors corresponding to these Black-Scholes approximations are denoted $\frac{BSS - w}{w}$ and $\frac{BSE - w}{w}$, respectively.

145

F I G U R E   7-4

Accuracy of the Black-Scholes Approximation for a European Equity
Warrant in a Levered Firm

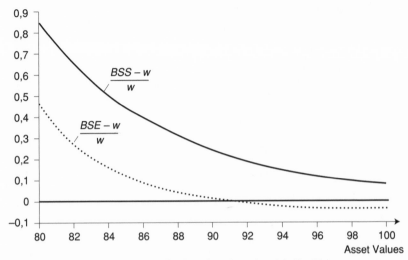

Parameter values and notations as in Table 7–2. This figure shows the results only for $T_1 = 0.2$ year.

price of an asset that is usually not traded, for example, the value of
the total assets of the firm.

In this chapter, we find the general conditions necessary for
deriving a PDE for complex contingent claims that is similar in
structure to the Black-Scholes PDE. This PDE is a function of the
security in terms of which the payoff for the complex contingent
claim is defined, and this security is more often traded than the
basic noncontingent security. In this PDE, the volatility parameter is
the volatility measure of the underlying (contingent) security and,
hence, is nonstationary. The nonconstant volatility for the underlying asset of the complex contingent claim is the major element in the
PDE that deviates from the conditions of BSM. Therefore, a closed-
form solution similar to a BSM cannot be obtained.

However, if the current volatility measure is a close approximation to its average over the life of the complex contingent claim,
BSM may provide a good approximation.

In the second part of the chapter we study several examples of
complex contingent claims and show, by simulations, the quality of
the approximation achieved by using BSM as if the current volatili-

ty measure for the underlying asset were a constant. The examples are, first, for an option on an option (e.g., a European call option on a share of a levered firm); second, for a warrant in an unlevered firm; and third, for a warrant in a levered firm. In all cases, the approximation for at- and in-the-money contingent claims is very good. Only for out-of-the-money contingent claims does the quality of the approximation deteriorate in percentage terms, while it becomes negligible in absolute terms.

REFERENCES

Bensoussan, A.; M. Crouhy; and D. Galai. "Black-Scholes Approximation of Warrant Prices. *Advances in Futures and Options Research* 8 (1995), pp. 1–14.

Black, F., and M. Scholes. "The Pricing of Options and Corporate Liabilities. *Journal of Political Economy* 81 (1973), pp. 637–54.

Cox, J., and M. Rubinstein. *Options Markets.* Englewood Cliffs, NJ: Prentice-Hall, 1985.

Crouhy, M., and D. Galai. "The Interaction between the Financial and Investment Decisions of the Firm: The Case of Issuing Warrants in a Levered Firm." *Journal of Banking and Finance* 18, no. 5 (1994), pp. 861–80.

Duffie, D. *Security Markets.* San Diego, CA: Academic Press, 1988.

Friedman, A. *Partial Differential Equation of Parabolic Type.* Englewood Cliffs, NJ: Prentice-Hall, 1964.

Galai, D., and R. Masulis. "The Option Pricing Model and the Risk Factor of Stock," *Journal of Financial Economics* 3 (1976), pp. 53–81.

Galai, D., and M. Schneller. "Pricing of Warrants and the Value of the Firm." *Journal of Finance* 33, no. 5 (1978), pp. 1333–42.

Geske, R. "The Valuation of Compound Options. *Journal of Financial Economics* 7, (1979), pp. 63–81.

Heston, S. L. "A Closed-Form Solution for Options with Stochastic Volatility with Applications to Bond and Currency Options." *Review of Financial Studies* 6, no. 2 (1993), pp. 327–43.

Hull, J., and A. White. "An Analysis of the Bias in Option Pricing Caused by a Stochastic Volatility." *Advances in Futures and Options Research* 3 (1988), pp. 29–61.

Jarrow, R., and A. Rudd. "Approximate Option Valuation for Arbitrary Stochastic Processes." *Journal of Financial Economics* 10 (1982), pp. 347–69.

Jarrow, R., and A. Rudd. Option Pricing. Homewood, IL: Irwin, 1983.

Jarrow, R., and J. Wiggins. "Option Pricing and Implicit Volatilities." *Journal of Economic Surveys* 3, no. 1 (1989).

Merton, R. C. "On the Pricing of Corporate Debt: The Risk Structure of Interest Rates." *Journal of Finance* 29, no. 2 (1974), pp. 449–70.

Merton, R. C. "Option Pricing When Underlying Stock Returns Are Discontinuous." *Journal of Financial Economics* 3 (1976), pp. 125–44.

APPENDIX 1

PROOF OF THEOREM 1

Note that $\sigma(C)$ is indeed a function of C, by replacing V by the solution of $C(V,t) = C$. By applying the chain rule for differentiating composite functions, it follows:

$$\psi_t = \varphi_t + \varphi_c C_t$$
$$\psi_v = \varphi_c C_v$$
$$\psi_{vv} = \varphi_c C_{vv} + \varphi_{cc}(C_v)^2.$$

Then, if ψ satisfies (4) it follows that:

$$-\psi_t - \frac{1}{2}\sigma^2 V^2 \psi_{vv} - rV\psi_v + r\psi \tag{29}$$

$$= -\varphi_t - \varphi_c C_t - \frac{1}{2}\sigma^2 V^2\left(\varphi_c C_{vv} + \varphi_{cc}(C_v)^2\right) - rV\varphi_c C_v + r\psi.$$

Using (3) and (2) to derive φ_t and C_t, respectively, we obtain for the right-hand side of (29):

$$= \frac{1}{2}\sigma(C)^2 C^2 \varphi_{cc} + rC\varphi_c - r\varphi$$

$$-\varphi_c\left(-\frac{1}{2}\sigma^2 V^2 C_{vv} - rVC_v + rC\right)$$

$$-\frac{1}{2}\sigma^2 V^2\left(\varphi_c C_{vv} + \varphi_{cc}(C_v)^2\right)$$

$$-rV\varphi_c C_v + r\varphi$$

$$= \frac{1}{2}\varphi_{cc}\left(\sigma(C)^2 C^2 - \sigma^2 V^2(C_v)^2\right),$$

which is equal to zero if

$$\sigma(C) = \sigma\frac{V}{C(V,t)}C_v, \tag{30}$$

which proves the necessary condition.

    If we now replace $\sigma(C)$ by expression (30) in equation (3), then (4) obtains, which proves the sufficient condition.

PROOF OF THEOREM 2

By the choice of $\sigma(C)$, the function $\psi(V,t) = \psi[C(V,t),t]$ satisfies the same PDE as F. Consider the process $V_0(t)$, which satisfies (1) with the initial condition:

$$V_0(t_0) = V_0.$$

From BSM, we have

$$\psi(V_0, t_0) = E\left\{\psi(V_0(T), T)e^{-r(T-t_0)}\right\}$$

$$F(V_0, t_0) = E\left\{F(V_0(T), T)e^{-r(T-t_0)}\right\}$$

Therefore, if $F(V,T) = \psi(V,T)$ $\forall V$ we get

$$\psi(V_0, t_0) = F(V_0, t_0),$$

and if $F(V,T) \leq \psi(V,T)$ $\forall T$, it follows that

$$F(V_0, t_0) \leq \psi(V_0, t_0).$$

V_0, t_0 being arbitrary, the desired result is proven.

APPENDIX 3

PROOF OF LEMMA 1

The results follow immediately from the property that the slope of the BSM call function in terms of the underlying asset price, is less than one.

More precisely, if τ denotes the option time-to-maturity:

$$\tau = T - t$$

$$BS(V,F,\sigma,r,\tau) = \int_{-\infty}^{+\infty} \left(Ve^{-\frac{\sigma^2}{2}\tau + \sigma\sqrt{\tau}y} Fe^{-r\tau} \right)^+ \frac{e^{-\frac{y^2}{2}}}{\sqrt{2\pi}} dy$$

$$BS(V+nK,F,\sigma,r,\tau) - nK = \int_{-\infty}^{+\infty} \left[\left((V+nK)e^{-\frac{\sigma^2}{2}\tau + \sigma\sqrt{\tau}y} - Fe^{-r\tau} \right)^+ \right] \frac{e^{-\frac{y^2}{2}}}{\sqrt{2\pi}} dy$$
$$\hspace{4cm} -nKe^{-\frac{\sigma^2}{2}\tau + \sigma\sqrt{\tau}y}$$

$$\leq \int_{-\infty}^{+\infty} \left(Ve^{-\frac{\sigma^2}{2}\tau + \sigma\sqrt{\tau}y} - Fe^{-r\tau} \right)^+ \frac{e^{-\frac{y^2}{2}}}{\sqrt{2n}} dy.$$

APPENDIX 4

PROOF OF LEMMA 2

From (17) and Lemma 1, it follows:

$$s(V,T_1) \geq \frac{BS(V + nK, F, \sigma, r, T - T_1)}{m + n} 1_{V \geq \bar{V}_1}$$

$$+ \frac{\left[BS(V + nK, F, \sigma, r, T - T_1) - nK\right]}{m} 1_{V < \bar{V}_1}$$

$$s(V,T_1) - K \geq \left[BS(V + nK, F, \sigma, r, T - T_1) - K(m + n)\right]$$

$$\left(\frac{1}{m + n} 1_{V \geq \bar{V}_1} + \frac{1}{m} 1_{V < \bar{V}_1}\right)$$

$$\left(s(V,T_1) - K\right)^+ \geq \frac{1}{m + n} \left[BS(V + nK, F, \sigma, r, T - T_1) - K(m + n)\right]^+$$

$$= w(V, T_1) \text{ from (18)}.$$

APPENDIX 5

PROOF OF LEMMA 3

From (18) we know that

$$(m+n)w(V,T_1) = \left[BS(V+nK,F,\sigma,r,T-T_1) - (m+n)K\right]1_{V \geq \overline{V}_1}. \quad (31)$$

From boundary condition (28) it follows that

$$E(V,T_1) \geq BS(V+nK,F,\sigma,r,T-T_1) - nK$$

and then,

$$E(V,T_1) - mK \geq BS(V+nK,F,\sigma,r,T-T_1) - (m+n)K$$

so that

$$\left(E(V,T_1) - mK\right)^+ \geq \left[BS(V+nK,F,\sigma,r,T-T_1) - (m+n)K\right]^+$$

where from (31) the desired result follows:

$$\left(E(V,T_1) - mK\right)^+ \geq (m+n)w(V,T_1).$$

A P P E N D I X   6

PROOF OF LEMMA 4

From (17) we have

$$s(V,T_1) = \frac{BS(V+nK,F,\sigma,r,T-T_1)-K(m+n)}{m+n}1_{V\geq\overline{V}_1}$$
$$+\frac{BS(V,F,\sigma,r,T-T_1)-Km}{m}1_{V<\overline{V}_1},$$

and from (28):

$$E(V,T_1)-mK = (BS(V,F,\sigma,r,T-T_1)-mK)1_{V<\overline{V}_1}$$
$$+[BS(V+nK,F,\sigma,r,T-T_1)-(m+n)K]1_{V\geq\overline{V}_1}.$$

Then,

$$(m+n)(s(V,T_1)-K) = [BS(V,F,\sigma,r,T-T_1)-K(m+n)]1_{V\geq\overline{V}_1}$$
$$+\frac{m+n}{m}[BS(V,F,\sigma,r,T-T_1)-Km]1_{V<\overline{V}_1}.$$

It follows for

$$V \geq \overline{V}_1 \text{ that } (m+n)(s(V,T_1)-K) = E(V,T_1)-mK$$

and for

$$V < \overline{V}_1 \text{ that } [E(V,T_1)-mK]^+ = [BS(V,F,\sigma,r,T-T_1)-mK]^+$$

but

$$(m+n)[s(V,T_1)-K]^+ = \frac{m+n}{n}[BS(V,F,\sigma,r,T-T_1)-Km]^+$$

so that,

$$[E(V,T_1)-mK]^+ \leq (m+n)[s(V,T_1)-K]^+$$

and therefore,

$$\frac{[E(V,T_1)-mK]^+}{m+n} \leq [s(V,T_1)-K]^+.$$

8

⑥ CONVERTIBLE BONDS AND PREFERRED SHARES

Izzy Nelken, President

Super Computer Consulting Corporation, Chicago

A CONVERTIBLE PRIMER

Many people love convertible cars. They offer the driver safety and convenience close to what a sedan offers coupled with the adventure and excitement of being close to the outdoors. In a similar fashion, convertible bonds offer the investor the safety of a fixed-income instrument coupled with participation in the upside of the equity markets. However, just as special care must be taken when driving convertible cars, special techniques must be used when managing investments in convertible bonds.

Essentially, convertible bonds (or simply *convertibles* or even *converts*) are bonds that, at the holder's option, are convertible into a pre-specified number of shares. Usually, but not always, these underlying shares are issued by the same entity that issued the convertible. So, when the stock rises, the convertible price rises in tandem with it and it becomes an "equity equivalent." However, when the stock tumbles, the convertible becomes equivalent to a normal bond and its price will not decline too much.

Figure 8–1 is a comparison of the value of a convertible bond and the underlying equity. Assume that the stock is currently trading at about $100. As the stock price increases, so does the price of the convertible that is said to be an equity equivalent. However, when the stock price declines, the convertible becomes a bond equivalent. The

FIGURE   8-1

Relationship of Convertible Bond Price to the Underlying Equity Value

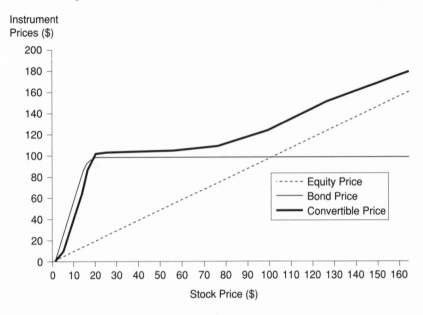

Stock Price ($)

share price can drop to almost $20 before the convertible holder feels a dramatic impact. When the share is in the range between $90 and $110, the bond is in the "hybrid region" and the impact of stock price movements on the price of the convertible is much subtler.

Market Conditions

As this chapter is written and 1995 draws to a close, stock markets are at record highs. Obviously, investors wish to participate in this meteoric rise. However, the fear of a major correction clouds this rosy picture. Some have labeled this mood as "cautious optimism." Such investors are considering investments in convertible bonds. Investor appetite is cited as one of the reasons for the resurgence in the convertible market. This is reassuring to many as 1994 was a dismal year in terms of new issues.

Figure 8–2 shows that issuance of new convertibles grew at a healthy rate between 1990 and 1993, then almost ground to a standstill in 1994. At that time, corporate America was "awash with cash." Most

F I G U R E   8–2

New Convertible Issues

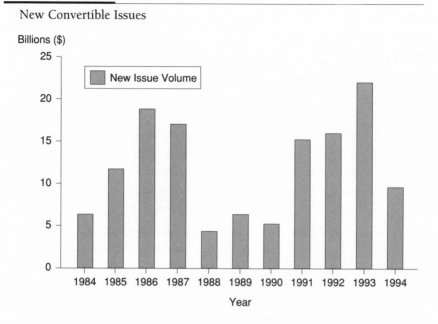

companies bought back bonds as well as stocks. Even if they needed to borrow, most creditworthy corporations found that spreads were razor thin, and they could do so at rates that were only slightly higher than Government yields. Unfortunately, exact figures for 1995 were not available at press time. However, it is well known that the convertible market has dramatically recovered from the lull of 1994.

At What Price Conversion?

From the issuer's point of view, conversion is a privilege granted to the investor in return for a lower coupon. So when issuers contemplate coming to market, they must determine the minimal coupon and conversion privilege that the market will bear. In times of low volatility, the issuer can bring a deal that is similar to a deal that was done in the past. However, when markets change rapidly, issuers must rely on theoretical pricing models.

Investors, however, have a variety of convertibles that are continuously being offered to them. We distinguish between two main types of investors:

- Money managers. They look at the universe of convertibles. Of these, they only consider issuers whose stock seems to be favorable. If they are bullish on the equity, they may purchase the corresponding convertible. There are many subcategories: convertible fund managers, fixed-income managers, risk-averse equity managers, income-oriented equity managers, and so on.

- Arbitrage specialists. They attempt to lock in profits due to misalignment between the equity market and the convertibles. They may be long the convertible bond and short the corresponding equity or vice versa. Since they maintain a close watch and a constant hedge, they are less concerned about the positive outlook for the equity.

All of these investors must be able to determine whether a particular deal is attractive. In addition, they must continually monitor their portfolios. In some cases, convertibles are illiquid instruments and it is difficult to obtain a recent market quote. Thus, in many cases, investors wish to "mark to model." They also need to determine risk measures and sensitivity parameters such as duration, convexity, key-rate duration, delta, gamma, the different vegas, and so on.

Some Complications

As the market matures, the structures are becoming more complex. Here is a sampling of some of the features found in recent convertibles.

Callability and Forced Conversion

To complicate matters further, many of the convertibles are also callable by the issuer. Assume that a certain convertible becomes callable by the issuer. The issuer decides to call the bond at par. However, the conversion value of the bond is $120. In this case, the investor would rather convert the bond into shares and receive $120 rather than wait for the call date and receive only $100. In this "forced conversion" scenario, the issuer forces the holder to convert the bonds into equity. Of course, the issuer knows if and when investors will choose to convert. We can almost think of this as a game between two opponents:

- The holder of the bond tries to maximize its value at all times.
- The issuer of the bond tries to minimize its value.

Protected Call and Unprotected Call

A certain bond may become callable by the issuer as of a certain date. This is known as an *unprotected call*. Another type of call is the *protected call*. In this case, the bond may only be called if the share price (or the average share price over the past 20 days) is above a certain barrier. Many bonds have some unprotected calls and some calls that are protected.

Conversion into Shares and Cash

Some bonds are convertible into a combination of shares and cash. In many cases, the conversion number as well as the cash amount vary as a function of time.

Put Features

Some convertibles have put features that could increase their value.

Dilution Effect

When an investor converts and receives shares, the shares may either be distributed from an existing stock or new shares might be printed. In the latter case, we have to account for a dilution effect—there are now more company shares for the same capital base adjusted by the debt. However, even when it is financially advantageous to do so, some investors may refrain from converting, perhaps due to tax considerations or maybe because they just forgot to do it. In these cases, we note a partial dilution.

Dual Currency

Some of the more recent issues are convertible into shares of different issuers who may be in different countries. This type of bond is also exposed to currency risk. For example, the underlying shares of several U.S. convertible bonds trade in Thai Bhat.

Step-Up Coupons

Many bonds exhibit step-up (or step-down) coupons in which the coupon rate varies with time.

Dividends

Dividends affect the share price and, as such, they impact the price of the convertible. At times we may want to model a certain dividend yield. In other circumstances, the yield may be a cash amount that is fixed regardless of the price. In many situations, the next few dividends may be modeled as known cash dividends and thereafter, it is more appropriate to model a dividend yield.

How to Model a Convert?

We distinguish among three generations of models:

1. The earliest methods compared the relative advantages of owning the convert versus owning the underlying shares outright. By subtracting the dividend yield from the coupon, the method computes a relative yield advantage. Then, it computes the time required for the yield differential to compensate for the initial conversion premium. In 1973, some institutions manufactured a plastic and carton circular slide rule that was used to compute relationships between various factors. It was able to manipulate the conversion value, conversion premium, conversion price, and stock price.

2. A more sophisticated approach considered the convertible as a combo of a regular (nonconvertible) bond plus a call option on the stock. The bond and call option are priced separately. Their prices are then summed together to form the price of the convertible. This method may work reasonably well when the convertible is either an equity equivalent or a bond equivalent. However, it is quite inaccurate in the hybrid region. This is unfortunate as most of the new issues are in that region. Also, this is where most of the opportunity and value in the convertible market are found.

3. The most advanced models consider the stochastic nature of both interest rates and share prices. This is the essence of a two-factor model. Almost everyone agrees that "Convertible bonds, for example, should be valued according to a model that considers both the behavior of interest rates and the issuer's stock price" (see "The Problem with Black, Scholes et al." by Andrew Kalotay, *Derivatives Strategy*, vol. 1, no. 1, November 1995). However, two-factor models are much more difficult to build and quite sophisticated to implement.

How to Check a Model

In addition to computing accurate results, a good software system must have the following characteristics:

1. It should be based on a two-factor algorithm.

2. It should be able to cope with all the complications mentioned in the previous sections and to accommodate some new "wrinkles" that the market may come up with in the future.

3. Since convertibles, by their very nature depend on a lot of data, it should offer good organization, intuitiveness, and user-friendliness.

4. A convertible system should also be able to handle preferred shares.

5. A good model should not be "grainy." One drawback of many of the models is their "graininess" or lack of continuity. Often, a user makes a small change to one of the input variables and discovers a large and inappropriate change in the value of the output. A good model should avoid this problem.

6. A model should not only compute the price of the convertible, but also all the relevant risk and sensitivity parameters.

7. A system should accommodate entire portfolios of convertible bonds. It also must be able to compare and sort a universe of bonds based on attractiveness. However, each individual bond must be modeled correctly.

8. The model should be able to automatically connect to a database or a data feed. There is too much information to maintain manually. Even if the database does not provide 100 percent of the required information, it will provide at least most of it.

9. In the case of bonds that do not exist yet or are not covered by the database, it should be simple to add details about them into the model.

10. Finally, the software should be able to handle nonconvertibles that are callable and putable. Therefore, it should have all of the characteristics required of any standard

bond-pricing algorithm, such as being arbitrage-free, easy to calibrate, and so on.

MODELING HYBRID INSTRUMENTS

Traditional Approaches

Next we review traditional methods used in valuing convertibles. The shortcomings of the traditional approaches have led us to develop more flexible and accurate evaluation methodologies.

Break-Even Period Analysis
This analysis compares two alternatives: owning shares versus owning convertibles. It first computes the ongoing *yield advantage*—coupon rate minus dividend rate—and then calculates the time required by the yield differential to fully compensate the initial *conversion premium*.[1]

Break-even period analysis only serves as a reasonable check on convertible securities. Convertible securities with a break-even period of less than three years generally are deemed to be acceptable investments. Break-even period analysis does not generate specific theoretical value or consider future dividend growth, certainty of dividend payment, option time value, or stock price volatility.

Discount Cash-Flow Analysis
Similar to the break-even period analysis, this analysis also is based on yield advantage, but it goes further and projects future cashflow—coupon income minus dividend income, with the possibility of incorporating dividend growth. This method adds net present value of the projected cash flows to the current stock price, then multiplies the sum by the conversion ratio to arrive at a "theoretical" convertible value.

Again, this method ignores the option time value and underlying stock price volatility. It is a better method than break-even period analysis because it actually values a convertible security. This approach is more applicable when the convertible is being evaluated as a debt rather than an equity instrument.

Synthetics (Bond Plus Equity Option)
This approach assumes that the value of a convertible is equal to the sum of two components: a straight bond of the same coupon and

---

1 Frank J. Fabozzi, *Bond Markets, Analysis and Strategies*, 2nd ed. (Englewood Cliffs, NJ: Prentice Hall, 1993), p. 376.

maturity, and a call option on the stock with the same exercise price. The bond component, in the absence of a comparable bond with the same coupon and maturity, can be valued by discounting all future coupons and the maturing principal by the appropriate risk-adjusted discount curve. The option will be valued independently with a long-term option model (see Fabozzi, 1993, footnote 1).

However, a closer look at the conversion feature reveals that the equality of a convertible to the sum of a straight bond and a call option on stock is inexact. There is a major difference between a straight freely traded equity option, which is exercisable by paying a known fixed exercise-price, and a convertible's converting feature, which is exercisable by turning in the value of a bond, which, at any point in time, depends on the value of the foregone coupons relative to the current yield curve.

Among the three approaches presented above, sophistication increases from one model to the next. Neither the break-even period analysis nor the discount cash flow analysis, can handle additional call or put features. The synthetics approach handles the option feature separately; though incorrect in valuation, it does try to account for the option time-value and volatility.

LYON Pricing

McConnell and Schwartz[2] have studied a liquid yield option note, which is a zero-coupon, convertible, callable, and puttable bond. They present the solution as a differential equation with a number of boundary conditions. The major difficulty with the LYON model is that it assumes a constant interest rate although it is well known that the term structure of interest rates is far from flat.

Quadro-Tree Approach

In light of numerous shortcomings in the traditional evaluation approaches, we have constructed a new convertible pricing model based on the concept of a quadro-tree—a combination of two binary trees, an interest rate binomial tree and a stock prices binomial tree. In this fashion, we model the price's dependency on the underlying stock price as well as on the prevailing interest rates.

---

2 John J. McConnell and Eduardo S. Schwartz, "LYON Taming," *The Journal of Finance* XLI, no. 3 (July 1986).

To explain the model, we first consider the separate construction of a tree of rates and a tree of stock prices. These have appeared elsewhere and so we only provide sketchy descriptions of the methods. If you are interested in more information, refer to the references given in footnotes.

Interest Rate Tree

A popular method of pricing a simple callable bond is to construct a tree of one-period future interest rates. We adopt the model developed by Kalotay, Williams, and Fabozzi,[3] who build a tree of future one-period rates beginning today:

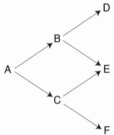

On each node is the one-year (or period) forward rate beginning at that time.

Node A   The one-period spot rate

Nodes B and C   Possible one-period forward rates one period from today.

Nodes D, E, and F   Possible one-period forward rates two periods from today.

In this case, a period could be one year or some other appropriate time frame.

Notice that only the present is determined. We know the information at node A—it is the one-year spot rate. However, since we are not sure of what the future will bring, there are a few possibilities for nodes B and C. For example, nodes B and C represent two possible one-year rates that may prevail one year from now. They are both equally likely and have equal probabilities. The further we go out into the future, the more possibilities we have. Hence we have one possible value for the current rates, two possible values for the one-

3 Andrew J. Kalotay, George O. Williams, and Frank J. Fabozzi, "A Model for Valuing Bonds and Embedded Options," *Financial Analysts Journal*, May/June 1993, p. 35.

year rate one year from now, three possibilities for the rate two years from now, and so on.

Given that the volatility of the short rate is σ, assume that the rate at C is r_1, then the rate at B is $r_1 e^{2\sigma\sqrt{\Delta t}}$ (in our case $\Delta t = 1$). We set the rate at node A to be equal to the one-year benchmark yield.

We choose r_1 so as to solve for the value of a two-year benchmark bond.

This is done as follows. Suppose the two-year benchmark bond, which has a coupon of 10 percent, is priced at P. For simplicity, and without loss of generality, we assume an annual-pay bond. Let's guess $r_1 = 7$ percent. Two years from now, the bond will mature at par and will also pay out its coupon. Assume that one year from now, the one-year rate will be $r_1 e^{2\sigma\sqrt{\Delta t}}$. We discount the maturity value of the bond, which is $110 at that rate, and obtain the price of the bond one year from today. We repeat the same procedure, but this time we assume that we are in node C and the one-year rate is r_1. We now have two possible prices for the benchmark one year from today.

However, the price of the bond today is its expected price one year from now plus the coupon payment, discounted back to today. Since we know the rate at node A, we can compute the average price of the bond at nodes B and C, add the coupon and discount it by the rate at node A. The price should be equal to the current market price of the two-year benchmark. If it is not, we should adjust our guess for r_1 until we obtain a match.

We then set the rate at F to r_2, the rate at E to $r_2 e^{2\sigma\sqrt{\Delta t}}$ and the rate at D to $r_2 e^{4\sigma\sqrt{\Delta t}}$. We choose r_2 so as to solve for the value of a three-year benchmark bond. We continue in this fashion until the entire tree is built.

We assume that there is an equal probability for an up move or a down move. The exact procedure for building the rate tree can be found in Kalotay, Williams, and Fabozzi (1993).

Stock Price Tree

A tree for stock prices in the future can easily be built as described by Hull.[4] The actual model is attributed to Cox, Ross, and Rubinstein.[5]

---

4 John C. Hull, *Options Futures and Other Derivative Securities,* 2nd ed. (Englewood Cliffs, NJ: Prentice Hall, 1993).

5 J. Cox, S. Ross, and M. Rubinstein, "Option Pricing: A Simplified Approach," *Journal of Financial Economics,* 7, (October 1979), pp. 229–64.

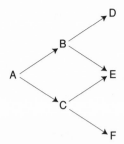

Node A—Today's stock price.

Nodes B and C—The stock price one year from today.

Nodes D, E, and F—the stock price two years from today. Since we are not sure of what the future will bring, there are a few possibilities.

The price at A is S

The price at B is Su and at C is Sd.

We assume that the probability of a move to B is p and of a move to C is $(1-p)$.

The price at D is Suu, the price at E is S, the price at F is Sdd.

u, d and p are easily calculated given the short rate r, the volatility of the stock price σ and the dividend rate q.

$u = e^{\sigma\sqrt{\Delta t}}$

$d = e^{-\sigma\sqrt{\Delta t}}$

$a = e^{(r-q)\Delta t}$

$p = (a-d)/(u-d)$

A Quadro-Tree

We will now combine the two approaches into a single quadranary or "quadro-tree." Each node will have four descendants.

Out of each node A, we will have four descendants: B, C, D, and E, defined as follows:

A
B—Stock up, rates up.
C—Stock up, rates down.
D—Stock down, rates up.
E—Stock down, rates down.

The price at maturity is 100. Then, moving backward in time, the instrument's price at A is computed as follows:

$$A = Z(0.5{*}p{*}B + 0.5{*}p{*}C + 0.5{*}(1-p){*}D + 0.5{*}(1-p){*}E + \text{coupon})$$

where Z is the discount factor, and

$$Z = e^{-r\Delta t}$$

Where r is the interest rate at node A.

We now subject the price at A to the following logic:

1. Define R = max (call price, N^* Stock Price). If the stock price is greater than the boundary at which the issuer may call and the instrument price is greater than R, then set the instrument price = R. If the issuer intends to call the instrument at the call price, then the holder gets the opportunity to convert to common shares. In most cases, the value of the shares is greater than the call price and so the issuer may "force conversion" on the holder.

2. If the instrument's price is smaller than N^*Stock Price, then set instrument price = N^*Stock Price. This is because the value of the bond cannot be smaller than its intrinsic value.

3. In all other cases, do not change the price at A.

Of course, other features of the bond (such as put options) may be modeled in this environment in a similar fashion. If the call and put features occur simultaneously, priority is given according to the prospectus.

CASE STUDY

A Convertible Bond that Is Callable Depending on the Current Stock Price

We used our model to price the bond of Abitibi-Price. It has a coupon of 7.85 percent and matures on March 1, 2003. It is an example of a bond that is both callable and convertible. These bonds are callable by the issuer at certain predetermined dates and at predetermined prices. However, the call option is enabled only if the price of the common stock of the issuer rises above a certain barrier. This type of bond is also convertible anytime at the holder's option into a certain predetermined number of common shares.

Of course, these benefits come at a price. We can assume that the price of a convertible is higher than the price of a similar regular bond. To make matters more complicated, the call option also has an impact on the price.

We used the above-described Quadro model to compute the fair value of this complicated instrument.

Pricing Challenges

As mentioned before, the bond has two embedded options. The call option means that if the common stock of the issuer is priced above a certain barrier, the issuer may call the bond at par. The barrier may change as maturity approaches. Under the conversion option, the holder may convert the bond into a predetermined amount of common stock at any time. The number of common stocks to which the bond can be converted may change as maturity approaches. There are no restrictions on this right of the holder.

It may happen that the issuer will notify the holder of an intention to call the bond. In that case, the holder might choose to convert. Thus, we may say that the issuer has the power to force the investor to convert. This is known as *forced conversion*.

Assumptions

Exercise Strategies We always assume that both the issuer and the holder will always follow a logical course of action when choosing whether to exercise their respective options. Further, the issuer and the holder are aware of each other and each one assumes that the other acts rationally. These are reasonable assumptions, as McConnell (1986, see footnote 2) makes clear. Acting rationally means that at all times the issuer tries to minimize the value of the instrument, and at all times the holder tries to maximize the value of the instrument.

Volatility of the Underlying Shares The volatility of the underlying shares is assumed constant over the life the bond. The user must estimate this volatility using either historical averages or implied volatility numbers from the option markets.

Volatility of Rates The volatility of the short rate is assumed constant over the life the bond. Although we recognize that this is a somewhat restrictive assumption, we felt that it was much less restrictive than assuming a constant interest rate.

No Arbitrage Like many other mathematical models, this is based on the assumption that no arbitrage conditions exist. Further, we assume frictionless markets, no bid/ask spreads, and that all information is available to everyone at the same time.

Computational Examples

We are now in the position to consider the Abitibi-Price callable convertible bond. The bond has a 7.85 percent coupon and matures in nine years. The following benchmark bond yields are assumed for a Canadian issuer with the same credit quality:

6 months 8.429%

1 year   8.751

2 years   9.970

3 years   10.210

5 years   10.920

7 years   11.360

10 years 11.580

The issuer can call the bond at par after two years provided that the stock price has gone above $18.75. Thereafter there is a declining barrier to the stock price. When the stock is above the barrier, the bond can be called. On the other hand, the holder can convert the bond at any time to 6.6666 stocks. We also assume that the dividend yield is 0 percent, the volatility of the stock price is 25 percent, and the volatility of the yields is 10 percent.

On March 30, 1994, the stock was trading at $17.375 and the bond was trading at $130. The theoretical price of the bond was $129.6161, which confirms that the model's price is close to the actual price.

CONCLUSION

We have presented a two-factor model-based methodology for valuing callable convertible bonds. This method has been extended for many other types of convertible bonds such as dual currency convertibles, preferred shares, and so on.

ⓖ   **A NEW APPROACH TO
EVALUATING MORTGAGE-
BACKED SECURITIES**

Gifford Fong, President,
Gifford Fong Associates

Dunmu Ji, Director of Research
Gifford Fong Associates

Daizhan Cheng, Research Associate
Gifford Fong Associates

It is well known that the major difficulty in pricing mortgage-backed securities is the uncertainty of the cash flows. This uncertainty is due to the fact that many mortgagors can prepay their loans at any time before maturity without a prepayment penalty. The mortgage-backed security investor then receives the scheduled payment, which consists of the coupon interest and the principal amortization, plus any additional prepayment of principal in the pool. The main issue in pricing mortgage-backed securities, therefore, is how to treat the uncertain cash flows and how to express the premium that an investor should demand as fair compensation for the extra risk from the unscheduled prepayments.

This chapter proposes a new evaluation method. This new method, called the mixed method, combines the characteristics of the closed-form model with a Monte Carlo simulation, and possesses two outstanding advantages:

1. It considers path-dependency of the prepayment rate of mortgage-backed securities by calculating price based on the expected value from various paths.

2. Since only prices over a few paths have to be calculated, the evaluation process is much faster than a Monte Carlo simulation.

We begin with an overview of the framework for valuing mortgage-backed securities that is based on contingent claims pricing theory.

CONTINGENT CLAIMS MODELS

As mentioned in the previous section, the difficulties in pricing mortgage-backed securities are cash flow uncertainties, caused by prepayment. Fortunately, prepayment behavior is not purely random. It depends on interest rates: prepayments tend to increase when interest rates are falling and vice versa. Contingent claims pricing theory provides models to describe the behavior of interest rates. We make the following assumptions:

1. The term structure of interest rates is driven by a single factor: the instantaneous spot rate. The instantaneous spot rate is a diffusion process.
2. The price movement of a security is a Markov process. In other words, the price of the security depends only on current and future interest rates.
3. The market is assumed to be efficient so that no profitable riskless arbitrage is possible.

Based on these assumptions, different models can be developed to evaluate contingent claims and determine their risk characteristics, such as duration, convexity, and the like.

One useful model is called the mean-reversion model (see Fabozzi and Fong [1994]). It assumes that the spot rate moves over time to keep pulling the short rate toward its long-term mean. The so called mean-reverting square-root diffusion process, a Wiener process, is described by:

$$dr = \alpha(\bar{r} - r)dt + \sigma\sqrt{r}dz \qquad (1)$$

where $\bar{r}$ is the long-run stable mean of the short rate, α is the speed of adjustment, and σ is the standard deviation of the instantaneous spot rate.

Assume the value of the security is a function of interest rates and time, $P = P(r,t)$. Then a closed form of the valuation equation, which is called Black-Scholes equation (see Hull [1989]), can be obtained as the following per Cox, Ingersoll, and Ross (1985):

$$\frac{\partial P}{\partial t} + \left[\alpha(\bar{r}-r)-qr\right]\frac{\partial P}{\partial r} + \frac{1}{2}\sigma^2 r\frac{\partial^2 P}{\partial r^2} + C - rP = 0 \qquad (2)$$

where q is the market price of risk and C is the coupon rate on the security. Adding suitable boundary conditions, Equation (2) can be solved numerically.

CLOSED-FORM VALUATION MODEL

For mortgage-backed securities, the prepayment rate depends on interest-rate paths (see Davidson and Herskovitz [1994]). For the time being, we ignore the path-dependency of the prepayment rate. The standard contingent-claims analysis method can then be used to generate different differential equations for mortgage-backed securities. The following model based on Fabozzi and Fong (1994) is what we used, and it is very similar to Equation (2):

$$\frac{\partial P}{\partial t} + \frac{\sigma^2}{2}\frac{\partial^2 P}{\partial r^2} + b\frac{\partial P}{\partial r} - rP - R(r)P + C + \left[1 - R(r)\right] = 0; \qquad (3)$$

$$P(r,T) = 0;$$

$$P(\infty,t) = 0;$$

where $P(r,t)$ is the price of the mortgage-backed security, r is the spread between the refinancing rate and the current mortgage rate, c is the coupon rate of the mortgage-backed security, b is the instantaneous expected change in interest rates, σ^2 is the instantaneous volatility of interest rates, $R(r)$ is the principal payment rate, t is the age of the mortgage, and T is the maturity date.

Equation (3) can be solved by a finite difference method, for example the finite element method.

Next, we consider duration and convexity. A straightforward numerical method to calculate duration and convexity is using the difference to approximate the derivative. That is, we can evaluate price on a basic term structure r_0, to get price P_0, then shift r_0 in a parallel manner up and down by h sequentially to get corresponding prices P_u and P_d. Then the duration and convexity can be evaluated approximately by the following two difference equations respectively:

$$\frac{dP}{dr} = \frac{P_u - P_d}{2h} \tag{4}$$

$$\frac{d^2P}{dr^2} = \frac{P_u - 2P_0 + P_d}{h^2}. \tag{5}$$

Then

Dollar Duration $= -dP / dr$;

Dollar Convexity $= d^2P / dr^2$.

In practice, we may improve the original deterministic model slightly by combining Equation (3) with Equations (4) and (5).

First of all, we assume interest rates have a normal distribution with a small variance (see Vasicek and Fong [1982]). We generate three paths by shifting the original term structure r_0 up and down by h sequentially and denote them as r_1 and r_{-1} respectively. Then we can calculate the corresponding prices P_i, where $i = -1, 0, 1$.

Using Hermite polynomial with $n = 3$ (see Abramovitz and Stegun [1972]), we estimate price P by EP, where

$$EP = \frac{H_1 * P_{-1} + H_0 * P_0 + H_1 * P_1}{\sqrt{\pi}} \tag{6}$$

with Hermite weight factors $H_1 = 0.295409$ and $H_0 = 1.181636$.

Note that since in Equations (4) and (5) h should be a small number, σ is also assumed to be small. Moreover h satisfies

$$\sqrt{2}\sigma x = h, \text{ where } x = 1.224745.$$

In general, if we want to use a Hermite polynomial with parameter n, then $3n$ paths are required to estimate duration and convexity.

Next, we sketch an example for a general approach to this model. Assume we use Hermite polynomial with $n = 5$. Then we need 15 paths: $P(r_i)$, $P(r_i \pm \delta_1)$, $P(r_i \pm \delta_2)$, for $i = -1, 0, 1$, where $r_{-1} = r_0 - h$, $r_1 = r_0 + h$, $\delta_1 = \sqrt{2}\ \sigma x_1$, $\delta_2 = \sqrt{2}\ \sigma x_2$, $x_1 = 0.95857$, $x_2 = 2.02018$, and

$$(EP)_i = \frac{H_2 P(r_i - \delta_2) + H_2 P(r_i + \delta_2) + H_1 P(r_i - \delta_1) + H_1 P(r_1 + \delta_1) + H_0 P(r_i)}{\sqrt{\pi}}, \tag{7}$$

for $i = -1, 0, 1$. The Hermite weight factors are $H_0 = 0.945309$, $H_1 = 0.393619$, and $H_2 = 0.019953$.

Choosing parameters $h = 0.01$ and $\sigma = 0.15$, we have

$$\frac{dP}{dr} = \frac{H_2}{2h\sqrt{\pi}} \left(\begin{array}{l} P\left(r_0 + h - \sqrt{2}\sigma x_2\right) + P\left(r_0 + h + \sqrt{2}\sigma x_2\right) \\ -P\left(r_0 - h - \sqrt{2}\sigma x_2\right) - P\left(r_0 - h + \sqrt{2}\sigma x_2\right) \end{array} \right) \tag{8}$$

$$+ \frac{H_1}{2h\sqrt{\pi}} \left(\begin{array}{l} P\left(r_0 + h - \sqrt{2}\sigma x_1\right) + P\left(r_0 + h + \sqrt{2}\sigma x_1\right) \\ -P\left(r_0 - h - \sqrt{2}\sigma x_1\right) - P\left(r_0 - h + \sqrt{2}\sigma x_1\right) \end{array} \right)$$

$$+ \frac{H_0}{2h\sqrt{\pi}} \left(P\left(r_0 + h\right) - P\left(r_0 - h\right) \right)$$

$$= 0.562869 \left(\begin{array}{l} P\left(r_0 - 0.418545\right) + P\left(r_0 + 0.438545\right) \\ -P\left(r_0 - 0.438545\right) - P\left(r_0 + 0.418545\right) \end{array} \right)$$

$$+ 11.103787 \left(\begin{array}{l} P\left(r_0 - 0.193744\right) + P\left(r_0 + 0.213344\right) \\ -P\left(r_0 - 0.213344\right) - P\left(r_0 + 0.193344\right) \end{array} \right)$$

$$+ 26.66667 \left(P\left(r_0 + 0.01\right) - P\left(r_0 - 0.01\right) \right)$$

and

$$\frac{d^2 P}{dr^2} = \frac{H_2}{h^2\sqrt{\pi}} \left(\begin{array}{l} P\left(r_0 + h - \sqrt{2}\sigma x_2\right) + P\left(r_0 + h + \sqrt{2}\sigma x_2\right) \\ -2P\left(r_0 - \sqrt{2}\sigma x_2\right) - 2P\left(r_0 + \sqrt{2}\sigma x_2\right) \\ +P\left(r_0 - h - \sqrt{2}\sigma x_2\right) + P\left(r_0 - h + \sqrt{2}\sigma x_2\right) \end{array} \right) \tag{9}$$

$$+ \frac{H_1}{h^2\sqrt{\pi}} \left(\begin{array}{l} P\left(r_0 + h - \sqrt{2}\sigma x_1\right) + P\left(r_0 + h + \sqrt{2}\sigma x_1\right) - 2P\left(r_0 - \sqrt{2}\sigma x_2\right) \\ -2P\left(r_0 + \sqrt{2}\sigma x_2\right) - P\left(r_0 + h - \sqrt{2}\sigma x_1\right) - P\left(r_0 - h + \sqrt{2}\sigma x_1\right) \end{array} \right)$$

$$+ \frac{H_0}{h^2\sqrt{\pi}} \left(P\left(r_0 + h\right) - P\left(r_0 - h\right) \right)$$

$$= 110.543 \left(\begin{array}{l} P\left(r_0 - 0.418545\right) + P\left(r_0 + 0.438545\right) - 2P\left(r_0 - 0.428545\right) \\ -2P\left(r_0 + 0.428545\right) + P\left(r_0 - 0.438545\right) + P\left(r_0 + 0.418545\right) \end{array} \right)$$

$$+ 2220.76 \left(\begin{array}{l} P\left(r_0 - 0.193744\right) + P\left(r_0 + 0.213344\right) - 2P\left(r_0 - 0.203344\right) \\ -2P\left(r_0 + 0.203344\right) + P\left(r_0 - 0.213344\right) + P\left(r_0 + 0.193344\right) \end{array} \right)$$

$$+ 5333.33 \left(P\left(r_0 + 0.01\right) - 2P\left(r_0\right) + P\left(r_0 - 0.01\right) \right).$$

MONTE CARLO SIMULATION

When we take the path-dependency of the prepayment rate into consideration, the prepayment rate becomes a function of the spread and of the relative portion of the pool prepaid. To accomplish this, the relative portion of the prepayment rate can be incorporated into the model through the pool factor. The pool factor becomes another state variable. Thus, we have two sets of partial differential equations: one for the price of the mortgage-backed security, the other for the pool factor. The property of path-dependency of the prepayment makes the solution process by finite difference method very complicated. Therefore, we must rely on the Monte Carlo simulation.

To use the Monte Carlo simulation method, we have to write the value of a mortgage-backed security into a stochastic integration form as:

$$P(r) = E \int_0^T e^{-\int_0^t r_\tau d\tau + R(r,t)} [1 - R(r,t) + c] dt \qquad (10)$$

where the expectation is taken over the possible interest rates in a risk-neutral world, and τ is the time such that $0 \le \tau \le t$. To calculate the value of $P(r)$ in Equation (10), the Monte Carlo simulation method generates a collection of paths by simulating the Wiener process of interest rates. We then take the weighted average as the expected price. This process is very time-consuming and requires a significantly large amount of computing capability.

Now the question is: Is it possible to calculate only a few paths and at the same time consider the path-dependency of the prepayment rate? To do this, we propose a new approach that combines the idea of the Monte Carlo simulation with the closed-form model. We call this new approach the mixed method, and it is presented in the next section.

NEW APPROACH FOR STOCHASTIC INTEGRAL

As we discussed before, the Monte Carlo method is one of the popular methods for calculating a stochastic integral. However, it is too slow for practical use in personal computers. What we propose here is a new method for calculating a stochastic integral.

The method can be adapted for the CIR model, Black model, Black-Derman-Toy model, Extended Vasicek model, and others. As an example, we illustrate the method via the Black model. In this section we describe the construction and derive formulas for the method. We will give the theoretical explanation in next section.

In the Black model, we assume

$$dr = f(t)dt + \sigma r dz \tag{11}$$

where $f(t)$ is the drift term, which is chosen to fit the current term structure. The new approach works in the following way: We first create a group of paths according to the model we have chosen. Note that it should be chosen carefully. Otherwise, a closed-form solution may not exist. Then we assign a suitable probability to each path according to the model. Finally, we sum the prices by probability to get the expected price.

The paths are chosen in the following way: First we choose a path along the current term structure. We call this path the central path. In fact, this path is

$$r(t) = r_0 e^{\int_0^t f(s)ds}.$$

Without confusion, we simply denote the central path by r_0.

Next, we generate several other paths. In the closed-form approach, all other paths are generated by shifting the basic path r_0 in a parallel manner up and down. In the Monte Carlo simulation, we assume $r(0) = r_0(0)$, and generate other paths by random numbers obtained through the probability distribution of interest rates. In this mixed approach we set a gate at time Δt and choose $2n + 1$ paths, based on Equation (11) as:

$$r_1 = r_0 \exp(i\Delta h), \ i = -n, \ -(n-1), \ \cdots, \ n-1, \ n \tag{12}$$

where $\Delta h = \mu \Delta t$.

Note that r_i is no longer a parallel shift of r_0.

Corresponding to each r_i we can work out P_i, for $i = -n, -(n-1)$, $\ldots, n-1, n$. Assuming the price is path dependent, to evaluate price P for any path we made the following assumptions:

1. For any two paths r_i, r_j, if $r_i(\Delta t) = r_j(\Delta t)$ at time Δt, then $P(r_i) = P(r_j)$.

2. $P(r)$ is piecewise linear.

In pricing mortgage-backed securities, we are only concerned about coupon dates, which are finite. If two paths have the same value at all coupon dates the prices over these two paths will be the same. That makes the first assumption reasonable. The second assumption is from the continuity of price with respect to spread. Additionally, we can increase the accuracy by increasing the number of paths.

Under these two assumptions we have:

$$P(r) = \begin{cases} P(r_{-n}), & 0 < r < r_{-n} \\ P_{i-1} + \dfrac{r - r_{i-1}}{r_i - r_{i-1}}(P_i - P_{i-1}), & r_{i-1} \le r < r_1, -n+1 < i \le n. \\ P(r_n), & r_n \le r < \infty \end{cases} \quad (13)$$

Since $r_i = r_0 \exp(i\Delta h)$, it follows that $P = P(r_0, r)$. Let $f_r(s)$ be the density function of r, which has a log-normal distribution (see Hull [1989]). Then

$$EP = \int_0^{r_{-n}} P_{-n} f_r(s)ds + \int_{r_n}^{\infty} P_n f_r(s)ds \qquad (14)$$
$$+ \sum_{i=-n+1}^{n} \int_{r_{i-1}}^{r_i} \left(P_{i-1} + \frac{r - r_{i-1}}{r_i - r_{i-1}}(P_i - P_{i-1}) \right) f_r(s)ds.$$

To convert it to a normal distribution, let $t = \log(r)$ or $r = \exp(t)$. Then we have

$$EP = \frac{1}{\sqrt{2\pi}\sigma} \int_{-\infty}^{\log(r_{-n})} P_{-n} e^{\frac{(\tau - \mu_t)^2}{2\sigma^2}} dt$$
$$+ \sum_{i=-n+1}^{n} \frac{1}{\sqrt{2\pi}\sigma} \int_{\log(r_{i-1})}^{\log(r_i)} \left(P_{i-1} + \frac{e^t - r_{i-1}}{r_i - r_{i-1}}(P_i - P_{i-1}) e^{\frac{(\tau - \mu_t)^2}{2\sigma^2}} \right) dt \quad (15)$$
$$+ \frac{1}{\sqrt{2\pi}\sigma} \int_{\log(r_n)}^{\infty} P_n e^{\frac{(\tau - \mu_t)^2}{2\sigma^2}} dt.$$

Note that

$$\mu_t = \log(\mu) - \frac{\sigma^2}{2}.$$

Skipping some tedious computation, we can show that

$$EP = P_{-n}N\left(\frac{\log\left(\frac{r_{-n}}{\mu}\right)}{\sigma} + \frac{\sigma}{2}\right) \tag{16}$$

$$+ \sum_{i=-n+1}^{n}\left(\frac{P_i r_i - 2P_i r_{i-1} + P_{i-1}r_{i-1}}{r_i - r_{i-1}}\right)\left(N\left(\frac{\log\left(\frac{r_i}{\mu}\right)}{\sigma} + \frac{\sigma}{2}\right) - N\left(\frac{\log\left(\frac{r_{i-1}}{\mu}\right)}{\sigma} + \frac{\sigma}{2}\right)\right)$$

$$+ \mu \sum_{i=-n+1}^{n}\left(\frac{P_i - P_{i-1}}{r_i - r_{i-1}}\right)\left(N\left(\frac{\log\left(\frac{r_i}{\mu}\right)}{\sigma} - \frac{\sigma}{2}\right) - N\left(\frac{\log\left(\frac{r_{i-1}}{\mu}\right)}{\sigma} - \frac{\sigma}{2}\right)\right)$$

$$+ P_n\left(1 - N\left(\frac{\log\left(\frac{r_n}{\mu}\right)}{\sigma} - \frac{\sigma}{2}\right)\right)$$

where

$$N(x) = \frac{1}{\sqrt{2\pi}}\int_{-\infty}^{x} e^{-\frac{s^2}{2}}\,ds.$$

Note that now we have price, duration, and convexity as:

$$\text{Price} = P(r_0) = EP(r_0, r); \tag{17}$$

$$\text{Dollar Duration} = -\left(\frac{\partial P}{\partial r_0}\right);$$

$$\text{Dollar Convexity} = \frac{1}{2}\left(\frac{\partial^2 P}{\partial r_0^2}\right).$$

Keeping in mind that r_i is a function of r_0, the following two formulas can be obtained through careful computation:

$$\frac{\partial}{\partial r_0} N\left(\frac{\log\left(\frac{r_i}{\mu}\right)}{\sigma} \pm \frac{\sigma}{2}\right) = \frac{1}{\sqrt{2\pi}} e^{-\frac{\left(\frac{\log\left(\frac{r_i}{\mu}\right)}{\sigma} \pm \frac{\sigma}{2}\right)}{2}} \left(\frac{1}{\sigma}\right)\left(\frac{1}{r_0}\right) \tag{18}$$

and

$$\frac{\partial^2}{\partial r_0^2} N\left(\frac{\log\left(\frac{r_i}{\mu}\right)}{\sigma} \pm \frac{\sigma}{2}\right) = \frac{1}{\sqrt{2\pi}} e^{-\frac{\left(\frac{\log\left(\frac{r_i}{\mu}\right)}{\sigma} \pm \frac{\sigma}{2}\right)^2}{2}} \left(-\frac{\log\left(\frac{r_i}{\mu}\right)}{\sigma^3 r_0^2} - \frac{c_\pm}{\sigma r_0^2}\right) \tag{19}$$

where $c_+ = \dfrac{3}{2}, c_- = \dfrac{1}{2}$.

Using Equations (18) and (19) repeatedly, we finally get the following formulas:

$$\frac{\partial P}{\partial r_0} = \frac{P_{-n}}{\sqrt{2\pi}\sigma r_0} e^{-\frac{\left(\frac{\log(r_{-n})}{\sigma} + \frac{\sigma}{2}\right)^2}{2}} \tag{20}$$

$$+ \sum_{i=-n+1}^{n} \left(\frac{P_i r_i - 2P_i r_{i-1} + P_{i-1} r_{i-1}}{(r_i - r_{i-1})\sqrt{2\pi}\sigma r_0}\right)\left(e^{-\frac{\left(\frac{\log(r_i)}{\mu} + \frac{\sigma}{2}\right)^2}{2}} - e^{-\frac{\left(\frac{\log(r_{i-1})}{\mu} + \frac{\sigma}{2}\right)^2}{2}}\right)$$

$$- \sum_{i=-n+1}^{n} \left(\frac{\mu(P_i - P_{i-1})}{(r_i - r_{i-1})r_0}\right)\left(N\left(\frac{\log\left(\frac{r_i}{\mu}\right)}{\sigma} - \frac{\sigma}{2}\right) - N\left(\frac{\log\left(\frac{r_{i-1}}{\mu}\right)}{\sigma} - \frac{\sigma}{2}\right)\right)$$

$$+ \sum_{i=-n+1}^{n} \left(\frac{\mu(P_i - P_{i-1})}{(r_i - r_{i-1})\sqrt{2\pi}\sigma r_0}\right)\left(e^{-\frac{\left(\frac{\log\left(\frac{r_i}{\mu}\right)}{\sigma} - \frac{\sigma}{2}\right)}{2}} - e^{-\frac{\left(\frac{\log\left(\frac{r_{i-1}}{\mu}\right)}{\sigma} - \frac{\sigma}{2}\right)}{2}}\right)$$

(continued)

(Equation 20 concluded)

$$-\frac{P_n}{\sqrt{2\pi}\sigma r_0}e^{-\frac{\left(\frac{\log\left(\frac{r_n}{\mu}\right)}{2}+\frac{\sigma}{2}\right)^2}{2}}$$

$$\frac{\partial^2 P}{\partial r_0^2} = \frac{P_{-n}}{\sqrt{2\pi}\sigma^3 r_0^2}e^{-\frac{\left(\frac{\log(r_{-n})}{\sigma}+\frac{\sigma}{2}\right)^2}{2}}\left(-\log\left(\frac{r_{-n}}{\mu}\right)-\frac{3\sigma^2}{2}\right) \tag{21}$$

$$+\sum_{i=-n+1}^{n}\left(\frac{P_i r_i - 2P_i r_{i-1} + P_{i-1}r_{i-1}}{(r_i - r_{i-1})\sqrt{2\pi}\sigma^3 r_0^2}\right)$$

$$\left(e^{-\frac{\left(\frac{\log\left(\frac{r_i}{\mu}\right)}{\sigma}+\frac{\sigma}{2}\right)^2}{2}}\left(-\log\left(\frac{r_i}{\mu}\right)-\frac{3\sigma^2}{2}\right)\right.$$

$$\left.-e^{-\frac{\left(\frac{\log\left(\frac{r_{i-1}}{\mu}\right)}{\sigma}+\frac{\sigma}{2}\right)^2}{2}}\left(-\log\left(\frac{r_{i-1}}{\mu}\right)-\frac{3\sigma^2}{2}\right)\right)$$

$$+\sum_{i=-n+1}^{n}\left(\frac{2\mu(P_i - P_{i-1})}{(r_i - r_{i-1})r_0^2}\right)\left(N\left(\frac{\log\left(\frac{r_i}{\mu}\right)}{\sigma}-\frac{\sigma}{2}\right)-N\left(\frac{\log\left(\frac{r_{i-1}}{\mu}\right)}{\sigma}-\frac{\sigma}{2}\right)\right)$$

$$-\sum_{i=-n+1}^{n}\left(\frac{2\mu(P_i - P_{i-1})}{(r_i - r_{i-1})\sqrt{2\pi}\sigma r_0}\right)\left(e^{-\frac{\left(\frac{\log\left(\frac{r_i}{\mu}\right)}{\sigma}-\frac{\sigma}{2}\right)^2}{2}}-e^{-\frac{\left(\frac{\log(r_{i-1})}{\mu}-\frac{\sigma}{2}\right)^2}{2}}\right)$$

$$+\sum_{i=-n+1}^{n}\left(\frac{\mu(P_i - P_{i-1})}{(r_i - r_{i-1})\sqrt{2\pi}\sigma^3 r_0^2}\right)$$

(continued)

(*Equation 21 concluded*)

$$
\begin{pmatrix}
e^{-\frac{\left(\frac{\log(r_i)}{\sigma}+\frac{\sigma}{2}\right)}{2}}\left(-\log\left(\frac{r_i}{\mu}\right)-\frac{\sigma^2}{2}\right) \\[4mm]
-e^{-\frac{\left[\frac{\log\left(\frac{r_{i-1}}{\mu}\right)}{\sigma}+\frac{\sigma}{2}\right]^2}{2}}\left(-\log\left(\frac{r_{i-1}}{\mu}\right)-\frac{\sigma^2}{2}\right)
\end{pmatrix}
$$

$$
-\frac{P_n}{\sqrt{2\pi}\sigma^3 r_0{}^2}e^{-\frac{\left(\log\left(\frac{r_n}{\mu}\right)+\frac{\sigma}{2}\right)^2}{2}}\left(-\log\left(\frac{r_n}{\mu}\right)-\frac{3\sigma^2}{2}\right).
$$

Equations (20) and (21) are our main result for calculating duration and convexity.

THEORETICAL EXPLANATIONS

First, we compare Equation (14) with Equation (10). In fact, the expectations in these two equations are different. Let

$R^+ = \{r \in R \mid r > 0\}$, where R is the set of real numbers

A = The σ-algebra generated by lognormal distribution

μ = The corresponding probability measure

The expectation of Equation (14) is taken over one gate; that is, it is taken over the probability space $\{R^+, A, \mu\}$.

Let $(R_t^+ = R^+, A_t = A, \mu_t = \mu, 0 \le t \le T$. Then we can see that the expectation of Equation (10) is taken over the product space

$$
\left\{ \prod_{0 \le t \le T} R_t^+, \quad \prod_{0 \le t \le T} A_t, \quad \prod_{0 \le t \le T} \mu_t \right\}
$$

because it is taken over all possible paths.

Since the product σ-algebra is generated by σ-algebra over finite gates(transactions) (see Halmos [1970]), when we take a large number of gates and then take the average over the gates, the expectation in Equation (14) will converge to that in Equation (10). In this sense, we can see that the mixed method is only an approximation.

We did not use a multigate approximation for two reasons:

1. If we increase the gate number from 1 to 2, we are still able to get a closed-form expression. But the corresponding formulas become extremely complex. Increasing the number of gates further makes the closed-form solution impractical.
2. Numerical results show that the one-gate approach provides reasonable results.

NUMERICAL RESULT

In this section we present two numerical results, obtained through the Genesis System as provided by Gifford Fong Associates. The following results are obtained by using Equations (16), (20) and (21) with parameters $n = 2$, $\mu = 0.1$ and $\sigma = 0.15$. The numerical results are very encouraging.

We chose 36 pass-through mortgage-backed securities reported from 13 different issuers. Our prices and market prices reported by Bloomberg are compared in Appendix 9–1. The average difference is 1.088 percent.

When we run the same data by using Equation (6), the average difference is about twice that.

An existing portfolio with 598 securities has been tested. Our durations and Lehman's durations are compared in Appendix 9–2. The average difference is 0.3288 year.

When we run the same data by using Equation (4), the average difference is about three times that.

CONCLUSION

This chapter presents a new approximation, called the mixed method, to evaluate mortgage-backed securities. As we know, the advantage of the closed-form model is that only a few paths have to be used to evaluate price, duration, convexity, and the like. The disadvantage of this model is that it ignores the path-dependency of the prepayment rate of mortgage-backed securities. However, a Monte Carlo simulation depends on paths. But since a large number of paths are required to evaluate price, it is very time-consuming. By choosing a few representative paths carefully, the mixed method takes path-dependency of the prepayment rate into consideration, and still provides a closed-form solution. In other words, the mixed method possesses advantages of both the closed-form model and the Monte Carlo simulation.

The theoretical argument of this new method is provided in the section "Theoretical Explanations." From there, we can see that the method is basically an approximation of existing models. Of course, any mathematical model in the financial field is an approximation of the real world. Our numerical results show that the new method is a good approximation of the real financial world.

REFERENCES

Abramovitz, M., and I. A. Stegun. Handbook of Mathematical Functions. New York: Dover, 1972.

Cox, J. C.; J. E. Ingersoll, Jr.; and S. A. Ross. "A Theory of the Term Structure of Interest Rates," *Econometrica,* 1985.

Davidson, A. S., and M. D. Herskovitz. *Mortgage-Backed Securities, Investment Analysis and Advanced Valuation Techniques.* Burr Ridge, IL: Irwin Professional Publishing, 1994.

Fabozzi, F. J., and G. Fong. *Advanced Fixed Income Portfolio Management.* Burr Ridge: Irwin Professional Publishing, 1994.

Halmos, P. R. *Measure Theory.* New York: Springer-Verlag, 1970.

Hull, J. *Options, Futures, and Other Derivative Securities.* 2nd ed. Englewood Cliffs, NJ: Prentice Hall, 1989.

Vasicek, O. A., and G. Fong. "Term Structure Modeling Using Exponential Splines," *Journal of Finance,* XXXVII, no. 2, May 1982.

APPENDIX 9-1

Price Comparison

	Cusip	Issue	Coupon	Market Price 7–31–95	GFA Calculated Price 7–31–95	Absolute Difference	Squared Difference
1	GI060338	GNSF	6.500	91.34375	89.22194	2.12181	4.50209
2	GI080298	GNSF	8.500	101.18750	101.29671	0.10921	0.01193
3	GI104261	GNSF	11.000	110.18750	111.07410	0.88660	0.78606
4	GM054161	GNJO	6.000	92.96875	90.79438	2.17437	4.72788
5	GM074150	GNJO	8.000	100.96875	99.85822	1.11053	1.23327
6	GM094098	GNJO	10.000	104.75000	105.26626	0.51626	0.26652
7	GT060334	G2SF	6.752	90.34375	91.14625	0.80250	0.64400
8	GT080317	G2SF	8.745	100.68750	102.26651	1.57901	2.49328
9	GT100273	G2SF	10.750	107.31250	109.85300	2.54050	6.45416
10	MC080170	FHLMC	8.889	100.06250	102.30372	2.24122	5.02308
11	MC100250	FHLMC	10.629	107.43750	107.82146	0.38396	0.14742
12	P3060335	FGLMC	6.676	91.96875	91.57794	0.39081	0.15273
13	P3080323	FGLMC	8.593	100.81250	101.02140	0.20890	0.04364
14	P3100283	FGLMC	10.607	108.18750	108.20799	0.02049	0.00042
15	P7054064	FGSB	6.229	95.31250	93.52607	1.78643	3.19133
16	P7074058	FGSB	8.065	101.00000	99.76401	1.23599	1.52766
17	P7094028	FGSB	10.003	102.43750	103.61693	1.17943	1.39105
18	PB050066	FNCX	5.667	92.53125	91.72588	0.80537	0.64862
19	PB070058	FNCX	7.555	99.93750	98.64794	1.28956	1.66298
20	PB090029	FNCX	9.000	102.46875	101.84828	0.62047	0.38499
21	PD054159	FNCI	6.198	93.34375	92.19315	1.15060	1.32389
22	PD074144	FNCI	8.040	100.71875	99.91359	0.80516	0.64828
23	PD094089	FNCI	10.155	104.81250	105.33057	0.51807	0.26839
24	PE054157	FGCI	6.169	93.40625	91.83259	1.57366	2.47639
25	PE074142	FGCI	8.079	100.75000	99.74820	1.00180	1.00361
26	PE094112	FGCI	10.137	104.46875	105.57474	1.10599	1.22322
27	PF060334	FNCL	6.705	91.90625	91.83700	0.06925	0.00480
28	PF080315	FNCL	8.562	100.78125	101.30936	0.52811	0.27890
29	PF100267	FNCL	10.621	108.43750	108.63134	0.19384	0.03757
30	PG050040	FGFB	5.734	95.96875	94.19472	1.77403	3.14717
31	PG090008	FGFB	9.564	101.75000	100.92353	0.82647	0.68305
33	PV094087	FHCI	10.207	103.84375	105.07495	1.23120	1.51584
34	PV100086	FHCI	10.708	103.78125	106.14015	2.35890	5.56440
35	GK064158	G2JO	7.250	96.25000	96.80207	0.55207	0.30478
36	GK080125	G2JO	8.750	101.21875	102.29943	1.08068	1.16787
37	GK094092	G2JO	10.250	103.50000	105.88460	2.38460	5.68631
	TOTAL SQUARED DIFFERENCE						60.62760
	AVERAGE ABSOLUTE DIFFERENCE						1.08772

APPENDIX 9-2

Duration Comparison

	Cusip	Issue	Lehman's Duration	Mixed Model Duration	Difference	Difference^2
1	FGB06093	FHLM	5.88432	5.08399	−0.80033	0.64053
2	FGB06094	FHLM	5.97535	5.0954	−0.87994	0.7743
3	FGB06493	FHLM	5.53573	4.86129	−0.67444	0.45486
4	FGB06494	FHLM	5.64559	4.8807	−0.76489	0.58506
5	FGB07092	FHLM	4.91231	4.50204	−0.41027	0.16833
6	FGB07093	FHLM	5.05666	4.58257	−0.47409	0.22476
7	FGB07094	FHLM	5.22724	4.61795	−0.6093	0.37124
8	FGB07487	FHLM	4.06499	3.70631	−0.35868	0.12865
9	FGB07489	FHLM	4.35562	4.0112	−0.34442	0.11863
10	FGB07491	FHLM	4.42172	4.11897	−0.30275	0.09165
11	FGB07492	FHLM	4.50736	4.16457	−0.3428	0.11751
12	FGB07493	FHLM	4.61418	4.22357	−0.3906	0.15257
13	FGB07494	FHLM	4.8059	4.26724	−0.53866	0.29016
14	FGB08077	FHLM	2.74448	2.77103	0.02655	0.0007
15	FGB08087	FHLM	3.64425	3.47511	−0.16914	0.02861
16	FGB08089	FHLM	3.87281	3.68801	−0.1848	0.03415
17	FGB08091	FHLM	3.92274	3.71682	−0.20591	0.0424
18	FGB08092	FHLM	3.99572	3.76857	−0.22715	0.0516
19	FGB08093	FHLM	4.08889	3.81751	−0.27138	0.07365
20	FGB08094	FHLM	4.32419	3.85195	−0.47224	0.22301
21	FGB08486	FHLM	3.12884	3.09717	−0.03167	0.001
22	FGB08487	FHLM	3.24051	3.18155	−0.05896	0.00348
23	FGB08488	FHLM	3.16889	3.22313	0.05424	0.00294
24	FGB08489	FHLM	3.25888	3.2699	0.01102	0.00012
25	FGB08490	FHLM	3.21922	3.25797	0.03875	0.0015
26	FGB08491	FHLM	3.31782	3.32073	0.00291	0.00001
27	FGB08492	FHLM	3.4289	3.38343	−0.04547	0.00207
28	FGB08493	FHLM	3.53652	3.43177	−0.10475	0.01097
29	FGB08494	FHLM	3.59761	3.44638	−0.15123	0.02287
30	FGB09085	FHLM	2.62822	2.76853	0.14031	0.01969
31	FGB09086	FHLM	2.62439	2.80053	0.17615	0.03103
32	FGB09087	FHLM	2.6814	2.8462	0.1648	0.02716
33	FGB09088	FHLM	2.46958	2.87465	0.40507	0.16409
34	FGB09089	FHLM	2.48258	2.89517	0.41259	0.17023
35	FGB09090	FHLM	2.49339	2.91599	0.4226	0.17859
36	FGB09091	FHLM	2.56708	2.9494	0.38232	0.14617
37	FGB09092	FHLM	2.73231	3.00782	0.27551	0.0759
38	FGB09484	FHLM	2.46229	2.51808	0.05579	0.00311
39	FGB09486	FHLM	2.2493	2.5731	0.32379	0.10484
40	FGB09487	FHLM	2.19576	2.59213	0.39637	0.15711
41	FGB09488	FHLM	2.35841	2.61	0.25159	0.0633
42	FGB09489	FHLM	2.36398	2.62865	0.26467	0.07005
43	FGB09490	FHLM	2.36946	2.64225	0.27278	0.07441
44	FGB09491	FHLM	1.93565	2.66585	0.7302	0.53319
45	FGB10086	FHLM	2.1323	2.37258	0.24028	0.05774
46	FGB10087	FHLM	1.9697	2.38727	0.41757	0.17437
47	FGB10088	FHLM	2.11018	2.40105	0.29087	0.08461
48	FGB10089	FHLM	2.08752	2.41178	0.32426	0.10515
49	FGB10090	FHLM	2.07627	2.41862	0.34235	0.1172
50	FGB10489	FHLM	1.86236	2.25157	0.38921	0.15149
51	FGD05493	FHLM	4.49001	4.12204	−0.36797	0.1354
52	FGD05494	FHLM	4.56863	4.14239	−0.42624	0.18168

53	FGD06093	FHLM	4.365	4.10238	−0.26262	0.06897
54	FGD06094	FHLM	4.49453	4.15997	−0.33456	0.11193
55	FGD06492	FHLM	3.98916	3.89752	−0.09164	0.0084
56	FGD06493	FHLM	4.17019	4.02113	−0.14907	0.02222
57	FGD06494	FHLM	4.36154	4.11323	−0.2483	0.06165
58	FGD07092	FHLM	3.76198	3.76033	−0.00165	0
59	FGD07093	FHLM	3.91287	3.87347	−0.0394	0.00155
60	FGD07094	FHLM	4.12932	4.01581	−0.11351	0.01289
61	FGD07491	FHLM	3.2901	3.44173	0.15163	0.02299
62	FGD07492	FHLM	3.40549	3.54007	0.13459	0.01811
63	FGD07493	FHLM	3.53916	3.66527	0.1261	0.0159
64	FGD07494	FHLM	3.80646	3.86128	0.05482	0.00301
65	FGD08087	FHLM	2.36836	2.46734	0.09899	0.0098
66	FGD08091	FHLM	2.89758	3.23103	0.33345	0.11119
67	FGD08092	FHLM	2.98733	3.3178	0.33048	0.10921
68	FGD08093	FHLM	3.13886	3.43854	0.29969	0.08981
69	FGD08094	FHLM	3.29953	3.62572	0.32618	0.1064
70	FGD08486	FHLM	1.97177	2.1826	0.21083	0.04445
71	FGD08487	FHLM	2.13568	2.34118	0.2055	0.04223
72	FGD08490	FHLM	2.40716	2.87831	0.47116	0.22199
73	FGD08491	FHLM	2.48489	2.98088	0.49599	0.24601
74	FGD08492	FHLM	2.5934	3.09621	0.50281	0.25282
75	FGD08087	FHLM	2.00831	2.24626	0.23795	0.05662
76	FGD09088	FHLM	2.0849	2.40228	0.31738	0.10073
77	FGD09090	FHLM	1.98271	2.67389	0.69118	0.47772
78	FGD09091	FHLM	2.03863	2.78201	0.74338	0.55261
79	FGD09490	FHLM	1.88049	2.55537	0.67488	0.45547
80	FGF05093	FHLM	2.87027	2.61589	−0.25437	0.06471
81	FGF05094	FHLM	3.13799	2.82336	−0.31463	0.09899
82	FGF05492	FHLM	2.30053	2.62199	0.32146	0.10333
83	FGF05493	FHLM	2.77239	3.1096	0.33721	0.11371
84	FGF05494	FHLM	3.07457	2.7913	−0.28327	0.08024
85	FGF06092	FHLM	2.27146	2.5624	0.29093	0.08464
86	FGF06093	FHLM	2.66855	2.42454	−0.244	0.05954
87	FGF06094	FHLM	2.99577	2.72821	−0.26756	0.07159
88	FGF06492	FHLM	2.14543	2.00402	−0.14141	0.02
89	FGF06493	FHLM	2.48096	2.29197	−0.189	0.03572
90	FGF06494	FHLM	2.98475	2.74545	−0.2393	0.05726
91	FGF07091	FHLM	1.73749	1.59442	−0.14307	0.02047
92	FGF07092	FHLM	1.96479	1.83389	−0.1309	0.01714
93	FGF07093	FHLM	2.32246	2.1461	−0.17636	0.0311
94	FGF07094	FHLM	2.9285	2.74136	−0.18714	0.03502
95	FGF07491	FHLM	1.58433	1.51109	−0.07324	0.00536
96	FGF07492	FHLM	1.88755	1.77199	−0.11556	0.01335
97	FGF08091	FHLM	1.28637	1.29869	0.01232	0.00015
98	FGF08092	FHLM	1.70658	1.66989	−0.03669	0.00135
99	FGF08491	FHLM	1.15859	1.22278	0.06419	0.00412
100	FGG05493	FHLM	3.51414	3.34784	−0.1663	0.02766
101	FGG05494	FHLM	3.73925	3.46745	−0.2718	0.07388
102	FGG06092	FHLM	3.03018	3.03914	0.00896	0.00008
103	FGG06093	FHLM	3.33528	3.28176	−0.05353	0.00287
104	FGG06094	FHLM	3.61824	3.44995	−0.1683	0.02832
105	FGG06492	FHLM	2.92161	2.99103	0.06942	0.00482
106	FGG06493	FHLM	3.16406	3.20449	0.04043	0.00163
107	FGG06494	FHLM	3.49407	3.41401	−0.08007	0.00641
108	FGG07092	FHLM	2.72043	2.85246	0.13203	0.01743
109	FGG07093	FHLM	2.88961	3.01342	0.12382	0.01533
110	FGG07094	FHLM	3.28564	3.36923	0.0836	0.00699
111	FGG07491	FHLM	2.35248	2.47569	0.12321	0.01518
112	FGG07492	FHLM	2.50124	2.65382	0.15257	0.02328

113	FGG07493	FHLM	2.68651	2.86358	0.17707	0.03135
114	FGG07494	FHLM	3.04975	3.253	0.20325	0.04131
115	FGG08091	FHLM	2.09885	2.29806	0.19922	0.03969
116	FGG08092	FHLM	2.27855	2.49059	0.21204	0.04496
117	FGG08491	FHLM	1.74759	1.7291	−0.01848	0.00034
118	FHA08075	FHLM	2.72276	2.80023	0.07746	0.006
119	FHA08076	FHLM	2.88459	3.00991	0.12532	0.01571
120	FHA08086	FHLM	3.68423	3.61628	−0.06795	0.00462
121	FHA08087	FHLM	3.63646	3.6537	0.01724	0.0003
122	FHA08277	FHLM	2.86753	2.94799	0.08046	0.00647
123	FHA08477	FHLM	2.89251	2.88814	−0.00437	0.00002
124	FHA08486	FHLM	3.10681	3.2065	0.09969	0.00994
125	FHA08677	FHLM	2.88692	2.7793	−0.10762	0.01158
126	FHA09085	FHLM	2.61625	2.83592	0.21967	0.04826
127	FHA09086	FHLM	2.60947	2.8969	0.28743	0.08261
128	FHA09089	FHLM	2.56137	3.02338	0.46201	0.21345
129	FHA09278	FHLM	2.91045	2.55088	−0.35957	0.12929
130	FHA09486	FHLM	2.2586	2.60361	0.34501	0.11903
131	FHA09487	FHLM	2.30117	2.64058	0.3394	0.1152
132	FHA09488	FHLM	2.46433	2.66272	0.19839	0.03936
133	FHA09489	FHLM	2.43555	2.67813	0.24258	0.05885
134	FHA09490	FHLM	2.4357	2.6876	0.2519	0.06345
135	FHA10087	FHLM	2.07425	2.37933	0.30508	0.09307
136	FHA10088	FHLM	2.19372	2.39164	0.19792	0.03917
137	FHA10089	FHLM	2.19001	2.39753	0.20752	0.04307
138	FHA10090	FHLM	2.17343	2.40767	0.23424	0.05487
139	FHA10489	FHLM	1.98088	2.20879	0.22791	0.05194
140	FHB06472	FHLM	2.42905	2.53097	0.10192	0.01039
141	FHB07072	FHLM	2.41166	2.50198	0.09032	0.00816
142	FHB07073	FHLM	2.44961	2.54519	0.09558	0.00914
143	FHB07076	FHLM	2.91511	3.07045	0.15534	0.02413
144	FHB07077	FHLM	3.04018	3.20682	0.16664	0.02777
145	FHB07087	FHLM	4.5444	4.31372	−0.23068	0.05321
146	FHB07476	FHLM	2.8558	2.9795	0.1237	0.0153
147	FHB07477	FHLM	3.05066	3.17607	0.12541	0.01573
148	FHB07486	FHLM	3.6741	3.66162	−0.01248	0.00016
149	FHB07487	FHLM	4.18284	4.08213	−0.10071	0.01014
150	FHB07677	FHLM	3.02035	3.0568	0.03645	0.00133
151	FHB08076	FHLM	2.72997	2.81336	0.08338	0.00695
152	FHB08077	FHLM	2.87117	2.9697	0.09852	0.00971
153	FHB08078	FHLM	2.97831	3.0405	0.06218	0.00387
154	FHB08085	FHLM	2.72725	2.97417	0.24692	0.06097
155	FHB08086	FHLM	3.38131	3.40829	0.02698	0.00073
156	FHB08087	FHLM	3.82971	3.83438	0.00467	0.00002
157	FHB08276	FHLM	2.78128	2.81133	0.03005	0.0009
158	FHB08277	FHLM	2.82284	2.88587	0.06304	0.00397
159	FHB08285	FHLM	2.66107	2.89568	0.23461	0.05504
160	FHB08287	FHLM	3.60957	3.59832	−0.01126	0.00013
161	FHB08476	FHLM	2.73783	2.70323	−0.0346	0.0012
162	FHB08477	FHLM	2.76739	2.75688	−0.01051	0.00011
163	FHB08478	FHLM	2.88445	2.81882	−0.06563	0.00431
164	FHB08485	FHLM	2.92029	2.99891	0.07861	0.00618
165	FHB08486	FHLM	3.1162	3.15938	0.04318	0.00186
166	FHB08487	FHLM	3.39893	3.42581	0.02688	0.00072
167	FHB08489	FHLM	3.17437	3.36318	0.18881	0.03565
168	FHB08490	FHLM	3.27343	3.43554	0.16211	0.02628
169	FHB08677	FHLM	2.76681	2.66054	−0.10627	0.01129
170	FHB08678	FHLM	2.82591	2.70195	−0.12397	0.01537
171	FHB09077	FHLM	2.77748	2.53704	−0.24044	0.05781
172	FHB09078	FHLM	2.81411	2.58673	−0.22737	0.0517

173	FHB09079	FHLM	2.88383	2.60415	−0.27968	0.07822
174	FHB09085	FHLM	2.74937	2.71738	−0.03198	0.00102
175	FHB09086	FHLM	2.78133	2.93136	0.15003	0.02251
176	FHB09087	FHLM	2.84487	2.9896	0.14472	0.02094
177	FHB09088	FHLM	2.56372	2.99207	0.42835	0.18348
178	FHB09089	FHLM	2.58731	3.02856	0.44125	0.1947
179	FHB09090	FHLM	2.63573	3.05691	0.42118	0.1774
180	FHB09278	FHLM	2.84674	2.50007	−0.34666	0.12017
181	FHB09279	FHLM	2.93558	2.51823	−0.41735	0.17418
182	FHB09478	FHLM	2.80534	2.4115	−0.39384	0.15511
183	FHB09479	FHLM	2.75206	2.3882	−0.36386	0.1324
184	FHB09486	FHLM	2.3839	2.63216	0.24825	0.06163
185	FHB09487	FHLM	2.35737	2.64364	0.28627	0.08195
186	FHB09488	FHLM	2.48787	2.66781	0.17993	0.03238
187	FHB09489	FHLM	2.49835	2.69071	0.19236	0.037
188	FHB09490	FHLM	2.08441	2.71206	0.62765	0.39394
189	FHB10079	FHLM	2.59828	2.20446	−0.39383	0.1551
190	FHB10086	FHLM	2.25697	2.35701	0.10004	0.01001
191	FHB10087	FHLM	2.09856	2.37493	0.27637	0.07638
192	FHB10088	FHLM	2.20418	2.3949	0.19072	0.03638
193	FHB10089	FHLM	2.21182	2.40062	0.1888	0.03564
194	FHB10090	FHLM	2.19483	2.40902	0.21419	0.04588
195	FHB10479	FHLM	2.46905	2.06625	−0.4028	0.16225
196	FHB10486	FHLM	2.26403	2.16929	−0.09474	0.00898
197	FHB10488	FHLM	1.99275	2.19538	0.20263	0.04106
198	FHB10489	FHLM	1.97255	2.20266	0.23012	0.05295
199	FHB10490	FHLM	1.88442	2.20447	0.32005	0.10243
200	FHB11089	FHLM	1.95109	2.10288	0.15179	0.02304
201	FHC06472	FHLM	2.77987	1.8429	−0.93697	0.87792
202	FHC08087	FHLM	4.45222	2.17972	−2.2725	5.16425
203	FHD07487	FHLM	2.6521	2.77643	0.12432	0.01546
204	FHD08087	FHLM	2.49391	2.69667	0.20276	0.04111
205	FHD08486	FHLM	2.13138	2.43995	0.30857	0.09522
206	FHD08487	FHLM	2.25421	2.60176	0.34754	0.12079
207	FHD09086	FHLM	1.97767	2.34446	0.36679	0.13454
208	FHD09087	FHLM	2.01624	2.46171	0.44548	0.19845
209	FHD09088	FHLM	2.0599	2.70695	0.64705	0.41868
210	FHD09089	FHLM	2.0679	2.92399	0.85609	0.73289
211	FHD09486	FHLM	1.90545	2.23176	0.32631	0.10648
212	FHD09487	FHLM	1.95843	2.39789	0.43946	0.19312
213	FHE07487	FHLM	2.5083	2.483	−0.0253	0.00064
214	FHE08486	FHLM	2.08922	2.18024	0.09102	0.00829
215	FHE09086	FHLM	1.89929	2.10838	0.20908	0.04372
216	FHE09087	FHLM	1.98732	2.26704	0.27972	0.07825
217	FHE09089	FHLM	2.23844	2.58333	0.34488	0.11895
218	FHE09487	FHLM	2.0478	2.20982	0.16201	0.02625
219	FHE09488	FHLM	1.96473	2.33139	0.36666	0.13444
220	FHE09489	FHLM	1.94909	2.45492	0.50583	0.25586
221	FNA05493	FNMA	6.0842	5.17883	−0.90537	0.81969
222	FNA06092	FNMA	5.62029	5.03387	−0.58642	0.34389
223	FNA06093	FNMA	5.87652	5.08711	−0.78942	0.62318
224	FNA06094	FNMA	5.9817	5.1001	−0.8816	0.77722
225	FNA06472	FNMA	2.75569	2.78459	0.02891	0.00084
226	FNA06491	FNMA	5.25267	4.77991	−0.47276	0.2235
227	FNA06492	FNMA	5.33996	4.82009	−0.51987	0.27026
228	FNA06493	FNMA	5.55067	4.86455	−0.68611	0.47075
229	FNA06494	FNMA	5.65085	4.88276	−0.76809	0.58996
230	FNA07072	FNMA	2.72603	2.74439	0.01836	0.00034
231	FNA07075	FNMA	3.27471	3.23947	−0.03524	0.00124
232	FNA07090	FNMA	4.84007	4.48342	−0.35665	0.1272

233	FNA07091	FNMA	4.85182	4.50525	-0.34657	0.12011
234	FNA07092	FNMA	4.93321	4.53994	-0.39326	0.15466
235	FNA07093	FNMA	5.0782	4.59208	-0.48612	0.23631
236	FNA07094	FNMA	5.24516	4.62098	-0.62418	0.3896
237	FNA07474	FNMA	2.96621	2.95361	-0.0126	0.00016
238	FNA07475	FNMA	3.07163	3.05244	-0.01919	0.00037
239	FNA07476	FNMA	3.1748	3.14641	-0.0284	0.00081
240	FNA07487	FNMA	4.19482	3.86485	-0.32997	0.10888
241	FNA07489	FNMA	4.41789	4.04438	-0.37352	0.13952
242	FNA07490	FNMA	4.40052	4.12733	-0.27319	0.07463
243	FNA07491	FNMA	4.42324	4.14307	-0.28017	0.07849
244	FNA07492	FNMA	4.5097	4.19465	-0.31506	0.09926
245	FNA07493	FNMA	4.61584	4.23658	-0.37926	0.14384
246	FNA07494	FNMA	4.79328	4.26457	-0.52871	0.27953
247	FNA08071	FNMA	2.52104	2.37593	-0.14511	0.02106
248	FNA08072	FNMA	2.60621	2.55643	-0.04978	0.00248
249	FNA08073	FNMA	2.71168	2.67904	-0.03264	0.00107
250	FNA08074	FNMA	2.82895	2.79945	-0.0295	0.00087
251	FNA08075	FNMA	2.92627	2.895	-0.03127	0.00098
252	FNA08076	FNMA	3.00291	2.97102	-0.03189	0.00102
253	FNA08077	FNMA	3.11577	3.07227	-0.04351	0.00189
254	FNA08078	FNMA	3.19845	3.14116	-0.05729	0.00328
255	FNA08086	FNMA	3.71006	3.53341	-0.17665	0.03121
256	FNA08087	FNMA	3.76155	3.58065	-0.1809	0.03273
257	FNA08088	FNMA	3.86431	3.6507	-0.21361	0.04563
258	FNA08089	FNMA	3.8574	3.66392	-0.19348	0.03743
259	FNA08090	FNMA	3.89364	3.71857	-0.17507	0.03065
260	FNA08091	FNMA	3.93185	3.75104	-0.18081	0.03269
261	FNA08092	FNMA	4.00661	3.79679	-0.20982	0.04402
262	FNA08093	FNMA	4.09471	3.8372	-0.25751	0.06631
263	FNA08094	FNMA	4.31537	3.85033	-0.46504	0.21626
264	FNA08474	FNMA	2.788	2.60425	-0.18374	0.03376
265	FNA08475	FNMA	2.80411	2.68336	-0.12075	0.01458
266	FNA08476	FNMA	2.89979	2.74949	-0.1503	0.02259
267	FNA08477	FNMA	2.99708	2.78926	-0.20782	0.04319
268	FNA08478	FNMA	3.06158	2.82195	-0.23963	0.05742
269	FNA08485	FNMA	3.28396	3.16824	-0.11572	0.01339
270	FNA08486	FNMA	3.26967	3.19123	-0.07844	0.00615
271	FNA08487	FNMA	3.31683	3.24206	-0.07476	0.00559
272	FNA08488	FNMA	3.19305	3.23604	0.04299	0.00185
273	FNA08489	FNMA	3.19275	3.24871	0.05596	0.00313
274	FNA08490	FNMA	3.26016	3.29609	0.03593	0.00129
275	FNA08491	FNMA	3.3491	3.35552	0.00642	0.00004
276	FNA08492	FNMA	3.44504	3.40752	-0.03752	0.00141
277	FNA08493	FNMA	3.54131	3.43995	-0.10136	0.01027
278	FNA08494	FNMA	3.62202	3.45787	-0.16415	0.02694
279	FNA09076	FNMA	2.82407	2.51845	-0.30562	0.0934
280	FNA09077	FNMA	2.93234	2.57571	-0.35663	0.12718
281	FNA09078	FNMA	2.91045	2.61314	-0.29731	0.08839
282	FNA09079	FNMA	2.96333	2.63905	-0.32427	0.10515
283	FNA09085	FNMA	2.73631	2.83369	0.09737	0.00948
284	FNA09086	FNMA	2.69807	2.85358	0.15551	0.02418
285	FNA09087	FNMA	2.72096	2.87992	0.15896	0.02527
286	FNA09088	FNMA	2.44221	2.88578	0.44357	0.19676
287	FNA09089	FNMA	2.4613	2.9126	0.4513	0.20367
288	FNA09090	FNMA	2.47458	2.92441	0.44983	0.20235
289	FNA09091	FNMA	2.56615	2.96635	0.4002	0.16016
290	FNA09092	FNMA	2.7094	3.0136	0.3042	0.09254
291	FNA09478	FNMA	2.75834	2.41188	-0.34646	0.12004
292	FNA09479	FNMA	2.75814	2.42294	-0.3352	0.11236

293	FNA09484	FNMA	2.29659	2.5675	0.27092	0.0734
294	FNA09485	FNMA	2.26266	2.58915	0.32649	0.1066
295	FNA09486	FNMA	2.21457	2.60326	0.38869	0.15108
296	FNA09487	FNMA	2.18505	2.61046	0.42541	0.18097
297	FNA09488	FNMA	2.32769	2.6229	0.29521	0.08715
298	FNA09489	FNMA	2.33587	2.56204	0.22617	0.05115
299	FNA09490	FNMA	1.8723	2.57357	0.70127	0.49178
300	FNA09491	FNMA	1.89885	2.59558	0.69673	0.48543
301	FNA10078	FNMA	2.55595	2.17735	-0.3786	0.14334
302	FNA10079	FNMA	2.59324	2.20079	-0.39245	0.15401
303	FNA10085	FNMA	2.03787	2.29818	0.26031	0.06776
304	FNA10086	FNMA	1.92332	2.30789	0.38457	0.14789
305	FNA10087	FNMA	1.8898	2.31846	0.42866	0.18375
306	FNA10088	FNMA	2.00917	2.32686	0.31768	0.10092
307	FNA10089	FNMA	2.00145	2.33399	0.33254	0.11058
308	FNA10090	FNMA	1.98057	2.34148	0.36091	0.13025
309	FNA10091	FNMA	1.96045	2.3462	0.38575	0.1488
310	FNA10479	FNMA	2.62896	2.08347	-0.5455	0.29757
311	FNA10487	FNMA	1.83807	2.16434	0.32627	0.10645
312	FNA10488	FNMA	1.88766	2.16989	0.28222	0.07965
313	FNA10489	FNMA	1.80713	2.17357	0.36644	0.13428
314	FNA10490	FNMA	1.71144	2.17773	0.46629	0.21742
315	FNA11085	FNMA	1.87256	2.07685	0.20429	0.04174
316	FNA11089	FNMA	1.74688	2.08633	0.33945	0.11523
317	FNB06072	FNMA	2.81646	2.78286	-0.0336	0.00113
318	FNB06271	FNMA	2.66871	2.65902	-0.0097	0.00009
319	FNB06471	FNMA	2.59082	2.60035	0.00953	0.00009
320	FNB06472	FNMA	2.77809	2.77871	0.00062	0
321	FNB06473	FNMA	2.99934	2.99264	-0.0067	0.00004
322	FNB07475	FNMA	3.23722	3.37444	0.13722	0.01883
323	FNB07477	FNMA	3.58918	3.6948	0.10562	0.01116
324	FNB08075	FNMA	3.14848	3.36901	0.22053	0.04863
325	FNB08076	FNMA	3.34862	3.59672	0.2481	0.06156
326	FNB08078	FNMA	3.54141	3.78022	0.23881	0.05703
327	FNB08476	FNMA	3.1632	3.42527	0.26207	0.06868
328	FNB08478	FNMA	3.50526	3.76029	0.25504	0.06504
329	FNB09078	FNMA	3.49615	3.72487	0.22872	0.05231
330	FNB09079	FNMA	3.51865	3.74646	0.22781	0.0519
331	FNB09479	FNMA	3.46683	3.70767	0.24084	0.058
332	FNB11080	FNMA	2.97825	3.50209	0.52384	0.27441
333	FNC05093	FNMA	4.65097	4.34919	-0.30178	0.09107
334	FNC05493	FNMA	4.51581	4.34462	-0.17119	0.02931
335	FNC05494	FNMA	4.63941	4.40254	-0.23687	0.05611
336	FNC06092	FNMA	4.15527	4.1258	-0.02947	0.00087
337	FNC06093	FNMA	4.40318	4.31731	-0.08587	0.00737
338	FNC06094	FNMA	4.53953	4.395	-0.14453	0.02089
339	FNC06492	FNMA	4.03768	4.10816	0.07048	0.00497
340	FNC06493	FNMA	4.20843	4.24691	0.03848	0.00148
341	FNC06494	FNMA	4.3962	4.38382	-0.01238	0.00015
342	FNC07091	FNMA	3.67052	3.85988	0.18937	0.03586
343	FNC07092	FNMA	3.8079	4.02787	0.21998	0.04839
344	FNC07093	FNMA	3.94819	4.16953	0.22135	0.049
345	FNC07094	FNMA	4.15981	4.35125	0.19145	0.03665
346	FNC07487	FNMA	2.64757	2.71388	0.06631	0.0044
347	FNC07491	FNMA	3.35018	3.74737	0.39719	0.15776
348	FNC07492	FNMA	3.45554	3.87843	0.42289	0.17883
349	FNC07493	FNMA	3.572	4.01908	0.44708	0.19988
350	FNC07494	FNMA	3.79519	4.25953	0.46435	0.21562
351	FNC08086	FNMA	2.37175	2.55963	0.18787	0.0353
352	FNC08087	FNMA	2.46252	2.63516	0.17264	0.02981

353	FNC08091	FNMA	2.95006	3.61007	0.66001	0.43561
354	FNC08092	FNMA	3.04444	3.73699	0.69255	0.47963
355	FNC08093	FNMA	3.17607	3.9019	0.72583	0.52684
356	FNC08094	FNMA	3.31705	4.12382	0.80677	0.65087
357	FNC08486	FNMA	2.11893	2.39455	0.27562	0.07597
358	FNC08487	FNMA	2.21555	2.5456	0.33005	0.10893
359	FNC08488	FNMA	2.30194	2.79227	0.49034	0.24043
360	FNC08489	FNMA	2.39139	3.05773	0.66634	0.44401
361	FNC08490	FNMA	2.3901	3.1824	0.7923	0.62774
362	FNC08491	FNMA	2.51725	3.3908	0.87355	0.76308
363	FNC08492	FNMA	2.62823	3.54373	0.9155	0.83814
364	FNC09086	FNMA	1.92259	2.30659	0.384	0.14746
365	FNC09087	FNMA	1.95401	2.49303	0.53903	0.29055
366	FNC09088	FNMA	1.97204	2.68082	0.70878	0.50236
367	FNC09089	FNMA	1.97705	2.89889	0.92184	0.8498
368	FNC09090	FNMA	1.97835	3.04373	1.06538	1.13504
369	FNC09091	FNMA	2.02774	3.19259	1.16484	1.35686
370	FNC09486	FNMA	1.83856	2.14036	0.3018	0.09108
371	FNC09487	FNMA	1.89148	2.35128	0.4598	0.21142
372	FNC09488	FNMA	1.88597	2.51387	0.62789	0.39425
373	FNC09489	FNMA	1.84501	2.66655	0.82154	0.67493
374	FNC09490	FNMA	1.83895	2.81235	0.9734	0.94752
375	FNC10088	FNMA	1.85943	2.32826	0.46883	0.2198
376	FNC10089	FNMA	1.80222	2.4205	0.61828	0.38227
377	FND05493	FNMA	3.58521	3.55923	−0.02598	0.00067
378	FND05494	FNMA	3.76959	3.74437	−0.02522	0.00064
379	FND06092	FNMA	3.09481	2.65255	−0.44227	0.1956
380	FND06093	FNMA	3.40387	3.43922	0.03534	0.00125
381	FND06094	FNMA	3.64284	3.70988	0.06705	0.0045
382	FND06492	FNMA	2.95594	2.98139	0.02545	0.00065
383	FND06493	FNMA	3.20435	3.29229	0.08795	0.00773
384	FND06494	FNMA	3.50896	3.69142	0.18246	0.03329
385	FND07092	FNMA	2.73234	2.79148	0.05914	0.0035
386	FND07093	FNMA	2.92624	3.08073	0.15449	0.02387
387	FND07094	FNMA	3.3437	3.74062	0.39692	0.15755
388	FND07491	FNMA	2.38768	2.43057	0.04289	0.00184
389	FND07492	FNMA	2.53699	2.60937	0.07239	0.00524
390	FND07493	FNMA	2.71297	2.87649	0.16352	0.02674
391	FND07494	FNMA	3.07899	3.59904	0.52005	0.27045
392	FND08091	FNMA	2.11489	2.21775	0.10285	0.01058
393	FND08092	FNMA	2.32589	2.46419	0.1383	0.01913
394	FND08491	FNMA	1.80861	1.68225	−0.12636	0.01597
395	FND09090	FNMA	1.16328	1.63637	0.47309	0.22381
396	FND09091	FNMA	1.40135	1.8597	0.45835	0.21008
397	FND09490	FNMA	1.03536	1.53427	0.49891	0.24891
398	GNA06093	FNMA	6.65098	5.6847	−0.96627	0.93368
399	GNA06094	FNMA	6.72339	5.69465	−1.02873	1.05829
400	GNA06471	FNMA	2.49733	2.49631	−0.00103	0
401	GNA06472	FNMA	2.73512	2.71736	−0.01777	0.00032
402	GNA06473	FNMA	2.96274	2.92458	−0.03815	0.00146
403	GNA06493	FNMA	6.31949	5.49329	−0.8262	0.68261
404	GNA06494	FNMA	6.40685	5.5117	−0.89516	0.80131
405	GNA06692	FNMA	5.98814	5.30573	−0.68241	0.46569
406	GNA07086	FNMA	5.32925	4.73184	−0.59741	0.3569
407	GNA07087	FNMA	5.34858	4.75244	−0.59614	0.35539
408	GNA07092	FNMA	5.6734	5.15534	−0.51806	0.26839
409	GNA07093	FNMA	5.79348	5.19814	−0.59534	0.35443
410	GNA07094	FNMA	5.91511	5.22662	−0.68849	0.47402
411	GNA07274	FNMA	3.14423	3.08774	−0.05649	0.00319
412	GNA07275	FNMA	3.28719	3.21625	−0.07094	0.00503

413	GNA07287	FNMA	5.2664	4.60641	−0.65999	0.43559
414	GNA07291	FNMA	5.41527	4.89678	−0.51849	0.26883
415	GNA07292	FNMA	5.49155	4.94716	−0.54439	0.29636
416	GNA07475	FNMA	3.26546	3.18312	−0.08234	0.00678
417	GNA07476	FNMA	3.45001	3.34832	−0.10169	0.01034
418	GNA07477	FNMA	3.55798	3.43803	−0.11994	0.01439
419	GNA07486	FNMA	4.87856	4.39747	−0.48109	0.23144
420	GNA07487	FNMA	4.91369	4.42594	−0.48775	0.2379
421	GNA07489	FNMA	4.91018	4.60378	−0.3064	0.09388
422	GNA07490	FNMA	4.91749	4.61215	−0.30533	0.09323
423	GNA07491	FNMA	5.01512	4.69747	−0.31765	0.1009
424	GNA07492	FNMA	5.08211	4.73586	−0.34625	0.11989
425	GNA07493	FNMA	5.17393	4.76786	−0.40608	0.1649
426	GNA07494	FNMA	5.29023	4.80137	−0.48886	0.23899
427	GNA07689	FNMA	4.72772	4.32294	−0.40479	0.16385
428	GNA07690	FNMA	4.82319	4.44206	−0.38113	0.14526
429	GNA07691	FNMA	4.8574	4.47718	−0.38022	0.14457
430	GNA08073	FNMA	2.77615	2.71192	−0.06424	0.00413
431	GNA08074	FNMA	2.84347	2.77095	−0.07252	0.00526
432	GNA08075	FNMA	3.07262	2.9777	−0.09492	0.00901
433	GNA08076	FNMA	3.28444	3.1605	−0.12394	0.01536
434	GNA08077	FNMA	3.44267	3.29123	−0.15144	0.02293
435	GNA08078	FNMA	3.51272	3.34208	−0.17065	0.02912
436	GNA08086	FNMA	4.36478	4.04315	−0.32163	0.10345
437	GNA08087	FNMA	4.40344	4.07074	−0.3327	0.11069
438	GNA08088	FNMA	4.23445	4.13028	−0.10417	0.01085
439	GNA08089	FNMA	4.27904	4.18115	−0.09789	0.00958
440	GNA08090	FNMA	4.33424	4.23459	−0.09964	0.00993
441	GNA08091	FNMA	4.39385	4.28506	−0.10879	0.01184
442	GNA08092	FNMA	4.4386	4.30836	−0.13024	0.01696
443	GNA08093	FNMA	4.53202	4.33394	−0.19808	0.03924
444	GNA08094	FNMA	4.67321	4.37586	−0.29735	0.08842
445	GNA08276	FNMA	3.16062	2.96707	−0.19355	0.03746
446	GNA08278	FNMA	3.49147	3.22031	−0.27116	0.07353
447	GNA08287	FNMA	4.15556	3.86259	−0.29297	0.08583
448	GNA08288	FNMA	4.07739	3.87482	−0.20258	0.04104
449	GNA08289	FNMA	4.13795	3.92331	−0.21464	0.04607
450	GNA08290	FNMA	4.19147	3.97784	−0.21363	0.04564
451	GNA08475	FNMA	2.98288	2.74835	−0.23453	0.05501
452	GNA08476	FNMA	3.05878	2.79928	−0.2595	0.06734
453	GNA08478	FNMA	3.4506	3.06638	−0.38421	0.14762
454	GNA08486	FNMA	3.8494	3.54773	−0.30166	0.091
455	GNA08487	FNMA	3.88422	3.57109	−0.31313	0.09805
456	GNA08488	FNMA	3.55789	3.61382	0.05593	0.00313
457	GNA08489	FNMA	3.63767	3.67016	0.03249	0.00106
458	GNA08490	FNMA	3.65502	3.6796	0.02458	0.0006
459	GNA08491	FNMA	3.73082	3.71894	−0.01188	0.00014
460	GNA08492	FNMA	3.80078	3.73812	−0.06265	0.00393
461	GNA08493	FNMA	3.85607	3.74828	−0.10779	0.01162
462	GNA08494	FNMA	4.02819	3.79242	−0.23577	0.05559
463	GNA08688	FNMA	3.44124	3.38852	−0.05272	0.00278
464	GNA09074	FNMA	2.91182	2.40622	−0.50559	0.25563
465	GNA09078	FNMA	3.44465	2.74243	−0.70222	0.49311
466	GNA09079	FNMA	3.48551	2.7686	−0.71691	0.51396
467	GNA09086	FNMA	3.33606	3.0708	−0.26526	0.07036
468	GNA09087	FNMA	3.3481	3.08651	−0.26159	0.06843
469	GNA09088	FNMA	2.80669	3.11936	0.31267	0.09776
470	GNA09089	FNMA	2.83318	3.15013	0.31695	0.10046
471	GNA09090	FNMA	2.8439	3.16008	0.31618	0.09997
472	GNA09091	FNMA	2.87802	3.18311	0.30509	0.09308

473	GNA09092	FNMA	2.92651	3.19163	0.26511	0.07029
474	GNA09093	FNMA	2.93067	3.20111	0.27044	0.07314
475	GNA09094	FNMA	2.93259	3.23129	0.2987	0.08922
476	GNA09479	FNMA	3.41511	2.47477	−0.94034	0.88425
477	GNA09486	FNMA	2.67329	2.65985	−0.01343	0.00018
478	GNA09487	FNMA	2.65445	2.67366	0.01921	0.00037
479	GNA09488	FNMA	1.77235	2.69112	0.91877	0.84414
480	GNA09489	FNMA	1.75171	2.70562	0.95391	0.90995
481	GNA09490	FNMA	1.74665	2.71771	0.97106	0.94296
482	GNA09491	FNMA	1.74708	2.72695	0.97986	0.96013
483	GNA09492	FNMA	1.7747	2.72606	0.95135	0.90507
484	GNA10079	FNMA	3.25705	2.21132	−1.04573	1.09355
485	GNA10080	FNMA	3.27053	2.22956	−1.04097	1.08363
486	GNA10085	FNMA	2.12792	2.31336	0.18544	0.03439
487	GNA10086	FNMA	2.09082	2.31704	0.22622	0.05118
488	GNA10087	FNMA	2.01243	2.33043	0.31799	0.10112
489	GNA10088	FNMA	0.81151	2.34061	1.5291	2.33815
490	GNA10089	FNMA	0.77352	2.34652	1.573	2.47432
491	GNA10090	FNMA	0.72418	2.35538	1.63121	2.66084
492	GNA10091	FNMA	0.70933	2.35862	1.64929	2.72016
493	GNA10485	FNMA	1.66922	2.0799	0.41069	0.16866
494	GNA10486	FNMA	1.64258	2.07934	0.43677	0.19076
495	GNA10487	FNMA	1.31943	2.09038	0.77094	0.59435
496	GNA10488	FNMA	−0.30103	2.09379	2.39482	5.73518
497	GNA10489	FNMA	−0.42572	2.0988	2.52451	6.37317
498	GNA10490	FNMA	−0.49827	2.10256	2.60083	6.76433
499	GNA11079	FNMA	2.92135	1.93852	−0.98283	0.96596
500	GNA11080	FNMA	2.93496	1.94626	−0.9887	0.97752
501	GNA11083	FNMA	2.0112	1.97489	−0.0363	0.00132
502	GNA11085	FNMA	1.81675	1.99007	0.17331	0.03004
503	GNA11086	FNMA	1.79598	1.98875	0.19277	0.03716
504	GNA11087	FNMA	1.69693	1.99742	0.30049	0.0903
505	GNA11088	FNMA	0.32355	1.99672	1.67317	2.7995
506	GNA11089	FNMA	0.22244	2.0013	1.77886	3.16435
507	GNA11480	FNMA	2.7669	1.93541	−0.83149	0.69138
508	GNA11483	FNMA	1.97789	1.95922	−0.01867	0.00035
509	GNA11485	FNMA	1.94592	1.9749	0.02898	0.00084
510	GNA12082	FNMA	2.18107	1.99619	−0.18488	0.03418
511	GNA12083	FNMA	2.19154	2.00285	−0.18869	0.0356
512	GNA12084	FNMA	2.21072	2.00814	−0.20258	0.04104
513	GNA12085	FNMA	2.22601	2.01567	−0.21034	0.04424
514	GNA12480	FNMA	2.83168	2.04017	−0.79151	0.62649
515	GNA12483	FNMA	2.32742	2.07884	−0.24859	0.06179
516	GNA12484	FNMA	2.34346	2.0843	−0.25915	0.06716
517	GNA12485	FNMA	2.35977	2.09198	−0.26779	0.07171
518	GNA13081	FNMA	2.95769	2.10658	−0.85111	0.72439
519	GNA13084	FNMA	2.47944	2.14866	−0.33077	0.10941
520	GNA13484	FNMA	2.57416	2.20521	−0.36895	0.13613
521	GNA15082	FNMA	2.69249	2.24276	−0.44972	0.20225
522	GNB06493	FNMA	6.2842	5.48648	−0.79772	0.63636
523	GNB06494	FNMA	6.39282	5.51883	−0.87399	0.76387
524	GNB07092	FNMA	5.65237	5.10273	−0.54964	0.3021
525	GNB07093	FNMA	5.76037	5.14302	−0.61734	0.38111
526	GNB07094	FNMA	5.86687	5.18178	−0.68509	0.46935
527	GNB07291	FNMA	5.46194	4.83656	−0.62538	0.3911
528	GNB07487	FNMA	4.97749	4.36611	−0.61138	0.37378
529	GNB07492	FNMA	5.07275	4.6593	−0.41346	0.17095
530	GNB07493	FNMA	5.15877	4.6938	−0.46497	0.21619
531	GNB07494	FNMA	5.2569	4.73191	−0.52499	0.27561
532	GNB07690	FNMA	4.85141	4.33372	−0.51769	0.268

533	GNB07691	FNMA	4.89132	4.37548	-0.51584	0.26609
534	GNB08086	FNMA	4.39396	3.89057	-0.50338	0.25339
535	GNB08087	FNMA	4.43959	3.92434	-0.51525	0.26548
536	GNB08090	FNMA	4.36205	4.09995	-0.2621	0.0687
537	GNB08091	FNMA	4.39627	4.11844	-0.27783	0.07719
538	GNB08092	FNMA	4.4724	4.14256	-0.32984	0.1088
539	GNB08093	FNMA	4.54874	4.1659	-0.38284	0.14657
540	GNB08094	FNMA	4.69385	4.21081	-0.48304	0.23333
541	GNB08486	FNMA	3.91462	3.37812	-0.5365	0.28784
542	GNB08487	FNMA	3.9142	3.38112	-0.53308	0.28418
543	GNB08491	FNMA	3.77164	3.52437	-0.24727	0.06114
544	GNB08492	FNMA	3.82977	3.54096	-0.28881	0.08341
545	GNB08493	FNMA	3.87892	3.55904	-0.31988	0.10232
546	GNB09086	FNMA	3.41957	2.81925	-0.60032	0.36039
547	GNB09087	FNMA	3.42127	2.82671	-0.59456	0.3535
548	GNB09088	FNMA	2.90159	2.85591	-0.04568	0.00209
549	GNB09090	FNMA	2.94571	2.8898	-0.05591	0.00313
550	GNB09091	FNMA	2.98411	2.90489	-0.07922	0.00628
551	GNB09092	FNMA	3.00528	2.92279	-0.08249	0.0068
552	GNB09486	FNMA	2.81217	2.32002	-0.49215	0.24221
553	GNB09487	FNMA	2.78885	2.32892	-0.45993	0.21154
554	GNB09488	FNMA	1.98859	2.33893	0.35034	0.12274
555	GNB09489	FNMA	1.98482	2.34886	0.36404	0.13253
556	GNB09490	FNMA	1.98511	2.35931	0.3742	0.14002
557	GNB09491	FNMA	1.98266	2.36398	0.38132	0.14541
558	GNB10086	FNMA	2.39882	2.02709	-0.37173	0.13818
559	GNB10088	FNMA	1.29095	2.03879	0.74784	0.55926
560	GNB10089	FNMA	1.25439	2.04383	0.78944	0.62322
561	GNB10090	FNMA	1.21586	2.04995	0.83409	0.69571
562	GNB10091	FNMA	1.19824	2.05332	0.85508	0.73117
563	GNB10489	FNMA	0.64155	1.88575	1.24421	1.54805
564	GNB11085	FNMA	2.35801	1.82984	-0.52817	0.27897
565	GND09286	FNMA	3.40413	4.24869	0.84456	0.71328
566	GND09479	FNMA	3.51596	3.64575	0.12979	0.01685
567	GNF05493	FNMA	4.66889	4.44119	-0.2277	0.05185
568	GNF05494	FNMA	4.74284	4.47331	-0.26953	0.07264
569	GNF06093	FNMA	4.63616	4.45651	-0.17965	0.03227
570	GNF06094	FNMA	4.72083	4.50501	-0.21582	0.04658
571	GNF06492	FNMA	4.28659	4.22839	-0.0582	0.00339
572	GNF06493	FNMA	4.49527	4.39685	-0.09841	0.00969
573	GNF06494	FNMA	4.67272	4.50977	-0.16294	0.02655
574	GNF07092	FNMA	4.14023	4.15156	0.01132	0.00013
575	GNF07093	FNMA	4.32913	4.31449	-0.01464	0.00021
576	GNF07094	FNMA	4.52463	4.45367	-0.07096	0.00504
577	GNF07487	FNMA	2.73209	2.7389	0.00681	0.00005
578	GNF07492	FNMA	3.84815	3.95208	0.10393	0.0108
579	GNF07493	FNMA	4.05113	4.13471	0.08358	0.00699
580	GNF07494	FNMA	4.27514	4.29066	0.01552	0.00024
597	GNF09488	FNMA	2.19077	2.47971	0.28894	0.08349
598	GNF09490	FNMA	2.14826	2.73126	0.583	0.33988

| | | | Sum of Squared Difference: | | | 128.54125 |
| | | | Average Absolute Difference: | | | 0.32881 |

10

⑥ INDEX, ASSET, AND MORTGAGE SWAPS*

Ravit Efraty, Vice President/Trader
Salomon Brothers, Inc., New York

WHAT ARE INDEX SWAPS?

Index swaps are swaps where one party pays the monthly total rate of return of an underlying index and the other party pays fixed- or floating-rate payments. This report will focus on interest-rate-related index swaps and notes.

Index swaps have many applications. For example, one common use of index swaps by institutional investors is as a means of matching or even outperforming a benchmark index. In addition, index swaps are also used as asset allocation tools by portfolio managers to overweight or underweight specific bond markets or sectors of bond markets. They also can be used by investors who seek to diversify the exposure of their portfolio to domestic or global markets. Finally, index swaps provide hedgers or investors with an effective way to get short a specific market.

This chapter was written for Salomon Brothers, Inc. by Ravit Efraty, Vice President/Trader.

* Although the information in this chapter has been obtained from sources that Salomon Brothers, Inc. believes to be reliable, we do not guarantee its accuracy, and such information may be incomplete or condensed. All opinions and estimates included in this chapter constitute our judgment as of this date and are subject to change without notice. This chapter is for information purposes only and is not intended as an offer or solicitation with respect to the purchase or sale of any security.

A typical example of an index swap would be where one party pays the monthly U.S. dollar total rate of return of the Salomon Brothers World Government Bond Index (WGBI)[1] while the other side pays one-month U.S. dollar LIBOR plus or minus a spread. Investors who cannot trade swaps can achieve a similar market exposure by embedding the swap in a note. For example, an investor can buy a note that pays coupons or principal that are linked to the total return of the WGBI instead of receiving the total return of the WGBI in an index swap.

Advantages of Index Swaps and Notes

- Index swaps allow investors to gain a *diversified* exposure to bond markets without the operational costs and difficulties associated with creating a diversified index. (The operational costs and difficulties would include tracking errors resulting from the liquidity of the market, the need to develop expertise in operating in many markets, setting up back-office systems for settling and tracking trades in diverse markets, or paying management fees to outside managers.)

- Investors who do not have access to a particular market can gain the market exposure through index swaps or notes.

- Index swaps allow portfolio managers with expertise in one bond market to diversify into different markets by paying the return on their assets and receiving the total return on the desired bond index.

- Receiving the total-rate-of-return in an index swap combined with the purchase of floating-rate assets can often provide investors with a spread over the index.

- Index swaps provide hedgers or investors with a way to effectively get short a specific market without the need to liquidate current holdings.

- For many investors, index swaps are off-balance-sheet transactions. Thus, they allow investors an exposure to the returns on an underlying index with a minimal capital requirement.

---

1 The WGBI is a market-capitalization weighted benchmark that tracks the performance of the government bond markets of Australia, Austria, Belgium, Canada, Denmark, France, Germany, Italy, Japan, the Netherlands, Spain, Sweden, the United Kingdom, and the United States. For more information, see *Salomon Brothers World Government Bond Index*, Salomon Brothers, Inc., October 1994; and Salomon Brothers Global Index Catalog, Salomon Brothers, Inc., January 1995.

• Global index swaps offer an effective way to participate in international bond markets and may provide tax benefits for fund managers who have difficulties reclaiming withholding tax on bonds in some markets.

Index Swap Mechanics

The mechanics of index swaps are similiar to those of plain vanilla interest-rate swaps. For example, both are documented using an ISDA master agreement and confirmation. In addition, the cash flows of both swaps are netted.

However, unlike a plain vanilla swap, if the return of the index is negative, then the total-rate-of-return receiver will have to pay the negative return that period as well as the LIBOR (or fixed) payment. This is completely analogous to borrowing the notional amount each period to buy the underlying bonds in the index. If the return is negative in any period, an investor owes interest on the money that was borrowed and has a mark-to-market loss on the bonds used to match the index.

As with plain vanilla interest rate swaps, investors can unwind index swaps prior to the swap's maturity date. However, the early termination cost can be high when compared to the bid/offer spread of a vanilla interest-rate swap. In practice, the bid/offer spread reflects the bid/offer in the securities used to hedge the index, along with financing and tracking uncertainties. Currently, investors can unwind some index swaps for approximately 25 basis points for each year of remaining life of the swap.

Applications of Index Swaps

Gaining Exposure to the Corporate Sector of the BIG Index
Index swaps can be used to increase or decrease an investor's exposure to a particular market. For example, investors who are underweighted in corporate bonds relative to the corporate sector of the Salomon Brothers Broad Investment Grade (BIG)[2] Bond Index can enter into a

---

2 The Salomon Brothers Broad Investment-Grade (BIG) Bond Index measures the monthly total-rate-of-return performance of institutionally traded U.S. Treasury/agency, investment-grade corporate and mortgage securities. For more information see *Introducing the Salomon Brothers Broad Investment-Grade Bond Index,* Salomon Brothers, Inc., October 1985.

swap to receive the total rate of return (see the local currency return computations in the Appendix to this chapter) of the corporate sector[3] of the BIG Index and pay one-month LIBOR plus a spread.

One strategy that is commonly used to outperform an index is to combine an index swap with an attractively priced floating-rate note. For example, investors may outperform the corporate index by combining the index swap in Figure 10–1 with a triple-A asset-backed security (ABS) currently yielding one-month LIBOR plus 14 bp. This combination (see Figure 10–2) creates a synthetic note that pays the total rate of return of the corporate index plus 4 bp.

Receiving a Sector of the WGBI in U.S. Dollars— Currency Unhedged

Investors can use index swaps to diversify the risks of their portfolios. For example, U.S.-based investors who seek an exposure to a foreign market can enter into a global index swap. This swap can be done so that the currency portion of the total return of the foreign bond index is hedged or unhedged against currency movements.

Figure 10–3 shows an example of a swap where an investor gains exposure to the interest rates and currencies of Germany, Holland, and Belgium. In this swap the investor receives the unhedged total rate of return of the Deutsche-mark-based-nations portion of the WGBI (Germany, Holland, and Belguim) and pays one-month U.S. dollar LIBOR plus 20 bp. In the unhedged case, the monthly U.S.-dollar-based total rate of return is calculated by multi-

---

F I G U R E   10–1

TRR Index Swap—Corporate Sector of the BIG Index

Settlement:	The beginning of next month
Maturity:	One year
Notional amount:	$100 mm
Investor receives:	TRR of corporate sector of the BIG index
Investor pays:	One-month LIBOR + 10 bp
Pay/reset Frequency	Monthly

bp (basis points); TRR (total-rate-of-return)
Source: Salomon Brothers, Inc.

---

3 The corporate sector of the BIG Index includes Utilities, Industrials, Financials, sovereign and provincial, and asset-backed/credit-enhanced securities.

FIGURE   10–2

Structure of Synthetic BIG-Index Investment

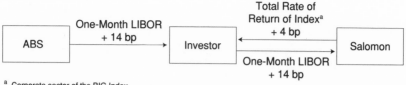

ᵃ Corporate sector of the BIG Index
Source: Salomon Brothers, Inc.

FIGURE   10–3

TRR Index Swap—DM-Based Nations Sector of WGBI

Settlement:	The beginning of next month
Maturity:	One year
Notional amount:	$100 mm
Investor receives:	[(End-of-period USD/DM)/(beginning-of-period USD/DM) × (1 + TRR of the DM block of WGBI) – 1] × 100
Investor pays:	One-month LIBOR + 20 bp
Pay/reset frequency	Monthly

Source: Salomon Brothers, Inc.

plying one plus the total rate of return of the index measured in the local currency (see the base currency return computations in the Appendix to this chapter) by the end-of-period currency exchange rate (U.S. dollar/local currency) divided by the beginning-of-period exchange rate. For example, if the local return is 5 percent, the beginning-of-period exchange rate is 0.7$/DM, and the end-of-period exchange rate is 0.8$/DM, then the unhedged total rate of return is $[0.8/0.7 \times 1.05 - 1] \times 100\% = 20\%$. Investors receiving the U.S.-dollar-based total rate of return can pay a fixed rate, a floating rate, or a different benchmark index.

Receiving a Sector of the WGBI in U.S. Dollars—After-Tax Currency Hedged

Withholding-tax issues can make it difficult for some market participants to invest in particular markets. Index swaps may provide a way for investors to efficiently access those markets. For example, a U.S.-based fund manager may seek a currency-hedged exposure to the Italian government bond market but cannot reclaim withholding tax on Italian bonds.[4] Currently, the investor can gain the desired exposure by entering into a swap to receive the after-tax currency-hedged total rate of return (see after-tax bond indexes in the Appendix) of the Italian sector of Salomon Brothers WGBI, and pay one-month LIBOR minus 50 bp (Figure 10–4). In addition, the investor may outperform the index by combining this swap with the purchase of a par priced, monthly pay, floating-rate asset that pays more than one-month LIBOR minus 50 bp.

In the case of a currency-hedged index swap, the total-rate-of-return payment is computed using one-month forward exchange contracts (see "Currency-Hedged Base Currency Return" in the Appendix). Because the face value of the forward contracts is an estimate of the bonds' market value plus reinvested cash flows at the end of the month, the receiver of the index's total rate of return does have some currency exposure. However, it should be substantially less exposure than using the swap with no currency hedge.

Tactical Asset Allocation

Investors who want to underweight, or get short, a specific market can enter into a swap to pay the total rate of return of the index and receive fixed- or floating-rate payments.

For example, investors who want to get short the U.S. mortgage market may enter into a swap to pay the return of the mortgage component of the BIG Index[5] and receive one-month LIBOR minus 35

Source: Salomon Brothers, Inc.

FIGURE 10–4

TRR Index Swap—Italian Sector of WGBI—After-Tax Currency Hedged

Settlement:	The beginning of next month
Maturity:	One year
Notional amount:	$100 mm
Investor receives:	After-tax currency hedged TRR of Italian sector of WGBI
Investor pays:	One-month LIBOR – 50 bp
Pay/reset frequency:	Monthly

4 If investors can repo, then they'll effectively reclaim the tax via the repo.
5 The mortgage component of the BIG Index comprises 30- and 15-year GNMA, FNMA and FHLMC securities, and FNMA and FHLMC balloon mortgages.

bp (see Figure 10–5 and "Mortgage Index Return" in the Appendix). This is an effective way to get short the mortgage market because mortgage index swaps provide diversification against pool-specific prepayment risk and reduce the operational difficulty of dealing with mortgage-backed securities (MBS).

Summary

Index swaps allow investors to gain a diversified exposure to a broad array of markets. They are typically used by institutional investors, whose performance is measured against an index, as a way to replicate and often outperform the benchmark index. In addition, index swaps may serve as effective asset allocation tools because they enable investors to take a short or long market position. Furthermore, global index swaps allow investors familiar with one set of markets to diversify into global markets.

INDEX SWAPS—APPENDIX

Salomon Brothers Indexes[6]

• **Broad Investment-Grade Bond Index**[SM]: The BIG Index is designed to cover the investment-grade universe of bonds issued in the United States. It includes institutionally traded U.S. Treasury, Government-sponsored (agency and supranational), mortgage, and corporate securities.

F I G U R E   10–5

TRR Index Swap—Shorting the Mortgage Sector of the BIG Index

Settlement:	The beginning of next month
Maturity:	One year
Notional amount:	$100 mm
Investor pays:	TRR of mortgage sector of the BIG Index
Investor receives:	One-month LIBOR – 35 bp
Pay/reset frequency:	Monthly

Source: Salomon Brothers, Inc.

---

6 For a complete description of Salomon Brothers indexes, please see *Salomon Brothers Global Index Catalog*, Salomon Brothers Inc, January 1995.

- **New Large Pension Fund (LPF) Bond Index^{SM}:** The new LPF provides an appropriate benchmark and/or tracking vehicle for pension funds seeking to establish long-term core portfolios that more closely match the longer durations of their nominal dollar liabilities.
- **High-Yield Indexes:** High-Yield Indexes capture the performance of below-investment-grade corporate bonds issued in the United States.
- **Brady Bond Index^{SM}:** The Brady Bond Index measures the performance of emerging market debt that has been restructured under Brady plans.
- **Emerging Market Mutual Fund (EMMF) Debt Index^{SM}:** The EMMF Debt Index provides the managers of regulated mutual funds with a more appropriate benchmark than the Brady Bond Index.
- **World Government Bond Index^{SM} (WGBI):** The WGBI is a market-capitalization-weighted benchmark that tracks the performance of the government bond markets of Australia, Austria, Belguim, Canada, Denmark, France, Germany, Italy, Japan, the Netherlands, Spain, Sweden, the United Kingdom, and the United States.
- **Eurobond Indexes:** The Eurobond Indexes provide a measure of performance of Eurodollar, Eurosterling, Euroyen, and Euro-Deutschemark bonds.
- **World Bond Index^{SM}:** The World Bond Index includes governments, Euro and/or foreign bond sectors for the following 10 currency sectors: Australian dollar, Canadian dollar, Deutschemark, Dutch guilder, European currency unit, French franc, Japanese yen, Swiss franc, U.K. sterling, and U.S. dollar.
- **World Money Market Index^{SM}:** The World Money Market Index approximates the performance of money market instruments of the following eight currencies, both in the domestic and Euromarkets: Canadian dollar, Deutschemark, Dutch guilder, French franc, Japanese yen, Swiss franc, U.K. sterling, and U.S. dollar.
- **Salomon Brothers World Equity Index^{SM} (SBWEI):** The SBWEI is a comprehensive top-down, float capitalization-weighted index that includes shares of about 6,000 companies in 22 countries. It includes all companies with available (float) market capitalization greater than US $100 million.

Return and profile information of Salomon Brothers Indexes are available by the third business day of each month and are published monthly in *Total Rate of Return Indexes* and weekly in *Bond Market Roundup: Abstract.* Information is also available through Salomon Performance Index Network at (212) 783-7746 and through a number of electronic data services including Telerate, Reuters, Bloomberg, and QUICK-10 (see Figure 10–6).

Return Computation

Index returns are calculated in *local currency* terms and in *base currency terms, unhedged* and *currency hedged.* For illustrative purposes, we calculate the base currency returns assuming a U.S. dollar base.

Local Currency Return

The local currency return for each bond is described in Figure 10–7. The local currency sector-return is the weighted average of the individual bond returns using each bond's beginning-of-month market value as its weight.

F I G U R E   10–6

Accessibility of Salomon Brothers Indexes

Index	Telerate	Reuters	Bloomberg	QUICK-10
Broad Investment-Grade Bond Index	2113–2116	SOLY-Z	SBI<GO>; SALO<GO>	SLBI
New Large Pension Fund Bond Index	2113–2116	SOLY-Z	SBI<GO>; SALO<GO>	SLBI
High-Yield Indexes	—	—	SBI<GO>; SALO<GO>	—
Brady Bond Index	1785(01) 1786(m)	BRDY	SBI<GO>; SALO<GO>	—
Emerging Market Mutual Fund Debt Index	1785(d) 1786(m)	BRDY	SBI<GO>; SALO<GO>	—
World Government Bond Index	2113–2118	SOLS-T;SOLY-Z	SBI<GO>; SALO<GO>	—
Eurobond Indexes	2117		SBI<GO>; SALO<GO>	—
World Bond Index	—	—	—	—
World Money Market Index	—	—	—	—
World Equity Index	—	—	SBI<GO>	—

Source: Salomon Brothers, Inc.

F I G U R E   10–7

Total-Rate-of-Return Calculation Methodology

Beginning-of-period value	= (Beginning price + beginning accrued) × beginning par amount outstanding
End-of-period value	= (Ending price + ending accrued) x (beginning par amount outstanding principal payments) + coupon payments + principal payments + reinvestment income
Total rate of return	= [(End-of-period value/beginning-of-period value) − 1] × 100

Source: Salomon Brothers, Inc.

Base Currency Return

The base currency sector-return, for example the U.S. dollar–base currency return for each sector, is calculated by multiplying the local currency sector-return by the end-of-period currency exchange rate (U.S. dollar/local currency) divided by the beginning-of-period currency exchange rate.

Currency-Hedged Base Currency Return

The calculation of the next total-return payment of a currency-hedged base return for individual bonds is as follows (see Figure 10–8):

• Find the market value (price plus accrued interest) in local currencies one month from today using today's bond yields.

• Convert that market value into U.S. dollars with today's one-month forward exchange rate contracts.

• The total-return payment will be this market value converted to U.S. dollars plus or minus any price change in the securities that occurs over the month, converted to U.S. dollars at the prevailing exchange rate at the end of that month.

The currency-hedged base currency sector return is computed by taking a weighted average of the individual bond return using each bond's beginning-of-month market value as its weight.

Salomon Brothers After-Tax Bond Indexes

The after-tax returns are computed from the point of view of a U.S. pension account and approximate the effect on total rate-of-return of withholding tax on coupon income. The markets that have with-

Currency-Hedged Return Calculation Methodology

Beginning-of-period value	= ((Beginning price + beginning accrued) × (beginning par outstanding)) × [beginning-of-period spot exchange rate (US$/Local Currency)]
End-of-period value	[(Yield with forward settle at the end of the month + expected change in accrued interest over one-month investment period + cash flow and reinvestment income) x beginning-of-period one-month forward exchange rate (US$/Local Currency)] + [change in market value of principal amount due to yield change x [end-of-period spot exchange rate (US$/Local Currency)]
Total rate-of-return	= [(End -of-period value/beginning-of-period value)-1] × 100

Source: Salomon Brothers, Inc.

holding taxes are displayed in Figure 10–9 along with our estimated withholding tax assumptions. The withholding tax assumptions are updated periodically in *Salomon Brothers Global Index Catalog.*

Mortgage Index Return

Most mortgage securities generate a cash flow made up of principal and interest. The index assumes that cash flow is reinvested at the monthly average of the daily one-month Treasury-bill rate. The return computation for mortgage securities is displayed in Figure 10–10.

WHAT ARE ASSET SWAPS?

An asset swap is a strategy that combines the purchase of a security and an interest rate or currency swap.[7] For example, an investor could buy a fixed-rate note and then pay a fixed rate in an interest rate swap to create a synthetic floating-rate note. The asset swap market, evolving since 1982, affords investors and issuers the following opportunities:

> • Asset swaps allow investors to take advantage of attractively priced sectors of the market by buying bonds with high relative value and swapping them into synthetic bonds with

---

7 Asset swaps can also be done with equity or commodity swaps.

FIGURE   10-9

Estimated Withholding Tax Assumptions for the After-Tax Indexes as of
January 1995

Market	Tax Rate	Calculation Assumption
Belgium	10.30% 12.75	Classical bonds only, rate depends upon issue date. Fully refundable with a 30-day delay to receipt of coupon income.
Japan	10.00	Nonrefundable
Italy	12.50	Nonrefundable
Switzerland	35.00	5% nonrefundable, 30% refundable three months following the January 1 or July 1 following the coupon payment date.
United Kingdom	25.00	Fully refundable. FOTRA stocks assume a 60-day delay to receipt of coupon income and Non-FOTRA stocks assume 120-day delay.

FOTRA (Free of Tax to Residents Abroad)
Source: Salomon Brothers, Inc.

more desirable risk/return profiles. For example, a common
strategy in the asset swap market is to buy an attractively
priced fixed-rate note and asset-swap it into a synthetic
LIBOR floating-rate note. This swap allows investors to create
synthetic LIBOR floaters that represent good relative value
when compared with the limited universe of floating-rate
notes. Investors can use asset swaps to transform inexpensive
bonds denominated in one currency into attractively priced
fixed- or floating-rate assets denominated in another.

• Asset swaps enable the creation of synthetic securities with
desired credit, interest rate, or currency characteristics that are
otherwise unavailable or expensive. For example, investors can
diversify their portfolios by creating synthetic floating-rate
notes for issuers that do not issue floating-rate debt.

• Asset swaps are important vehicles for trading structured
products (inverse floaters, step-up callables, CMT-indexed
floaters, etc.) in the secondary market. Dealers frequently buy
structured notes with the intention of reselling them together
with an interest-rate swap (that is, as an asset swap), converting the package into a plain-vanilla LIBOR floater.

F I G U R E   10–10

Return Calculation for Mortgage

Total Return (%) = $[((C + X) \times (1+Rm/200)N/180 + (EP + EA)$
$(1 - (X/100)))/(BP + BA) -1] \times 100$

BP   Beginning price
EP   Ending price
X   Principal payment as percent of beginning balance
C   Coupon rate/12
Rm   Reinvestment rate on intra-month payment (average of daily one-month
     Treasury Bill rate)
N   Number of days between date of receipt of coupon and principal payment and
     calendar month-end
BA   Beginning accrued interest
EA   Ending accured interest

- Corporations whose debt is trading cheaply in the secondary market often can use asset swaps to lower their cost of funds.[8] Suppose, for example, that a corporation issues a fixed-rate note and swaps it into a floating-rate liability at issuance. If, at some later date, this debt issue is trading cheaply, the corporation can buy back the debt in the secondary market and unwind the original swap position. The corporation then can issue another type of debt that appeals to the market (such as callable debt) at more attractive levels.[9]

A variety of investors—such as banks, insurance companies, corporate cash managers, and other short-term cash managers—use asset swaps. In addition, a range of security types typically underlie asset swaps, including corporates, mortgages, asset-backed securities, and structured notes. However, approximately 80 percent to 90 percent of the swaps in the asset swap market involve the creation of LIBOR floaters from other assets.

In this section of the chapter, I explain the different ways and different vehicles used to execute asset swaps and provide a variety of examples to demonstrate how investors are using asset swaps.

---

8 The issuer needs to consider tax and accounting effects of the refinancing.
9 The swap used by the issuer is technically a liability swap.

Structuring Asset Swaps

An asset swap can be done directly with a counterparty that is able to execute interest-rate swaps or can be securitized for customers that cannot execute swaps. Securitization is achieved by placing an asset in a special purpose vehicle (SPV), usually a trust, and entering into a swap with the SPV. The SPV then issues a security whose cash flows are identical to the net cash flows of an asset swap. Thus, investors that cannot execute swaps still can benefit from the asset-swap market by purchasing the securities issued by the SPV.

Similarly, investors can use a corporation that is able to issue debt securities that are not subject to any withholding tax and that is established in a country with effective double-tax treaties with numerous other countries (for example, Luxembourg) as a vehicle with which to invest globally. This strategy allows investors to invest in foreign bond markets based on credit and on gross yields without having to rely on an effective treaty between the investor's country of residence and the relevant foreign country.

Various vehicles are now available in the market place, including Salomon Brothers' Trust Investment Enhanced Return Securities[10] (TIERS[SM]) and Swap Enhanced Asset Linked Securities (SEALS[SM]).[11]

Although the net cash flows of an asset swap and a securitized asset swap are the same, the accounting treatment, liquidity, and credit ratings may differ. In addition, a synthetic security is likely to be more liquid than the asset swap package and may be traded on the secondary market.

Par Asset Swaps versus Market Value Asset Swaps

Asset swaps generally are executed either at par or at the market value of the underlying asset. In a par asset swap, the investor pays par for the asset swap package regardless of the underlying asset price, thereby lending the discount to, or borrowing the premium from, the swap counterparty at settlement. In a market value swap, the investor pays the market value for the underlying asset and receives that same amount when the bond and the swap mature.

---

10 For more information about TIERS, see *Trust Investment Enhanced Return Securities (TIERS)*, Salomon Brothers Inc, March 30, 1995.

11 Trust Investment Enhanced Return Securities, TIERS, and Swap Enhanced Asset Linked Securities, SEALS, are service marks of Salomon Brothers Inc.

Therefore, investors can shift credit exposure between the asset issuer and the swap counterparty. Investors should base their decisions to effect a market value or a par value asset swap on their counterparties' credit-risk preferences as well as on tax- or accounting-treatment preference.

The Mechanics of Par Asset Swaps

In a par asset swap, the investor always pays par for the net investment, but the value of the underlying asset may be greater than or less than par. Figure 10–11 shows the three types of par asset swaps—for par, discount, and premium assets of different credits—in which a fixed-rate asset may be swapped into a floating-rate asset. The various spreads to LIBOR reflect the differences in the issuers' credit.

Figure 10–11(a) illustrates the cash flows of a par asset swap when the underlying asset is a five-year, fixed-rate bond priced at par (in this case a par asset swap is the same as a market value asset swap). Thus, the investor buys the fixed-rate bond at par and enters

F I G U R E   10–11

Par Asset Swaps of (a) Par Asset, (b) Discount Asset, and (c) Premium Asset

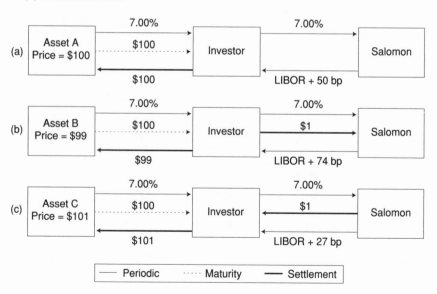

Source: Salomon Brothers, Inc.

into a swap to pay the coupon on the bond and receive three-month LIBOR plus 50 basis points (quarterly). At maturity, the investor receives back the asset's par value from the issuer.

If the underlying asset's value is not par, then the swap counterparty will adjust for the difference between par and the actual bond price either by lending the premium to the investor or by borrowing the discount from the investor. This lending or borrowing is reflected in the swap payments that the investor receives. If the underlying asset value is at a discount, then the discount is amortized over the life of the swap and is added to the swap payments that the investor receives. If the underlying asset value is at a premium, then the premium amount is amortized over the life of the swap and is subtracted from the swap payments that the investor receives. For example, in Figure 10–11(b) the price of the underlying fixed-rate asset is $99. At settlement of a par asset swap, the investor pays par. Thus, the $1 discount is effectively paid to the swap counterparty and is amortized over the five-year life of the swap [24 basis points for the dollar value of 1 bp change in yield (DV01) of 0.042]. Therefore, the floating-rate coupon received by the investor is LIBOR plus 74 basis points. Because this type of asset swap involves the purchase of a bond plus a single-currency interest-rate swap, no principal is exchanged between the swap counterparties. At maturity, the investor receives the $100 of principal.

If the asset is traded at a premium, the swap counterparty lends the premium to the investor. Figure 10–11(c) illustrates a premium asset swap. The DV01 of the swap, as well as the financing rate at which the swap counterparty borrows money, determine the spread to LIBOR.[12]

The Mechanics of Market Value Asset Swaps

In a market value asset swap, the investor pays the market value on the underlying asset and enters into a swap. The swap counterparty adjusts for the difference between par and the asset price at the maturity of the swap. That is, the swap counterparty pays the premium to the investor or receives the discount at the swap maturity (the investor receives at maturity the same amount invested at settlement). As in a par asset swap, the investor passes along the coupon received from the underlying asset on the whole notional to the

---

12 Therefore, the asset swap level cannot be obtained simply by subtracting the swap spread from the underlying bond's spread to Treasuries.

swap counterparty. However, the swap floating payments received by the investor are based on the initial market value (which can be the flat or full price[13]) of the asset.

Figure 10–12(a) shows an example of an asset swap in which the underlying fixed-rate asset has a market value of $101. At settlement, the investor pays the $101 market value of the asset and therefore receives floating-rate payments that are based on a notional amount of $101. The fixed-rate payment of the swap is equal to the coupon received from the underlying asset. At maturity, the investor receives back the asset's par value and the $1 premium from the swap counterparty. (In this example, the swap counterparty has borrowed $1 over the life of the asset swap.)

Examples of Asset Swaps

Cross-Currency Asset Swaps

Investors commonly use asset swaps to alter the currency denomination of an investment. For example, U.S. commercial banks buy

F I G U R E   10–12

Market-Value Asset Swaps of (a) Premium Asset and (b) Discount Asset

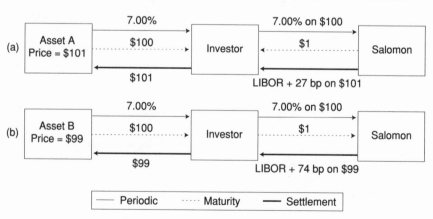

Source: Salomon Brothers, Inc.

---

13 In a flat-market-value asset swap, the swap counterparty lends the investor the accrued interest at settlement.

foreign currency denominated bonds and asset-swap them into U.S. dollar-denominated LIBOR-indexed floating rate notes. In contrast, money managers often use currency asset swaps to create fixed-rate bonds denominated in a desired foreign currency. In either case, the investor buys an asset and enters into a cross-currency swap to convert the cash flows, both interest and principal, into the desired currency denomination.

We illustrate an example of an asset swap involving a currency swap in Figure 10–13. The underlying investment is a two-year yen Government bond with a par coupon of 1 percent. A currency swap is used to create a synthetic U.S. dollar floating-rate note, yielding six-month LIBOR plus nine basis points.[14] The investor initially exchanges $0.96 million for ¥100 million to pay for the bond at an exchange rate of 104.17¥/US$. Over the subsequent two years, the investor passes on the coupon on the Japanese bond in exchange for U.S. dollar LIBOR plus nine basis points on $0.96 million. At the end

F I G U R E   10–13

Cross-Currency Asset Swap—Cash Flow Diagram

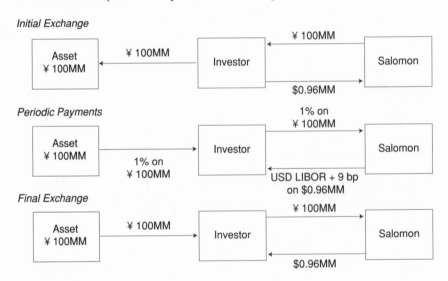

Source: Salomon Brothers, Inc.

14 Note that on cross-currency swaps, U.S. dollar LIBOR plus nine basis points is not equivalent to yen LIBOR plus nine basis points because of the difference in DV01 and basis cost.

of two years, the investor and the swap counterparty exchange the initial principal amount. We describe in detail the cash flows from the investor's perspective in Figure 10–14.

Structured Note Asset Swaps

Many structured notes are created with highly customized views of a market built into them. As the market moves over time, the view embedded in such a note may no longer be of interest to market participants. Therefore, the universe of buyers may be limited for this security in its original form. Thus, structured notes are likely to be traded based upon the value of the LIBOR floater that can be created by asset-swapping them. In this case, the ability to asset-swap the structured note into a plain vanilla LIBOR floater greatly enhances the liquidity of the structured note.

Figure 10–15 shows an example of asset-swapping a structured note. In this example, the underlying note is a callable agency inverse floater that pays a coupon of 10.55 percent minus six-month LIBOR. The note is callable at par on any coupon date. The price of the bond is 87.40 percent.

An investor entering into this par asset swap pays par for the package of the bond plus the swap (see Figure 10–16). Similar to a fixed-rate asset swap, the investor passes along the full coupon received from the inverse floater bond to the swap counterparty. The investor receives floating-rate payments of three-month LIBOR plus five basis points. These payments reflect the 12.60 percent discount of the bond. When the bond is called or matures, the swap terminates and the investor receives par from the asset.

Tax-Immunized Asset Swaps

When investors purchase a bond that is subject to withholding tax and are able to reclaim this tax via a double-tax treaty, they are exposed to financing risk if either the time taken to receive the tax refund increases or the tax rate rises. Salomon Brothers can immunize investors against both of these risks. In this case, the investor pays Salomon Brothers the coupon net of withholding tax on the coupon date and Salomon Brothers pays LIBOR plus a spread (see Figure 10–17). The investor, who is responsible for filing all requisite tax forms in a timely manner, pays Salomon Brothers the refunded withholding tax when received.

FIGURE 10-14

Detailed Cash Flows of a Cross-Currency Asset Swap (Yen and U.S. Dollars in Millions)

Investor's Date		Asset	Payment	Swap		Swap	
					Payment	Payment	Net
Settlement	Oct 95	¥-100	¥100	US$-0.96		US$-0.96	Act/360
	Apr 96	Act/365x1%x100	-Act/365x1%x100	Act/360x(LIBOR+9bp)x0.96		Act/360x(LIBOR+9bp)x0.96	Act/360
	Oct 96	Act/365x1%x100	-Act/365x1%x100	Act/360x(LIBOR+9bp)x0.96		Act/360x(LIBOR+9bp)x0.96	Act/360
	Apr 96	Act/365x1%x100	-Act/365x1%x100	Act/360x(LIBOR+9bp)x0.96		Act/360x(LIBOR+9bp)x0.96	Act/360
Maturity	Oct 97	100+Act/365x1%x100	-100+Act/365x1%x100	0.96+Act/360x(LIBOR+9bp)x0.96		0.96+Act/360x(LIBOR+9bp)x0.9	0.96+Act/360

LIBOR (London Interbank Offered Rate)

Source: Salomon Brothers, Inc.

FIGURE   10–15

Par Asset Swap of a Callable Inverse Floater

Swap	
Investor Pays	Par for the bond and the swap coupons on the bond described below.
Investor Receives	3-Month LIBOR + 5bp reset and paid quarterly, on an Act/360-day-count basis.
Bond	
Issuer	Agency
Settlement	October 2, 1995
Maturity Date	September 22, 1997
Market Price	87.40%
Coupon	10.55%—6-Month LIBOR
Coupon Payment/Reset	Semiannual/Semiannual
Call Option	Bond is callable at par on coupon payment dates provided that 30 days notice is given
Day Count Convention	30/360

LIBOR (London Interbank Offered Rate)
Source: Salomon Brothers, Inc.

FIGURE   10–16

Par Asset Swaps of a Callable Inverse Floater—Cash Flows Diagram

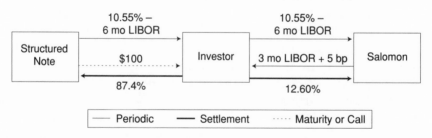

Source: Salomon Brothers, Inc.

Investors resident in jurisdictions that do not have suitable double-tax treaties still can benefit from Salomon Brothers' willingness to assume tax risk. However, such investors require that the investors' bonds be held by an entity resident in a country with a suitable double-tax treaty. Thus, the investor must purchase the credit either in a note issued by an SPV—such as SEALS—or in the form of a credit-

FIGURE   10–17

Tax Related Asset Swaps — Cash Flows

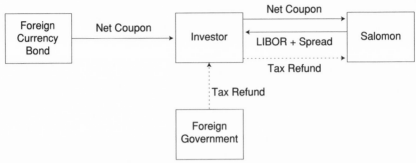

Source: Salomon Brothers, Inc.

linked note. A credit-linked note is issued by a highly rated entity, and payments on the note are indexed to the credit performance of the underlying bond. Both of these notes can be issued in any currency that the investor chooses and in a fixed or a floating format.

Convertible Bond Asset Swaps

A convertible bond can be separated into a conventional bullet bond plus an option exercisable by the investor to convert the bond into stock at a specified exchange ratio. However, the convertible bond may trade more cheaply than the conventional bullet bond plus the conversion option, creating an arbitrage opportunity for investors. In addition, for certain companies, convertible bonds may represent the only issued debt in a particular maturity sector. Therefore, convertible bond asset swaps may be the only means to purchase a conventional debt of a particular issuer.

In convertible bond asset swaps, the investor sells the conversion option embedded in the convertible bond in exchange for receiving a higher coupon on the swap. Figure 10–18 illustrates an example of a convertible bond asset swap. This swap is structured as a market value asset swap in which the investor initially pays the cost of acquiring the asset in the secondary market.

The investor purchases a $20 million face amount of a 4 percent convertible bond on October 2, 2000, for a full price of 85 percent of par ($17 million). The investor simultaneously enters into a swap with Salomon Brothers to pay a fixed rate of 4 percent on a $20 mil-

FIGURE   10–18

Convertible Bond Asset Swap

Settlement:	October 2, 1995
Maturity:	October 2, 2000
Investor pays:	4.00% on a $20-million notional amount
	Paid semiannually
	30/360 Daycount
Investor receives:	3-Month LIBOR + 125bp on a $17-million notional amount
	Paid/reset quarterly
	Act/360 daycount
Reference convertible bond:	$20-million face amount ($17-million initial market value) of 4.00% on October 2, 2000
Early termination:	Salomon Brothers may call the reference convertible bond and terminate the swap on any floating-rate reset date. In the event of an early termination, the investor receives $17 million and pays the proceeds from the sale of reference convertible bond.
Final exchange on October 2, 2000 if there is no early termination:	Investor receives $17 million. Investor pays the greater of $20 Million or the proceeds from the sale of the reference convertible bond

Source: Salomon Brothers, Inc.

lion notional amount and receive three-month LIBOR plus 125 basis points on a $17 million notional amount (see Figure 10–19). By purchasing the convertible bond and entering into the asset swap, the investor has created a $17 million face amount of a synthetic floater that pays three-month LIBOR plus 125 basis points.

A conventional bond with the same issuer, coupon maturity, and price as the convertible bond would asset-swap at three-month LIBOR plus 110 basis points. Therefore, by effectively selling the conversion option embedded in the convertible bond, investors receive an additional 15 basis points in coupon than if they swapped the conventional bond.

Salomon Brothers can terminate the convertible bond asset swap at each floating rate reset date. In the event of an early termination, the investor will receive the initial $17 million paid for the convertible bonds and will pay the proceeds of the convertible bond sale.

F I G U R E   10–19

Convertible Bond Asset Swap—Cash Flows

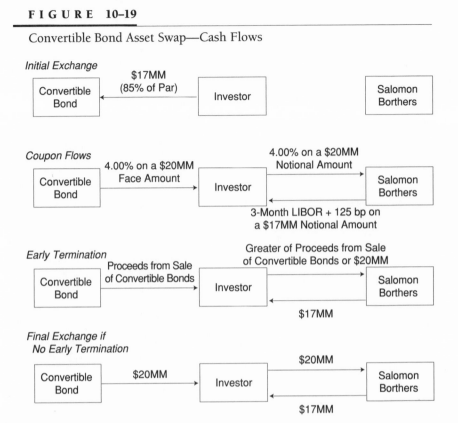

Source: Salomon Brothers, Inc.

Amortizing Asset Swaps

Amortizing swaps can be created to mimic the cash flows of an amortizing asset. The most popular amortizing asset swaps are executed using tranches of collateralized mortgage obligations (CMOs) or asset-backed securities as the underlying assets. Typically, in the case of CMOs, the investor receives the coupon on the CMO based on the actual remaining mortgage balance and pays the CMO coupon on an amortizing notional amount of the swap (and receives LIBOR plus a spread on the amortizing notional balance). Therefore, the investor remains exposed to prepayment risk to the extent that the mortgage balance does not match the swap notional amount. When creating an asset swap using CMOs, the following are the three most common ways to handle the prepayment uncertainty of the underlying asset over time:

- Calculate the CMO amortization schedule (using an estimated prepayment speed) and then combine the CMO with an amortizing interest-rate swap that has the same estimated amortization schedule.

- Use the first method while retaining the option to cancel all or part of the interest rate swap at any time before maturity, should rates fall. This strategy mitigates the investor's exposure to accelerating prepayments in a rally, but the investor must pay for an option. The option premium is amortized over the life of the swap and subtracted from the swap payments received by the investor.

- Use an index principal swap (IPS) to swap the underlying asset's coupons from fixed to floating, or vice versa. An IPS amortizes based on the movements of an index such as Constant-Maturity Treasury rates or LIBOR. Thus, an IPS can be structured to have similar weighted-average-life sensitivities to changes in interest rates as a CMO. To the extent that the amortization of the CMO can be approximated using a particular interest rate and amortization schedule, this method more efficiently reduces amortization mismatches relative to the first two alternatives.

Mortgage Swaps

The following example illustrates an asset swap that is sensitive to the prepayment speed of the underlying asset. The investor buys FHLMC 1722 PG backed by Gold 7s priced at 94.98 percent. The CMO pays a monthly fixed coupon of 6.50 percent and has a PAC range of 95 percent to 255 percent PSA. The weighted-average life (WAL) of the fixed-rate PAC schedule is 6.75 years and the scheduled maturity is 5/2003. The investor simultaneously enters into an interest rate swap to convert the coupon from a 6.50 percent fixed rate into a floating rate of one-month LIBOR plus 26 basis points. The notional amount of the swap amortizes at the same rate as the CMO at 200 percent PSA.

If prepayments come inside the PAC range, then the coupons on the remaining mortgage balance offset the fixed payments on the swap, and the investor's net cash flows are the floating-rate payments received on the swap. However, if prepayments come outside the PAC range, then the mortgage balance and the swap notional amount will decline at different rates. When prepayments are faster than 255 percent PSA, the investor receives back the principal on the CMO faster than expected; thus, the remaining balance of the mortgage will be lower than the swap notional amount. To correct this mismatch, the investor can reinvest the excess principal received in additional mortgages. Therefore, the investor benefits from fast prepayments if the underlying mortgage trades at a discount. However, market rallies usually accompany fast prepayments, and thus the underlying mortgage is likely to trade at a premium. Similarly, when prepayments are slow, the remaining mortgage balance is higher than the swap notional amount. If the PAC trades at a premium, then the investor can benefit from selling the difference between the remaining mortgage balance and the swap notional amount. High interest rates usually accompany slow prepayments, however; thus, the PAC is likely to trade at a discount.

And Much More . . .

The variations on asset swaps are endless, allowing investors to rearrange cash flows of any underlying assets into more desirable structures. Here are some examples:

- A zero-coupon bond can be converted into a floating-rate bond[15] if the investor finds the zero-coupon bond attractively priced but wishes to shorten its duration.
- An investor that finds a perpetual floating-rate note with an attractive spread to LIBOR can convert it into a fixed-rate asset for a known period of time. For example, an asset swap can convert the perpetual into a fixed-rate note for 10 years and into a LIBOR floater thereafter.
- Basis swaps are used in floating-to-floating asset swaps in which, for example, a LIBOR-based floating-rate note is converted into a synthetic floating-prime-rate note.
- Investors can overlay options on asset swaps to enhance yield. For instance, a floating-rate investor can buy a fixed-

---

15 The investor can purchase the zero-coupon bond and enter into a zero-coupon interest-rate swap.

rate asset and swap it into a floating rate with a periodic cap. Similarly, underlying assets with embedded options such as convertible or callable bonds can be asset-swapped so that the embedded option in the underlying bond is effectively bought back. An investor can effect this transaction by entering into a swap that terminates whenever the underlying asset is called or converted.

Conclusion

Asset swaps allow market participants to alter the cash flows of an investment to achieve a more desirable risk/return profile. Thus, these transactions have implications for investors. Investors can create attractive securities by buying securities with good relative value and asset-swapping them into the desired currency and risk/return profile. Investors can overlay options on asset swaps to enhance yield or buy back options on attractively priced secondary-structured products. Alternatively, investors can create synthetic securities with customized characteristics that are unavailable in the market place. SPVs can be used by investors that cannot execute swaps or that want to invest globally without relying on an effective tax treaty.

WHAT ARE MORTGAGE SWAP AGREEMENTS?

Mortgage swap agreements (MSAs) are interest rate swaps (fixed versus floating) that replicate the economics of long or short positions in mortgage-backed securities (MBS). The notional amount of the swap amortizes according to the principal paydowns of a reference set of passthroughs that all have the same fixed coupon. Fixed-rate receivers in MSAs have the equivalent of a financed long position in an MBS. They receive the fixed coupon of the reference set of passthroughs, experience the gains or losses due to principal paydowns, and have a termination adjustment (payment or physical delivery) when the swap matures, reflecting the change in the market value of the reference set of passthroughs. The floating payments represent the cost of financing the MBS. Because receiving fixed in a swap is equivalent to financing a long position in an MBS, paying fixed on the MSA is equivalent to being short a cash MBS.

Salomon Brothers started the MSA market in 1987, and it has grown significantly since then. MSAs typically are one- to three-year swaps. Figure 10–20 shows indicative MSA offering levels referencing Federal National Mortgage Association (FNMA) passthroughs. The fixed-rate coupon is equal to the coupon of the reference passthroughs and the swap levels for MSAs are quoted as LIBOR less a spread.

MSA Advantages

Entering into an MSA and, thus, creating a long or short synthetic MBS may have significant advantages over being long or short cash MBS, as follows:

- **MSAs provide diversification protection against pool-specific prepayment risk** because the reference group of securities underlying the mortgage swap is a large set of agency passthroughs.
- Fixed-rate receivers in MSAs effectively have locked in sub-LIBOR funding levels. Conversely, fixed-rate payers have locked in implied repo rates that are often higher than those that the collateral market offers. In either case, **MSAs allow investors or hedgers to remove funding uncertainty from their decision making.**
- For most customers, **MSAs are off–balance-sheet transactions**[16] MSAs allow hedgers to short mortgages and allow investors to own synthetic mortgages with a minimal capital requirement.
- **MSAs significantly reduce operational difficulty** in dealing with MBS. While cash MBS can include as many as three

FIGURE   10–20

Indicative Mortgage Swap Agreement Offering Levels, as of 13 Sep 94

	FNMA 7s	FNMA 8s	FNMA 9s
1 Year	1-Mo. LIBOR - 10bp	1-Mo. LIBOR - 25bp	1-Mo. LIBOR - 60bp
2 Year	1-Mo. LIBOR - 10	1-Mo. LIBOR - 25	1-Mo. LIBOR - 45
3 Year	1-Mo. LIBOR - 10	1-Mo. LIBOR - 20	1-Mo. LIBOR - 25

bp (basis points). FNMA (Federal National Mortgage Association). LIBOR (London Interbank Offered Rate).
Note: Pricing date — September 13, 1994; 2% variance.
Source: Salomon Brothers, Inc.

16 The accounting treatment of MSAs may vary across customers.

pools per $1 million, the swap refers to one large pool of mortgages.

• MSAs used in conjunction with floating-rate assets can **provide nonleveraged investors with incremental returns that have minimal additional risk** compared with passthrough investments.

Mortgage Swap Agreement Mechanics

A simple example of a two-year MSA indexed off FNMA 8s illustrates the basic mechanics of MSAs (see Figure 10–21).

In an MSA, there is an exchange of a fixed and a floating cash flow at each monthly reset. However, unlike conventional interest-rate swaps, MSAs have a monthly adjustment to the regular fixed/floating payment because of principal paydowns. For MSAs indexed off of discount or premium mortgages, the monthly adjustment is added to the fixed-rate payment or the floating-rate payment, respectively. Finally, at the maturity of the swap there is a termination adjustment either in cash or in the form of physical delivery that accounts for the change in the mortgage value over the life of the swap (see Figure 10–22).

Fixed-Rate Payments

The fixed-rate payment is equal to the coupon received on the reference passthroughs times the remaining balance. **Thus, this fixed-**

FIGURE   10–21

Example of a Mortgage Swap Agreement

Reference security	All FNMA 8s maturing in 2023
Initial notional amount	$100 million
Effective date	25 Sep 94
Maturity date	25 Sep 96
Initial price (full price)	98-19 plus 24 days of accrued interest = 99.127%
Fixed rate	8%
Floating rate	One-Month LIBOR less 25bp; (currently 4.625%)
Variance at termination	2%

FNMA (Federal National Mortgage Association). LIBOR (London Interbank Offered Rate).
Note: Pricing date—September 13, 1994.
Source: Salomon Brothers, Inc.

FIGURE   10–22

Monthly Cash Flow Diagram of a Mortgage Swap Agreement

Source: Salomon Brothers, Inc.

rate payment is exactly the coupon that the cash mortgage holder receives. For example, the first fixed-rate payment of the MSA in Figure 10–21 will be one-twelfth of the 8 percent coupon times the balance ($100 million), which is $666,667 (see Figure 10–23).

Floating-Rate Payments

The monthly floating-rate payment is one-month LIBOR less a spread times the initial price (market price plus accrued interest of the reference security) times the remaining balance. **The financing cost of an MBS purchase is the floating-rate payment.** Continuing with the example from Figure 10–21, the first monthly floating-rate payment will be $382,052, which is the initial price (99.127 percent) times the floating rate (4.625 percent in the first month) times $100 million (see Figure 10–23).

Monthly Adjustment for Discount and Premium Mortgages

To account for principal repayments, there is a monthly adjustment equal to the discount or the premium of the initial price times the principal paydowns. **For discount mortgages, this adjustment represents the gain that the holder of an actual mortgage realizes when receiving the prepayments and the scheduled principal;** therefore it is paid by the fixed-rate payer. In a premium MSA, the adjustment replicates the loss of a long position in a cash MBS when receiving principal paydowns. Therefore it is paid by the fixed-rate receiver.

Suppose that the first-month principal paydown for the reference security in Figure 10–21 is $417,570. Because the full price of the mortgage is below par, the fixed-rate payer will pay an additional $3,645. This figure is determined by multiplying the 0.873 percent discount (100 percent – the initial price of 99.127) times the $417,570 that has been paid down (see Figure 10–24a). Figure 10–24b shows a pre-

Fixed-and Floating-Rate Payments

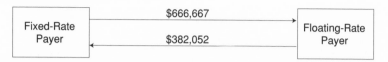

Fixed-Rate Payments = Remaining Balance x Reference Security Coupon x 30/360
Floating-Rate Payments = Remaining Balance x Initial Price x (1-month LIBOR – Spread) x Act/360

Source: Salomon Brothers, Inc.

mium adjustment for FNMA 9s priced at 103–10 (full price of 103.91 percent). In this case, the premium adjustment paid by the fixed-rate receiver for a projected principal paydown of $442,600 is $17,306.

Termination Payment or Physical Delivery at Maturity
Finally, **a lump sum cash settlement may be paid when the swap terminates to reflect the change in the price of the reference passthroughs.** The terminal payment depends on the final price and is applied to the final MBS balance plus or minus the variance.

The **final price** is the full price of the reference security based on Salomon Brothers's market price.[17] The swap may permit **variance,** which is similar to the delivery variance of to-be-announced mortgage forward contracts. If the swap does permit variance, the fixed-rate payer holds an option that allows it to set the termination balance at plus or minus the variance percentage of the MBS final balance. For example, if the final MBS balance is $88,802,810 and the variance is 2 percent, then the fixed-rate payer can set the termination balance at anywhere between $87,026,753 and $90,578,866.

If the final price is greater than the initial price, then the fixed-rate payer must pay the difference times the final amount. If the final price is less than the initial price, then the fixed-rate receiver must pay the fixed-rate payer. For example, if the final price is one point higher than the initial price and the final remaining balance is $88,802,810, then the fixed-rate payer likely will set the final amount to $87,026,753 (98 percent of the final MBS balance) and pay $870,268 to the fixed-rate receiver (see Figure 10–25). Figure 10–25 shows the termination payment if the final price is one point lower

17 Salomon will bid as a fixed-rate payer and will offer as a fixed-rate receiver.

F I G U R E   10–24

Discount and Premium Adjustments to Monthly Cash Flows

(a) Monthly Discount Adjustment of the MSA

Discount Adjustments = Paydowns × (100% − Initial Price)

(b) Monthly Premium Adjustment of an MSA Indexed off a Premium Mortgage

Discount Adjustments = Paydowns × (Initial Price − 100%)

MSA (Mortgage swap agreement).
Source: Salomon Brothers, Inc.

than the initial price (same final remaining balance) assuming that the fixed-rate payer sets the final amount to $90,578,866 (102 percent of the final MBS balance).

The termination payment may be replaced with physical delivery. In that case the fixed-rate payer will sell the final balance (plus or minus the variance) of the reference securities to the fixed-rate receiver **at the initial price.**

Figure 10–26 shows the monthly sample cash flows of the MSA over the term of the swap. The principal paydowns are based on the Salomon Brothers' prepayment model projections. The MBS balance is used to calculate the fixed- and floating-rate payments. The monthly floating-rate payments, however, also depend on one-month LIBOR levels. Figure 10–26 shows these payments assuming that one-month LIBOR rises by one-sixteenth every month. The monthly discount adjustments (paid by the fixed-rate payer) are calculated according to the principal paydowns.

For example, on October 25, the remaining balance is $99,582,430 and one-month LIBOR is 4.9375 percent. Thus the fixed- and floating-rate payments on November 25 are $663,882 and

F I G U R E   10–25

Termination Payment of a Mortgage Swap Agreement

(a) Terminal Cash Flow if the Final Price is Higher than the Initial Price (by One Point)

Termination Payment = (Final Balance+/– Variance) × (Final Price – Initial Price)

(b) Terminal Cash Flow if the Final Price is Lower than the Final Price (by One Point)

Termination Payment = (Final Balance+/– Variance) × (Initial Price – Final Price)

Source: Salomon Brothers, Inc.

$365,033, respectively. The principal paydown for that month is $365,010 ($99,582,431 minus $99,190,080); therefore, the discount adjustment on November 25 is $3,425. As a result, the net cash flow for the fixed-rate receiver on November 25 is $302,275. Finally, the termination payment of the swap at maturity is $870,268 on a final price one point higher than the initial price and a final remaining balance of $88,802,810 minus 2 percent variance ($87,026,753).

SUMMARY

MSAs replicate the economics of short or long positions in MBS. However, MSAs provide diversification protection against pool-specific prepayment risk because they are indexed off of a large set of passthroughs. Fixed-rate receivers can own synthetic mortgages with attractive funding levels and minimal capital expenditure. Furthermore, by overlaying MSAs on floating-rate assets, fixed-rate receivers may earn incremental returns. Fixed-rate payers have short positions in MBS and often can lock in repo rates that are higher than those that the collateral market offers.

F I G U R E 10–26

Sample Monthly Cash Flows of a Mortgage Swap Agreement

Date	CPR	LIBOR	MBS Balance	Fixed-Rate Payments	Floating-Rate Payments	Discount Adjustments	Fixed-Rate Receiver's Net
25 Sep 94		4.8750%	$100,000,000				
25 Oct 94	4.2%	4.9375	99,528,430	$666,667	$382,052	$3,645	$288,260
25 Nov 94	3.9	5.0000	99,190,080	663,882	365,033	3,425	302,275
25 Dec 94	3.6	5.0625	98,825,070	661,267	348,231	3,187	316,222
.	.	.	.	.	.	.	.
.	.	.	.	.	.	.	.
.	.	.	.	.	.	.	.
25 Aug 96	8.1	6.3125	89,523,460				
25 Sep 96	8.4		88,802,810	596,823	463,276	6,291	1,025,051
25 Sep 96	**Termination Payment**			870,268			

CPR (constant prepayment rate). LIBOR (London Interbank Offered Rate). MBS (mortgage-backed securities).
Source: Salomon Brothers, Inc.

11

⑥ PRICING DERIVATIVES ON RISKY BONDS AS APPLIED TO EMERGING MARKETS

P. Calderini, V. Finkelstein, and B.Y. Gelfand

J. P. Morgan

In this chapter we address some aspects of pricing and hedging derivative instruments on the sovereign debt of emerging market countries. We consider debt denominated in global currencies, in particular the U.S. dollar. The most important feature of this foreign country debt is the possibility of restructuring. This event is treated as an event of default. In this sense, emerging markets (EM) debt is similar to corporate and municipal debt. In the case of sovereign debt, the possibility of default arises from the budgetary constraints that prevent a sovereign from printing foreign currency, as well as from the political and technical limitations of inflationary finance. All these restrictions were in place at the beginning of the 1980s, when after years of heavy borrowing, some developing nations entered into a serious fiscal and balance of payments crisis that led them into default on a large part of their commercial bank loans. At the beginning of the 1990s, a rescue package called the Brady plan was devised to restructure the then-defaulted loans into new bonds. These packages were set up for those countries that were willing to implement sound monetary and fiscal policies. This plan gave rise to the Brady market. Today, the total size of the EM debt market is about $434 billion. Of this, $152 billion are Brady bonds, 90 percent of which are dollar denominated. The rest of the market is mostly

Eurobonds and "local" dollar-denominated debt. The options market is in Bradies, with some exceptions.

Brady Bond Market

Brady restructuring has already taken place in Argentina, Brazil, Bulgaria, Costa Rica, the Dominican Republic, Ecuador, Jordan, Mexico, Nigeria, Philippines, Poland, Uruguay, and Venezuela. Forthcoming Brady restructurings are expected for Russia and Peru.

The general structure of any Brady deal consists of exchanging the outstanding loans plus the due and unpaid interest for bonds. Some of these bonds are partially collateralized by U.S. Treasuries and/or AA-rated deposits. The first Brady exchange was organized for Mexico in March 1990. In this particular case, two main U.S. dollar bonds were issued. One is the Mexican Par Bond with the following structure:

Maturity: December 2019.

USD denominated.

6.25% coupon, semiannual.

Bullet amortization.

Guarantees: Face value fully collateralized by U.S. Treasury zero-coupon bond, and three coupon payments collateralized by AA-rated paper on a rolling basis.

The other Brady exchange is the Mexican Discount Bond due December 2019, which has a somewhat different structure:

Maturity: December 2019.

USD denominated.

LIBOR + 13/16 coupon, semiannual.

Bullet amortization.

Guarantees: Face value fully collateralized by U.S. Treasury zero-coupon bond, and 15 percent collateralized by rolling AA-rated guarantees (approximately five coupon payments).

In general, Brady bonds come in a wide variety of "shapes" and "flavors," leading to additional complexity for pricing and hedging derivative instruments. An example of a different "flavor" is the Argentina FRB:

Maturity: March 2005.

USD denominated.

LIBOR + 13/16 coupon, semiannual.

Amortizing starting March 1994.

Guarantees: none.

Volumes in Brady bonds and Brady bond options have increased constantly since the market started. For 1994, the total estimated trading volumes are U.S.$ 2,760 billion for cash and U.S.$ 142 billion for plain-vanilla options. These figures represent increases of 40 percent and 148 percent, respectively, from 1993 volumes. Despite these relatively large volumes, bid/offer spreads are still quite high, with 25 bp being the minimum price spread (given the disparity in asset prices, the actual percentage cost could range from 0.625 percent to .25 percent).

Options Market

The options market is relatively liquid for the plain vanilla at-the-money (ATM) options under one year (these are traded on live screens). The wide cash bid/offer spreads translate into wide volatility spreads in the options market. It is not unusual to see 300 bp volatility bid/offer for 90-day ATM options.

The variety of exotic derivative instruments traded over the counter (OTC) is gradually increasing; for example, there are barrier options, spread options on price or yield, digital options, currency-protected options, and so on. In particular, spread options are quite popular, as they allow investors to take a view directly on the country credit spreads. Many options are traded implicitly through structured notes.

An important feature of EM option prices observed in the market is the difference in implied volatility across strikes. In particular, there is a very well-defined inverse relationship between strike level and implied volatility associated with pricing using the Black-Scholes framework. A number of reasons for the occurrence of the so-called volatility smirk can be given. In order of importance they are:

1. Default is equivalent to a large jump downward with some probability. In the case of zero recovery value, a deep out-of-the-money put option is essentially equivalent to a contingent contract that pays the strike price if and only if

there is a default. Then, as follows from later discussion, the price of such a put option decreases linearly rather than exponentially with decreasing strike, which leads to a substantial volatility smirk.

2. It is generally true that a market that trades down is associated with nervousness and hence with more volatility. The converse is true for markets trading up (see Figures 11–1 through 11–4). In this environment, market markers prefer to have long vega positions in a bear market and short vega positions in a bull market.

The smirk could be as pronounced as a 10 percent volatility difference between a 10 percent delta put and a 10 percent delta call.

Theoretical Framework

Various theoretical approaches to pricing derivatives on assets that may default (called risky assets below) have been discussed in a number of papers (see the references at the end of the chapter). In this article we base our analysis on an approach first introduced by Jarrow and Turnbull (1992). In particular, in pricing derivatives on risky assets we assume that default is a "sudden death" event with no return. Within a risk-neutral framework, we model the default process as Poisson characterized by time-dependent pseudo-probability (which we refer to simply as probability) per unit time $s(\tau)$, where τ is the time that default occurs, with value date set equal to zero. Then, the probability that default does not occur between time moments t and T is given by

$$p(t,T) = \exp\left(-\int_t^T s(\tau)d\tau\right). \qquad (1)$$

We also assume that each risky bond can be characterized by a recovery value for its risky cash flows and that these values are known in advance. In the next two sections we assume that $s(\tau)$ is deterministic. In reality $s(\tau)$ is itself stochastic, and in the last section we extend our modeling to the case of stochastic default probability.

The outline of this chapter as follows: In "Basic EM Bond Mathematics" we review some basic bond math as it relates to emerging markets; in "Modeling Derivatives on Risky Assets in Closed

Form" we develop a closed-form analytical approach for pricing derivatives on bonds with default risk; and in "Beyond Default-Adjusted Black-Scholes" we discuss a more general tree model that relies on the same basic methodology, but incorporates stochastic default probability and allows us to price a wider range of options.

BASIC EM BOND MATHEMATICS

Credit Spreads

As any other fixed-income instrument, Bradies can be described by a vector that represents a stream of cash flows:

$$C = \{c_{t1}, c_{t2}, \ldots, c_{tn}\}. \tag{2}$$

The present value PV of C could be determined by simply multiplying C by the "present value" vector:

$$Z = \{z_{t1}, z_{t2}, \ldots, z_{tn}\}, \tag{3}$$

where z_{ti} is the value today of \$1 payable at t_i if and only if the risky cash flow c_{ti} is actually paid. For the present value of a stream of cash flows in Equation (2), we have

$$PV = Z \bullet C, \tag{4}$$

where PV is the bond "dirty" price. As an example, if each c_{ti} is fully collateralized by U.S. Treasuries, then, $z_{ti} = \exp(-r_{ti}t_i)$, where r_{ti} is the risk-free rate between today and t_i. However, in reality, most of the c_{ti} are risky—they're subject to default. Under this scenario the prices z_{ti} will have to compensate for this risk. We could then define the price of a risky cash flow as:

$$z_{ti} = \exp\left[-\left(r_{ti} + S(0,t_i)\right)t_i\right], \tag{5}$$

where $S(0,t_i)$ is the spread or excess return required by investors to bear the default risk embedded in c_{ti}.

In emerging markets, it is hard to find zeroes or "strips" like the one described in Equation (5), since most of EM fixed-income instruments are long-dated coupon bonds. The value of such bonds is represented in the market using a flat spread over the U.S. yield curve. Several spread definitions are used in the market. The two most popular are:

- Blended spread, which is computed as the risky bond yield minus the appropriate on-the-run U.S. Treasury yield.
- Stripped spread, which is computed as a flat spread over the U.S. yield curve when the bond is "stripped" from its collateral.

One particular example of stripped and blended spreads is shown in Figure 11–1. We can see that the two spreads may differ dramatically for EM bonds with substantial guarantees. A minor complication arises in determining the spread of bonds having floating-rate coupons such as the Argentina FRB (Figure 11–2).

To understand this, consider doing the usual swap from floating to fixed in order to set the unknown coupons. In this event the occurrence of default will leave us with an open swap position. It is then important to consider the correlation between swap rates and spreads to determine the risk-adjusted value of a risky floating cash flow (the spread shown in Figure 11–2 *does not* take this correlation into account).

F I G U R E   11–1

Blended and Stripped Spreads for Mexico Par Bond
(offer-side daily close)

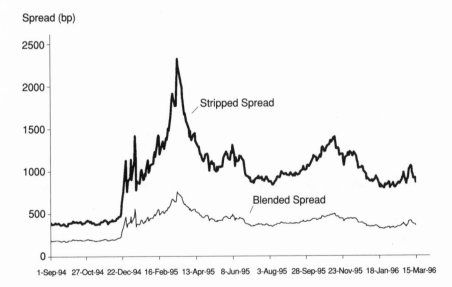

Source: J. P. Morgan

FIGURE 11–2

Stripped Spreads for Argentina FRB Bond
(offer-side daily close)

Spread (bp)

Source: J. P. Morgan

Default Probabilities

Under the approach described above, *any future cash flow can be viewed as a "portfolio" of contingent cash flows corresponding to different default scenarios and weighted by the probabilities of these scenarios.* In this section, if not stated specifically, we assume that an event of default is not correlated with underlying prices and that probability of default is a deterministic function of time.

We assume that any risky cash flow can be analyzed in terms of default probabilities. That is, the only reason for this cash flow to be priced today below default-free (risk-free) cash flow having the same maturity is the possibility of default.

To illustrate the relation between a credit spread of a risky bond, discussed in the previous section, and the risk-neutral probability of default, consider the following example. Assume we know the market prices for risky zero-coupon bonds of maturities T_1 and T_2, as well as the corresponding prices $Z_{r-free}(0,T_1)$, $Z_{r-free}(0,T_2)$ for risk-free bonds.

In a case of default between value date (today) and maturity date T_1, at maturity an investor receives α_1 dollars (recovery value) where $\alpha_1 \leq 1$ with probability $[1 - p(0,T_1)]$, while in a case of no-default the investor receives \$1 with probability $p(0,T_1)$. Discounting both outcomes with risk-free rates, we have for a price of a risky zero bond

$$Z_{risky}(0,T) = [(1-\alpha_1)p(0,T_1) + \alpha_1] * Z_{r-free}(0,T_1). \qquad (6)$$

Thus, for given bond prices and recovery rate, the probability of no-default is given by

$$p(0,T_1) = \frac{Z_{risky}(0,T_1)/Z_{r-free}(0,T_1) - \alpha_1}{1-\alpha_1}. \qquad (7)$$

Taking into account Equations (4) and (5) and introducing the probability of default

$$p_D(0,T_1) = 1 - p(0,T_1). \qquad (8)$$

we have

$$p_D(0,T_1) = \frac{1 - \exp[-S(0,T_1)T_1]}{1-d_1}. \qquad (9)$$

Obviously, for no-default probability to have a positive value smaller than 1, bond prices should satisfy a condition

$$1 > Z_{risky}(0,T_1)/Z_{r-free}(0,T_1) > \alpha_1. \qquad (10)$$

From Equation (7) it is clear that the implied probability of no-default is a function of assumed recovery value. As will be seen later, pricing and hedging of derivatives on risky bonds depend on the implied risk-neutral probabilities of default. It is then clear that pricing and hedging may depend substantially on recovery value assumptions.

Taking into account Equation (1) and assuming for the sake of simplicity that forward probability of default per unit time, $s(\tau)$, is constant between value date and T_1, we can easily determine this forward probability using Equation (7). Applying the same approach to the bonds with maturity T_2, we have

$$p(0,T_2) = \frac{Z_{risky}(0,T_2)/Z_{r-free}(0,T_2) - \alpha_2}{1-\alpha_2} \qquad (11)$$

where

$$1 > Z_{risky}(0, T_2) / Z_{r-free}(0, T_2) > \alpha_2. \qquad (12)$$

Taking into account that

$$p(0, T_2) = p(0, T_1) \exp\left(-\int_{T_1}^{T_2} s(\tau) d\tau\right), \qquad (13)$$

and assuming $s(\tau)$ to be constant between T_1 and, T_2 we can calculate the forward probability of default between these dates. This calculation is very similar to the standard method of "boot-strapping" applied in generating a discount yield curve from a par yield curve. Using the data for default-free bond prices (United States) and risky bond prices for a specific country, for example Argentina, we can determine the term structure of forward probabilities of default $s(\tau)$.

We may encounter difficulties when constructing a consistent and reasonable forward spread curve using traded EM bonds. One of the reasons may be lack of liquid instruments in some maturity ranges. Another may be large differentials in credit-spread premiums between instruments with nearby maturities. For example, the two bonds described below have very similar structures. However, because of market perceptions concerning safety of respective investments, these bonds have been priced using very different spreads. For example on March 14, 1996 we had

	Coupon	Maturity	Spread over Treasury
Bote II	L	09/01/97	225 bp
BONEX 87	L	09/07/97	110 bp

Thus we need to make a choice of which bond to use to generate a forward default-probability term structure. In general, this decision should be based on a choice of instruments to be used for hedging.

MODELING DERIVATIVES ON RISKY ASSETS IN CLOSED FORM

To price derivatives on assets with embedded default risk, we first need to determine market data to be used in pricing. Any model should be calibrated to satisfy this data; that is, it should be marked to market. In this treatment we assume that the following market information is available:

- Term structure of U.S. dollar default-free rates.
- Structure of cash flows for risky bonds and their prices in U.S. dollars.
- Volatilities of options on default-free bonds.
- Spot volatilities of risky bonds.

As usual, for the first two types of data it is assumed that zero-coupon bonds of all maturities are available for pricing and hedging. It is also assumed that default is a "global" event; that is, all the risky cash flows of all maturities are subject to default simultaneously.

Forward Bond Price

To illustrate the approach with some examples, first consider a forward contract on a bond of maturity T with a single guaranteed rolling coupon and a guaranteed principal (e.g., a simplified analog of an Argentina par Brady bond).

Let us consider the specific example. A risky bond with maturity of 26 years is paying an annual coupon of 7 percent. It has a single guaranteed rolling coupon and a guaranteed payment of principal. The spot price is equal to $B_{spot} = 49.0$ percent. Consider a forward contract on this bond that expires in one year, just after the next coupon. Assume that a price of a risk-free zero-coupon bond is $Z_{r-free} = 93$ percent. The forward contract can be replicated using traded instruments. By taking a long position in the risky bond and financing this position by shorting the guaranteed coupon and a needed amount of one-year risk-free zero bond, we have

$$F(0,1) = \frac{B_{spot} - c * Z_{r-free}(0,1)}{Z_{r-free}(0,1)} = 45.69\%. \tag{14}$$

It is easy to show that a general approach employing probabilities of default brings about the same result. Indeed, if the contract is expiring at time t just after the next coupon, the forward price is given by

$$F(0,t) = p(0,t) * B_{no-def}(t,T) + (1 - p(0,t)) * B_{def,0}(t,T), \tag{15}$$

where $B_{no-def}(t, T)$ is the expected bond price conditional on no default over time t, and $B_{def, 0}(t, T)$ is the expected defaulted bond value with no guaranteed coupons left.

Assume that recovery value for risky cash flows is equal to zero, and that prices of relevant risky and risk-free bonds are known. In particular, assume that

$$Z_{risky}(0,1) = 79\%, \text{ and } Z_{r-free}(0,26) = 15.1\%.$$

Using Equations (7), (11), and (13) we find that default probability between value and expiration dates is equal to 0.15, while annualized default probability between years 1 and 26 is 0.125. Taking into account that the present value of the guaranteed coupon is 6.51 percent, we arrive at $B_{no-def}(1, 26) = 50.91$ percent and $B_{def, 0}(1, 26) = 16.24$ percent. As a result, according to Equation (15) the price of the forward contract is given by

$$F(0,1) = 45.69\%. \tag{16}$$

The reason the results of Equations (14) and (16) coincide is pretty clear. Default probabilities used in Equation (15) are implied by the bond prices and can be replicated exactly and statically.

If there is at least one coupon payment before the contract expiration, and time period δ from the last coupon before expiration to expiration time t is nonzero, we arrive at

$$F(0,t) = p(0,t) * B_{no-def}(t,T) + \left(p(0,t-\delta) - p(0,t)\right) * B_{def,1}(t,T) \tag{17}$$

$$+\left(1 - p(0,t-\delta)\right) * B_{def,0}(t,T),$$

where $B_{def,n}(t,T)$ is the expected defaulted bond value with guaranteed coupons left. Forward price of the bond is a portfolio of three forward contingent bonds, one corresponding to a no-default scenario, and two to various default situations. Note that here again the probability of default is assumed to be deterministic.

It is not difficult to show that, as in Equation (14), the price for the forward contract given by Equation (17) can be expressed as

$$F(0,t) = \frac{B_{spot} - A(0,t)}{Z_{r-free}(0,t)}, \tag{18}$$

where $A(0,t)$ is a present value of $(n + 1)$ coupons paid before expiration of the contract given by

$$A(0,t) = c \sum_{i=0}^{n} \tilde{Z}(0, t - \delta - fi), \tag{19}$$

where

$$\tilde{Z}(0,\tau) = \frac{Z_{risky}(0,\tau-f)}{Z_{r-free}(0,\tau-f)} Z_{r-free}(0,\tau) \qquad (20)$$

is the PV of a \$1 coupon with a rolling guarantee paid at time τ, f is a period between coupon payments, and $f(n+1) > t - \delta > fn$.

Equation (18), obvious as it might seem, has a twist. If probability of default (that is, a credit spread) does not vary with time, hedging coupons [Equation (19)] is straightforward. We need to shorten

$$c\left[p(0,\tau-f)/p(0,\tau)\right] \qquad (21)$$

of a risky zero bond Z_{risky} $(0, \tau)$. If default occurs before a previous coupon has been paid, the value of this short position goes to zero together with a hedged coupon payment. If default does not happen over this time period, the coupon payment at time τ is guaranteed, and at time $(\tau - f)$ the short position (Equation (21)) in the risky zero bond Z_{risky} $(\tau - f, \tau)$ should be switched to a short position of c units of the risk-free zero bond Z_{r-free} $(\tau - f, \tau)$ having identical value at time $(\tau - f)$. However, if the spread is volatile, the amount of risky bond needed at time $(\tau - f)$ is uncertain. Thus hedging a coupon with a rolling guarantee now requires dynamic rebalancing of a short position in a risky bond. This brings about an exposure to correlation between the credit spread and the level of risk-free interest rates. As a result of this exposure, Equation (20) takes the form

$$\tilde{Z}(0,\tau) = \frac{Z_{risky}(0,\tau-f)}{Z_{r-free}(0,\tau-f)} Z_{r-free}(0,\tau)\exp\left[.5\rho\hat{\sigma}_{sp}\hat{\sigma}_{r-free}f(\tau-f)^2\right], \quad (22)$$

where $\hat{\sigma}_{sp}$ and $\hat{\sigma}_{r-free}$ are, respectively, basis point volatilities of the credit spread and the risk-free interest rate with correlation coefficient ρ.

Forward Contract on a Risky Bond Conditional on No-Default

In this section we consider a forward contract on a risky bond that is canceled in the case of default prior to the expiration date.

Bond without Guarantees

In this case the price of a contract is given by an expected forward price of the bond $B_{no-def}(t,T)$ conditional on no default over time t, that is

$$F_{no-def}(0,t) = B_{no-def}(t,T) \tag{23}$$

For a bond with no guarantees, replication of the contract is simple. In particular, one needs to take a long position in a risky bond B_{spot}, and take short positions in F units of short-term risky zero bond Z_{risky} $(0,t)$ and risky cash flows corresponding to coupon payments prior to expiration of the contract. This portfolio provides a needed payoff in the case of no default and disappears in the case of default. To make a position self-financing, we need to have

$$F_{no-def}(0,t) = \frac{B_{spot} - A(0,t)}{Z_{risky}(0,t)}. \tag{24}$$

Comparing Equation (24) to Equation (18), we can see that for a given spot bond price a contract conditional on no-default is more expensive than a regular contract, just as a short-term risky bond is cheaper than a risk-free one. At the same time, this is fully consistent with the obvious fact that a forward expected value for the bond in

FIGURE   11–3

Implied Price Volatility for 30-Day Option on Mexican Par Bond, Midmarket

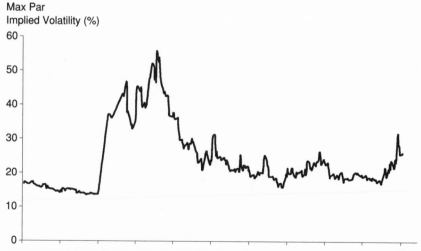

Max Par
Implied Volatility (%)

Source: EuroBrokers

Implied Price Volatility for 30-Day Option on Argentina FRB Bond, Midmarket

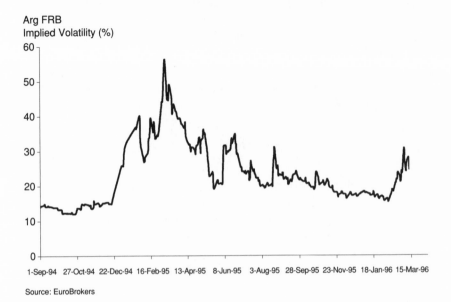

Source: EuroBrokers

the case of no default is higher than a forward expected value that takes into account all default scenarios (see Equations (15) and (23)).

Bond with Guarantees
Consider now a contract conditional on no default on a bond from the example in the section above, and that expires just after the next coupon. Although the principal for a bond is guaranteed, under this contract it is paid only in the case of no default. Then the price of the contract is given by

$$F_{no-def}(0,1) = \tag{25}$$

$$\frac{B_{spot} - c * Z_{r-free}(0,1) - Z_{r-free}(0,26) * \left[1 - Z_{risky}(0,1)/Z_{r-free}(0,1)\right]}{Z_{risky}(0,1)}$$

$$= 50.91\%.$$

Once again, the contract is self-financing. Although replication is more complicated than for a bond with no guarantees, for deterministic default probabilities replication is still static. In particular, one has to take the following positions:

Long	1 unit of	risky bond B_{spot}
Short	$F(0,1)$ units of	$Z_{risky}(0,1)$
Long	$\dfrac{1}{p(1,26)} = \dfrac{Z_{r-free}(0,26)Z_{risky}(0,1)}{Z_{risky}(0,26)Z_{r-free}(0,1)}]$ units of	$Z_{risky}(0,26)$
Short	c units of	$Z_{r-free}(0,1)$
Short	1 unit of	$Z_{r-free}(0,26)$

This hedging portfolio provides the needed pay-off in the case of no-default and completely disappears in the case of default.

If the stripped spread is volatile, hedges are no longer static. In particular, position in a long-term risky zero bond must be rebalanced. In the case of a highly volatile credit spread, we might prefer to take an additional long position in a short-term risky zero bond initially given by

$$\frac{Z_{r-free}(0,26)}{Z_{r-free}(0,1)},$$

and rebalance it as interest rates change, rather than taking a position in a long-term risky zero bond. Similar to the case illustrated by Equation (22), the portfolio is sensitive to the correlation between interest rates and the stripped spread. As the premium F is paid by a counterparty only in the case of no default, the contract should include some sort of mark-to-default provision. That is, expenses related to dynamic hedging should be reimbursed over the life of the contract or as a special fee.

Forward Contract on the Yield of a Risky Bond

In this subsection we consider another type of a forward contract that clearly demonstrates the difference between the pricing of derivative instruments on risky and risk-free underlyings.

For both risky and nonrisky bonds, a forward contract on a bond yield is a contract on a nontraded asset. As a result of the non-linear relation between yield and bond price, hedging of the contract involves dynamic rebalancing of hedging positions in traded instruments (bonds). That in turn leads to the so-called convexity adjustment $C(0, t)$ for the forward yield given by

$$C(0,t) \approx \frac{C_F}{2D_F} Y_F^2 \sigma_Y^2 t \qquad (26)$$

where C_F and D_F are, respectively, convexity and duration of the forward bond, Y_F is the forward yield, and σ_Y is implied yield volatility. However, for a bond exposed to the possibility of default, there is an additional complication. As we demonstrated above, a forward risky bond can be considered as a portfolio of two contingent bonds corresponding to different default scenarios. Similarly, the forward yield of this bond also can be treated as a portfolio of yields contingent on different default scenarios. Each of these yields corresponds to a contingent forward bond price. As a result, the yield of the bond under a no-default scenario may be relatively low, while the yield corresponding to a defaulted forward bond can be very high. In particular, for a bond with no guarantees and zero recovery value, this yield is actually infinite, which puts some restrictions on a structure of the contract in this case. Meanwhile, conventional calculations of the forward yield for a given forward bond price would give the value that corresponds to the yield of the portfolio of bonds rather than the portfolio of yields on contingent bonds. Thus, for a given forward bond price we can expect the price of the contract on the forward bond yield to be somewhat higher for a risky bond than for a risk-free one. Assuming no additional complications related to rolling guarantees, the price of the contract is given by

$$F(0,t) = p(0,t) * Y_{no-def}(t,T) + \big(1 - p(0,t)\big) * Y_{def,0}(t,T) \qquad (27)$$

In Equation (27) each yield is calculated using the corresponding forward contingent bond price and includes convexity adjustment given by Equation (26) that drives the price of the contract up. In addition, as discussed above, in the portfolio of yields (Equation 27)) the contribution by the yield corresponding to a defaulted bond can be very high. The result may lead to a substantial spread between the value of this contract and the forward yield. We call this price increase resulting from the possibility of default the *Super-Convexity Effect*. To give an example, consider the price of a one-year contract on the yield of a risky bond of 26-year maturity with a single annual rolling guaranteed coupon and a guaranteed principal. The contract expires right after the next coupon payment. Using the numbers from the example considered earlier we get

$Y_{no-def}(1,\ 26) = 14.26\%$ and $Y_{def}(1,\ 26) = 43.12\%$.

Assuming that volatilities of risky and risk-free bonds are given by

$$Vol_{risky}(1,\ 26) = 25\%,\quad Vol_{r-free}(1,\ 26) = 13\%,$$

we arrive at the strike 19.43 percent for the contract. The "conventional" forward yield is equal to 15.81 percent. The spread of 3.62 percent can be explained by a combination of convexity adjustment of 0.84 percent and a super-convexity adjustment of 2.78 percent.

This additional value can be extracted by dynamically hedging using risky and nonrisky bonds. Additional expenses related to the correlation of the stripped spread with interest rates may require an up-front or mark-to-default premium.

Option on a Risky Bond

To price an option on a risky bond we can treat it as a portfolio of options on default and no-default contingent bonds. This is quite different from a naive approach that employs the Black formula and treats the forward bond with the forward price (see Equation (14)) as the option underlying. Since a risky bond can be viewed as a portfolio of default and no-default contingent bonds, the difference between the two approaches is the difference between pricing a portfolio of options and an option on a portfolio. However, call-put parity has the same form in both cases, that is

$$call - put = Z_{r-free}(0,t)\big[F(0,T) - X\big], \tag{28}$$

where $F(0,t)$ is the forward bond price given by Equation (14) if coupons due prior to expiration are guaranteed, and X is an option strike price.

The European call option can be represented as a default-probability-weighted portfolio of contingent payoffs

$$\text{Payoff} = p(0,t) * \max\big[B_{no-def}(t,T) - X, 0\big] \tag{29}$$
$$+ \big(1 - p(0,t)\big) * \max\big[B_{def,0}(t,T) - X, 0\big].$$

Assuming that the default value of the bond is always lower than the strike price (which is usually the case), we can neglect the second term in Equation (29). Assuming for the sake of simplicity that the forward no-default bond behaves as a lognormal stochastic variable, we can price the option in Equation (29) analytically under the Black-Scholes assumptions and arrive at

$$Call = Z_{risky}(0,t) * \left[F_{no-def}(t,T)N(d_1) - XN(d_2) \right] \qquad (30)$$

where $F_{no-def}(t,T)$ is the bond-forward-price conditional on no default (see for example Equations (23) or (24)), and

$$N(d) = \frac{1}{\sqrt{2\pi}} \int_0^d e^{-x^2/2} dx,$$

$$d_1 = \frac{1n\left[F_{no-def}(t,T)/X \right]}{\sigma\sqrt{t}} + \frac{1}{2}\sigma\sqrt{t} \quad \text{and} \quad d_2 = d_1 - \sigma\sqrt{t},$$

where σ is the implied volatility of the forward bond conditional on no default.

Combining Equations (28) and (30) for a put option we have

$$Put = Z_{risky}(0,t) * \left[XN(-d_2) - F_{no-def}(t,T)N(-d_1) \right] \qquad (31)$$

$$+ \left[Z_{r-free}(0,t) - z_{risky}(0,t) \right] \left[X - F_{def}(t,T) \right].$$

The naive approach that treats the entire forward bond as a lognormal variable leads to

$$Call = Z_{r-free}(0,t) * \left[F(t,T)N(\tilde{d}_1) - XN(\tilde{d}_2) \right] \qquad (32)$$

$$Put = Z_{r-free}(0,t) * \left[XN(-\tilde{d}_2) - F(t,T)N(-\tilde{d}_1) \right], \qquad (33)$$

where $F(t,T)$ is a bond forward price (see for example Equation (18)), and

$$\tilde{d}_1 = \frac{1n\left[F(t,T)/X \right]}{\tilde{\sigma}\sqrt{t}} + \frac{1}{2}\tilde{\sigma}\sqrt{t} \text{ and } \tilde{d}_2 = \tilde{d}_1 - \tilde{\sigma}\sqrt{t},$$

with $\tilde{\sigma}$ being the implied volatility of the forward bond.

Consider one-year call and put options on the bond having the same characteristics as in the previous examples.

Strike	50%
Price	49%
Forward price	45.69%
Forward no-default price	50.91%
Forward default price	16.24%
Bond volatility	25%

Using Equations (31) and (32) to calculate option prices, we get

	Default Term	No-Default Term	Full Price
call	0	4.33%	4.33%
put	4.72%	3.62%	8.34%

To match the prices shown above using the naive method we need to use a much higher implied volatility of 35 percent. Another interesting effect related to this implied volatility is a pronounced volatility smirk associated with naive pricing. In particular, the implied volatility $\tilde{\sigma}$ is a monotonically decreasing function of the strike price for a given volatility σ of a bond conditional on no default (see Figure 11–5). As mentioned above, this smirk is the direct result of a possible default of the underlying bond.

If we analyze hedging positions that correspond to the two approaches, the difference is even more striking.

	Hedge			
	Naive	Default	No-Default	Correct
Short Call				
B_{spot}	.406	0	.578	.578
$Z_{risky}(0,1)$	0	0	.145	−.145
$Z_{r-free}(0,1)$	−.185	0	−.120	−.120
$Z_{r-free}(0,26)$	0	0	−.087	−.087
Short Put				
B_{spot}	−.593	0	−.422	−.422
$Z_{risky}(0,1)$	0	−.337	.192	−.145
$Z_{r-free}(0,1)$	0.385	.362	.088	.450
$Z_{r-free}(0,26)$	0	−.150	.063	−.087

Comparing the first and the last columns, we can see that for naive pricing there is no hedging position in a short-term risky zero bond and a long-term risk-free bond. Thus, in a case of default we

F I G U R E   11–5

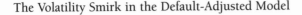

The Volatility Smirk in the Default-Adjusted Model

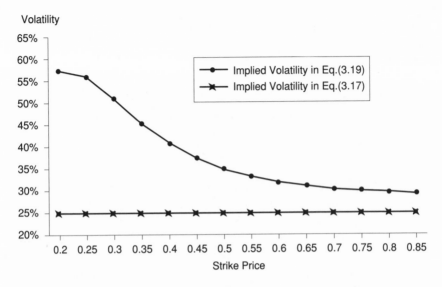

are left with a considerable loss as the bond price collapses and the put option goes into the money. In contrast, for the pricing that takes into account the possibility of default the position is hedged completely under all scenarios. This is achieved by using risky as well as risk-free bonds as hedging instruments.

BEYOND DEFAULT-ADJUSTED BLACK-SCHOLES

The model for options on risky bonds described above has the virtue of analytical and conceptual simplicity, but also has some significant shortcomings and limitations. Most obvious is the assumption of lognormal bond-price distribution in the event of no default. It is clearly more reasonable and consistent to model the yield as lognormal. Further, we are using the total bond price volatility and ignoring the fact that it is actually a combination of interest rate volatility and credit spread volatility. The latter can be very large, and the case of emerging markets often accounts for most of the observed price volatility. The most dramatic example of this is in the case of risky floaters. These factors can have a considerable effect on the shape of the bond price distribution. Also, by treating credit spreads as deterministic we ignore the correlation between bond price and default probability. Finally, most of the options traded in this market are American, which require a tree-based model for valuation. Increasing demand for more complicated derivatives products also requires a flexible tree model.

To address these problems we introduce a model where the term structure of riskless rates and the term structure of credit spreads are both diffused. We model the default process as a Poisson process with a time-dependent stochastic transition probability (default rate) per unit time, $s(t)$. We also treat the riskless instantaneous interest rate $r(t)$ as a stochastic variable. We assume that the instantaneous riskless interest rate $r(t)$ and the instantaneous default probability $s(t)$ are both lognormal stochastic variables with correlation ρ:

$$\frac{dr}{r} = \mu_r(t)dt + \sigma_r dW_1 \tag{34}$$

$$\frac{ds}{s} = \mu_s(t)dt + \sigma_s dW_2$$

where expected values are given by $E(dW_i) = 0$, $E(dW_i^2) = dt$ and $E(dW_1 dW_2) = \rho dt$. The third stochastic variable is, of course, the default transition itself, which by our assumption is described by a two-state Poisson process: {No Default (ND), Default (D)}, where Prob (ND->D) = $s(t)dt$ over interval dt and Prob(D->ND) = 0. Actually, for bonds with rolling interest guarantees, default will consist of several discrete states characterized by the number of remaining guaranteed coupons, with transitions between these states occurring at coupon payment dates.

The spot term structure of riskless interest rates is related to the instantaneous stochastic interest rate $r(t)$ by the expectation

$$Z_{risk-free}(t,T) = E_r\left[\exp\left(-\int_t^T rdt\right)\right] \tag{35}$$

where $Z_{risk-free}(t,T)$ is the spot price of a riskless zero maturing at T, and $E_r[\ldots]$ is the average over the stochastic process $r(t)$.

Given our definition of recovery α, the risky term structure is given by

$$Z_{risky}(t,T) = (1-\alpha)E_s E_r\left[\exp\left(-\int_t^T (r+s)dt\right)\right] + \alpha Z_{risk-free}(t,T) \tag{36}$$

where $Z_{risky}(t,T)$ is the spot price of a *risky* zero maturing at time T. We make the model arbitrage-free within the Treasury market by calibrating the drift rate μ_s to match the riskless term structure, and we calibrate the drift rate μ_r to match the risky term structure, making our model arbitrage-free with respect to the set of risky bonds used to construct the credit curve. In particular, our model must correctly reproduce the market price of the underlying risky bond.

The price of a hedgeable option is just the risk-neutral expectation of the payoff. In this model we need to take the expectation over r, s and the default states. For example, for a European option expiring at time T with payoff $H(B)$, where B is the price of the risky bond at expiration (no rolling guarantees) the premium is given by

$$V(t) = E_r E_s \left[e^{-\int_t^T r d\tau} \left[e^{-\int_t^T s d\tau} H\big(B_{ND}(r,s,T)\big) + \left(1 - e^{-\int_t^T s d\tau}\right) H\big(B_D(r,T)\big) \right] \right] \quad (37)$$

where $B_{ND}(r, s, T)$ is the price of the bond at T in the no-default state (this is a stochastic variable that depends on r and s at time T), and $B_D(r,T)$ is the price of the bond at T in the default state (a stochastic variable depending on r). For an American option this pricing is modified by introducing the usual optimal early exercise conditions. Note that Equation (37) for the option price has the structure of a portfolio of options on nondefaulted and defaulted bonds.

Tree Implementation

A reasonable tree realization of the above model is a two-dimensional trinomial tree for $r(t)$ and $s(t)$ with a state variable to handle default transitions. In this tree each node is characterized by the triplet (r_i, s_j, d), where $d = \{ND, D_{g\,max}, D_{g\,max-1}, \ldots, D_1, D_0\}$ is the default state variable (g_{max} is the total number of rolling guarantees). The transitions between different r and s values are given by the nine trinomial transition probabilities chosen to satisfy drift, volatility, and correlation constraints. Transitions between different default states are given by the local instantaneous default probability:

ND	$\to ND$	$\text{Prob} = 1/(1+s_j)^{\Delta t}$
ND	$\to D_{g\,max}$	$\text{Prob} = 1 - 1/(1+s_j)^{\Delta t}$
$D_{g\,max}$	$\to D_{g\,max-1}$	$\text{Prob} = 1$ at coupon payment date, $= 0$ otherwise
$\cdots D_1$	$\to D_0$	$\text{Prob} = 1$ at coupon payment date, $= 0$ otherwise

Volatility Calibration

The tree volatility parameters are the instantaneous riskless interest-rate volatility σ_r and the spread volatility σ_s. The interest rate volatility is taken as an external input from the Treasury option or swaption market. The spread volatility can be input by the trader or, alternatively, calibrated against the forward price volatility of the underlying risky bond. The Brady bond options trade in terms of price volatility; hence we follow the latter approach. Within our model the forward price volatility of the risky bond at option expiration T_{exp} is defined by

$$
\sigma_p^2 = Z_{risk-free}(t,T)p(t,T)\frac{E_r E_s\left[e^{-\int_t^T r d\tau}e^{-\int_t^T s d\tau}B_{ND}^2(T_{exp})\right]}{\left(E_r E_s\left[e^{-\int_t^T r d\tau}e^{-\int_t^T s d\tau}B_{ND}(T_{exp})\right]\right)^2} - 1. \tag{38}
$$

In other words, it is the price volatility conditional on no default. Hence for a given bond we have some relation $\sigma_p = f(\sigma_r, \sigma_s)$, and we can use Newton-Rhapson to calibrate the model against a given price volatility. This calibration procedure, naturally, significantly increases computation time, since it requires recalculating the tree several times.

Hedging

As discussed in the section above on modeling derivatives, to hedge an option on risky bonds we need positions in the underlying bond and in short-dated risky zeros. It was demonstrated that if risk-free bonds and risky bonds of all relevant maturities were available as hedging instruments and recovery values were known, we would be able to hedge market risk and default risk simultaneously. This can be achieved for a simple reason: Although an event of default is a jump, this jump is characterized by known direction and amplitude. Only the timing of this jump is unknown. As a result of these restrictions, risky bonds in a hedging portfolio would provide adequate protection against the jump.

When using the tree model we can obtain the required hedges by "tweaking" the term structures of risk-free and risky interest rates. Risky zeros usually are not available in the market. However, as long as some risky bond of similar maturity is available, a reasonable hedge can be constructed. Unfortunately, we are often faced with a complete lack of liquid hedging instruments in the required maturity range. If the set of hedging instruments is incomplete, the hedge portfolio must be optimized to reduce the overall risk exposure. In our case, this entails tradeoffs between default exposure and market exposure, and the hedge will depend on the risk-aversion of the hedger. Also, insofar as the option cannot be completely hedged, risk-aversion will affect pricing.

CONCLUSIONS

In this chapter we discussed an approach to pricing fixed-income derivatives in emerging markets, focusing particularly on the issue of default risk. We presented a simple analytical model based on modified Black-Scholes and outlined a more accurate and general modeling framework based on a two-factor tree. The main practical difficulty with managing default exposure is a lack of liquid risky instruments of appropriate maturities. It is hoped that as these markets grow and become more sophisticated, the set of hedging alternatives will widen. In particular, synthetic credit instruments (credit derivatives) could fill some of the gap. Until then, the players in this market will have to rely on diversification and careful book management to minimize the risks.

REFERENCES

Duffie, D., and K. J. Singleton. "Econometric Modeling of Term Structures of Defaultable Bonds." Working paper, Graduate School of Business, Stanford University, 1995.

Hull J., and A. White. "The Impact of Default Risk on the Prices of Options and Other Derivative Securities." Working paper, Faculty of Management, University of Toronto, 1992.

Hull, J., and A. White. "The Price of Default." *Risk,* 5, 1992, pp. 101–3.

Jarrow, R.; D. Lando; and S. Turnbull. "A Markov Model for the Term Structure of Credit Spreads." Working paper, Graduate School of Management, Cornell University, 1993.

Jarrow, R., and S. Turnbull. "Pricing Options on Financial Securities Subject to Default Risk." Working paper, Graduate School of Management, Cornell University, 1992.

Longstaff, F.A., and E. S. Schwartz. "Valuing Risky Debt: New Approach." Working paper, Anderson Graduate School of Management, University of California at Los Angeles, 1993.

12

⑥ INTEREST RATES AND LIFE INSURANCE

J. P. Hunziker and P. Koch-Medina
Winterthur Insurance Group, Winterthur, Switzerland

In a book, such as this, an explanatory word might be called for when including a chapter on life insurance products. After all, at first sight a life insurance contract is nothing but a straightforward investment vehicle with some additional death coverage. In reality though, life insurance contracts such as endowments or annuities, to be defined later on, have a variety of embedded options that render hedging them a difficult task. Consequently, in today's world of volatile capital markets they require serious consideration more than ever. Moreover, life insurance products themselves are becoming increasingly popular. The reason for this development is twofold. First of all, people are turning more and more to private insurance companies to cover their basic economic needs after completion of their productive lives. This is because traditional means of financing pensions (on a pay-as-you-go basis) are proving to be inadequate as a consequence of the shift in the demographic structure in most countries (fewer payers than receivers). Second, the privileged tax treatment received by life insurance contracts all over the world combined with ever more innovative products—a result of a global trend towards deregulation in the insurance markets—make insurance policies an attractive alternative to investment products offered by other financial institutions. In the following pages, we give an overview of some of the problems arising in the world of life insurance. The aim is to make the reader aware of the issues, not to treat these problems exhaustively.

Most single-premium life insurance contracts can be viewed as structured products: They can be decomposed into first, a zero-bond type of benefit; second, a part having the character of an option; and third, a part consisting of a policy covering an insurable risk (death, longevity, invalidity, etc). In the building-block approach to which we subscribe, the price is determined by adding up the prices of the individual components. We shall give a quick review of how death coverage is hedged. This will allow us to identify the different components clearly. It will become evident that life insurance products contain a myriad of embedded financial options, which are often not taken into account in the usual actuarial pricing method. These options should be priced by specifying a self-financing replicating portfolio consisting of investment instruments available in the financial market, and then determining its value. What is often straightforward (at least in theory) in the case of investments products calls for special arguments in the case of life insurance policies since some of the options embedded in them will not always be exercised rationally.

INSURABLE RISKS

In this section we will briefly describe the funding of two pure risk components a life insurance contract may have[1]: death coverage and longevity. Both of these risks have the property of being *insurable:* By pooling a large enough number of independent contracts, the insurer will be able to charge each individual contract its share of the expected losses of the whole pool. This approach to risk management essentially relies on the validity of the law of large numbers, which ensures that a large pool of uncorrelated contracts will display the behavior predicted by statistical tables. Therefore, for this type of funding to function properly, reliable statistics on the insured events are needed. Of course, the risk remains that the pool of contracts will not behave in accordance with the statistical model. However, this risk, which is usually referred to as underwriting risk, can be hedged by resorting to reinsurance or can be minimized by built-in margins.

---

1 Compare Williams, Smith, and Young (1995) or Witzel (1995).

Pure Death Coverage

One of the basic building blocks of life insurance products is a contract paying the beneficiary a prespecified sum in case of death of the insured person during the term of the contract. To illustrate the pricing mechanism, take for example a pool of contracts with a maturity of five years and paying $CR(t)$ dollars if the insured person were to die within the year t for $t = 1, \ldots, 5$. The amount $CR(t)$ is called the *capital at risk* at time t.

Let $L(0)$ be the initial number of insureds. Assume now that $L(t)$ is the number of remaining insureds at time t and that $p(t)$ is the percentage of insureds that will die within the year t ($p(t)$ is based on a suitable mortality table). Then, by definition, we have $L(t) = [1 - p(t)] \cdot L(t-1)$ for $t = 1, \ldots, 5$. Therefore, if $D(t)$ denotes the number of deaths in the pool of insureds at time t, the evolution of $D(t)$ over time is described by the Table 12–1.

Denote by $P(t)$ the benefits to be paid by the insurer at time t due to the mortality behavior of the pool of insureds within the year t. It follows that the evolution of $P(t)$ over time will be described by Table 12–2.

We call $P(t)$ the *natural risk* premium for the year t. By present-valuing this cash flow and ignoring costs, we obtain the single premium needed to finance the pattern of benefits offered by the policy.

The premiums due for an individual contract are calculated in the following way: Let x be the age of the insured person and $s(x, t)$ the probability that a person of age x will die at age $x + t - 1$ for $t = 1, \ldots, 5$. The individual share of the expected collective loss in year t will then be the amount $s(x, t) \cdot CR(t)$.

Annuities

Another typical contract, the annuity, will provide the insured person with a prespecified yearly income as long as the insured lives and the contract has not matured. Again, the risk arising from this

T A B L E   12–1

t	0	1	2	3	4	5
$D(t)$	0	$p(1) \cdot L(0)$	$p(2) \cdot L(1)$	$p(3) \cdot L(2)$	$p(4) \cdot L(3)$	0

TABLE   12–2

t	0	1	2	3	4	5
$P(t)$	0	$D(1) \cdot CR(1)$	$D(2) \cdot CR(2)$	$D(3) \cdot CR(3)$	$D(4) \cdot CR(4)$	$D(5) \cdot CR(5)$

kind of contract is insurable and can in principle be hedged by pooling many individual policies.

LIFE INSURANCE CONTRACTS I:
THE CLASSICAL ENDOWMENT

The classical *endowment* is probably the oldest single-premium life insurance product with a built-in investment component. The savings part may be characterized as an investment in the portfolio of assets of the insurance company, an investment with several guarantees. The terms of a typical endowment contract are determined by the following data:

Maturity	T
Single premium	E
Insured capital	D
Technical interest rate	i percent (generally much lower than market rates)

The basic guarantee offered by the policy is that in case the insured person either lives at maturity or dies during the lifetime of the contract, the beneficiary will receive the *insured capital D* (either at maturity or at the end of the year of the insured's death), which depends on the technical interest rate as explained next.

Define the *net premium NP* as that part of the single premium to be invested in the insurer's portfolio; in other words, NP is the single premium net of costs and risk premium for death coverage. Compounded until maturity at the *technical interest rate i* percent, the net premium NP will yield D. For $t = 0,1, \ldots, T$ the book-value of the savings component will be $A(t) := (1+i\%)^t \cdot NP$. The book-value is considered to represent an asset on which the insured has a claim. Hence, without taking the surplus (to be defined below) into account, the insured owns exactly the book-value of the contract. From the point of view of the policyholder, this is equivalent to investing in the insurer's portfolio while holding an American put and writing an American call on the portfolio, both options having a time-dependent strike $K(t):=A(t)$ for $t = 1, 2, \ldots, T$. A peculiarity of this pair of options is the fact that the call is automatically exercised at the moment the insured exercises the put. We shall call this pair of options the *surrender* option.

The meaning of the surrender option is that the insured has at any time the choice of selling the contract back to the insurer (surrendering the contract in insurance jargon) at book-value[2] or letting it mature. Although the insured will be able to exercise the option at his or her discretion, it is well-known that holders of insurance policies will not always exercise this option rationally. Just as in the case of early repayment of mortgages, a variety of other reasons can lead to early surrender. Among them are liquidity problems or a change in the policyholder's need for death coverage. But as we shall see shortly, this option is also exercised in case of death of the insured person.

Before turning to the last building block of the savings component, we now describe the part corresponding to the death coverage. The capital at risk for each year will be given by $CR(t):=D - A(t)$ for $t = 1, \ldots, T$. The idea is that the investment part of the contract already provides for $A(t)$ at any time. Hence the only part that has to be covered by a standard policy covering premature death is $CR(t)$ for $t = 1, \ldots, T$, and is depicted in Figure 12–1. From this, the premium for death coverage is determined as explained above. Note that this risk premium only accounts for the difference between the insured capital D and the book-value of the savings component of the contract. Therefore, the surrender option is exercised automatically in case of death of the insured.

We now come to an additional investment benefit provided by the contract: the *bonus*. Since the technical interest rate i is considered to be a conservative lower bound for the annual growth rate of the portfolio, the insurer will be expected to realize a higher annual yield than i percent. When realized, this expected surplus will be credited yearly to the contract in the form of a bonus. This means that the policyholder holds a string of European call-options on the asset-portfolio of the insurance company with strikes $K(t):=A(t)$ for $t = 1, 2, \ldots, 5$.

Although all options described up to now look fairly standard save for the exercise oddities of the surrender option, some additional

---

2 Minus applicable charges if surrendered before maturity.

FIGURE 12-1

Capital at Risk

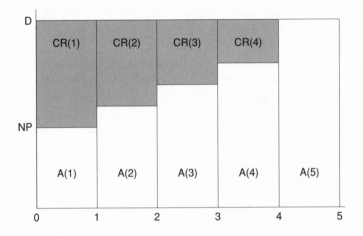

difficulties lay hidden. These difficulties have to do mostly with the nature of an insurer's portfolio and the method of its valuation. An insurer's portfolio usually consists of a mixture of fixed-income securities, stock, and real estate. The difficulties in valuing real estate are evident. Moreover, in many countries regulators require that stock be valued according to the principle "cost or market, whichever is lower" and fixed-income instruments valued at "amortized cost." In any case, we have a portfolio that is valued artificially, at least partly. It is already difficult to write options on the market value of such a portfolio, let alone on one that is artificially valued. This problem should certainly be of major concern to insurers: It leads to nonnegligible difficulties in the determination of the correct price of the endowment, one of the most popular life insurance products. The rationale for artificial valuation is that it should lead to values of the insurer's portfolio that are on the safe side, making it easier to ensure the solvency of the company. This, however, is a fallacy: Besides being the only measure for the real worth of the portfolio, the market value can be on either side of the artificial value of the portfolio. Therefore, the regulatory value could just as well understate or overstate the value of the portfolio. All of these valuation issues can only be resolved by adopting a market value approach.

LIFE-INSURANCE CONTRACTS II:
THE GUARANTEED INVESTMENT CONTRACT (GIC)

Insurance markets all over the world have experienced a trend towards deregulation and have been confronted with rapidly changing financial markets. This had led to increased competition among insurers themselves and has encouraged other financial institutions to try for a share of this market. On the side of the consumers, there is a growing awareness of the possible alternatives in the investment sector. All this has brought about the creation of a myriad of new life insurance products. Among them, the guaranteed investment contract, or GIC for short, has become popular both in the United States and in Europe. It is basically an investment instrument that looks very much like a bank account but that has relatively high crediting rates. The determinants of a GIC are the following:

Maturity	T
Single premium	E
Insured capital	D
Guaranteed crediting rate	i percent (generally near market rates)

The GIC is basically a zero-bond with face value D maturing at time T. As in the classical endowment, the net premium NP is defined as the single premium net of costs. The net premium grown at the guaranteed crediting rate until maturity equals the insured capital D. In case of death in the year t, the beneficiary receives the *book-value* $ZB(t)$ of the contract, which is defined as $ZB(t):= NP \bullet (1 + i\%)^t$ for $t = 0, 1, \ldots, T$. The insured may also surrender the contract at any time, receiving the book-value of the zero-bond minus applicable surrender charges. In many cases the insurer guarantees the crediting rate during part of the lifetime of the contract, keeping the option to reset it at the end of the guarantee period. We shall not consider this issue here.

Again we have a similar situation as in the classical endowment: The policyholder is long an American put and short an American call on the zero-bond with time-dependent strike equal to its book-value. Also in this case both options are exercised at the same time at the discretion of the policyholder or in case of the insured's death. Here, as in the case of the classical endowment, "at the discretion of the policyholder" is not to be interpreted in the sense that the investor will always exercise this option rationally. In fact, as already mentioned, a variety of other individual reasons such as the need for liquidity, and the like, can lead to early lapses.

LIFE-INSURANCE CONTRACTS III: INDEX-LINKED INSURANCE PRODUCTS

Both of the products described above have some features that increase costs (or, more precisely, would increase costs if properly priced) and that are not clearly a necessity. If the investment objective of a life insurance buyer is, as generally assumed, long term, it makes sense to argue that the surrender option is of limited value to the policyholder. Although most regulations force the insurer to grant the option of surrendering the contract, it is not clear that this must be done at book-value. This critique does not pertain to surrender in case of death: This type of exercise is needed in order to correctly price the death coverage. But in all other instances, surrender could probably be granted at market value, as long as the regulators agree to it. A second point concerning a classical endowment that we already made above is that inherent difficulties arise when trying to determine the fair price of all of a contract's embedded options. Both of these critiques already suggest a way to construct a product that has all of the features expected of a life insurance policy, while at the same time being accessible to a financial analysis consistent with capital markets. We shall illustrate this point using index-linked products as an example.

The index-linked contract would be described by the following data:

Maturity	T
Single premium	E
Insured capital	D
Bonus	B (an option granting participation on some market, e.g., a stock-exchange-index option)

First of all, the contract would guarantee the payment of the insured sum at maturity or in case of premature death of the insured (a zero-bond with face value D). Second, the bonus would be specified as an option on an appropriate index (for instance a clicket structure such as a string of calls on the yearly performance of the local stock exchange index throughout the lifetime of the contract). The surrender option on the book-value of the zero-bond would be exercised only in case of death of the insured. All other surrenders would be executed at market-value. Currently, such products are becoming increasingly popular, especially in Europe.[3]

From the point of view of the client, these products offer a solution to the problem of the lack of transparency of the classical endowment perceived by the policyholder (due to the fact that the insured is not completely aware of the structure of the insurer's portfolio). Moreover, the risk preferences of the policyholder can be taken into account individually by an appropriate choice of the underlying index. From the point of view of the insurer, these products are designed in such a way that their hedging will represent no additional difficulties.

TARGETING A ZERO-BOND

We have seen that one of the basic building blocks of a single-premium life insurance product is a zero-bond. In most countries, the market for this kind of instrument is fairly illiquid so that they have to be "produced" by resorting to what is available in the market, say coupon-bearing bonds. It is also well-known that *dedication* is not viable:[4] No single portfolio of coupon-bearing bonds will be able to exactly replicate a zero-bond on a buy-and-hold basis. The only chance of tracking the present value of a zero-bond over time is by periodically rebalancing the portfolio to accommodate for changes in the interest rate environment. This leads to strategies such as *immunization*. Broadly speaking, to immunize a zero-bond liability is to implement a dynamic investment strategy that is, in a certain way, self-financing: For all rebalancing dates and "in all possible states of the world," the portfolio must contain enough wealth so as to be able to finance the portfolio for the next period. In one of its formulations, immunization tries to achieve this by matching the interest rate sensitivities (duration and convexity matching). In a practical setting, the phrase "in all possible states of the world" would more appropri-

---

3 Compare Hunziker and Koch-Medina (1994).
4 Compare Leibowitz (1992).

ately mean "under a large enough set of representative interest rate scenarios." Finding the immunizing strategy would entail solving an optimization problem.

Both dedication (when possible) and immunization have a certain objective character: They try to replicate on the asset side, in a mechanical way, the incurred liabilities. On the other hand, a third strategy could also be adopted: *actively managing* the asset portfolio. Here, the subjective expectation of the portfolio manager plays the central role and a mismatch between the asset and liability sides may be conciously taken with the aim of taking advantage of a correctly anticipated market move. While dedication is the safest of all strategies, it fails to be practicable. When striving for a safe strategy the most widely used method is that of immunization (in one of its many guises).[5] However, immunization, due to its dynamic character, can prove to be cost intensive in terms of transaction fees; so that even within an immunizing strategy, it might pay to switch to active management in market situations where the portfolio manager feels confident enough.

THE SURRENDER OPTION: EXERCISE BY DEATH

We shall now turn to the issue of the valuation of the surrender option in GICs and in index-linked contracts. In order to introduce the basic idea, we address in this section the case of an index-linked product where the surrender option is exercised only in case of premature death of the insured.

We are given a zero-bond with face value of $1 and a maturity of, say, five years. The market price $S(0)$ of the zero-bond at issuance date grown until maturity at the internal rate of return i percent will thus yield $1. The book-value of the zero-bond is defined as $ZB(t) := S(0) \bullet (1+i\%)^t$ for $t = 0, 1, \ldots, 5$ with i fixed throughout the lifetime of the bond. We are confronted with the task of determining the fair value of the payoff resulting from a long position in an American put and a short position in an American call on a zero-bond with time-dependent strike $K(t)$ equal to the book-value $ZB(t)$. The peculiarity of this option is that it will be exercised only in case of death of the policyholder. This means that the risk resulting from the exercise of the option will occur for each contract independently. We

---

5 Compare Leibowitz (1992), Noris and Epstein (1989), and Miller, Shimpi, and Rajan (1989).

have already remarked that in such situations pooling a large amount of contracts will result in an effective hedge.

As previously stated, let $L(0)$ be the initial number of insureds, denote by $L(t)$ the number of insureds still alive at time t and denote by $p(t)$ the death frequency of insureds at time t based on the information contained in mortality tables. The evolution of $D(t)$, the number of deaths in the pool at time t, is again described by Table 12–1.

We have already said that each contract consists of a zero-bond and that we have to hedge the book-value for the pool of contracts. Denote by $SP(t)$ the payments due to the exercise of the surrender option at the level of the pool: $SP(t)$ accounts at the pool level for the difference $R(t)$: $= S(t) - ZB(t)$ between the market and book-value of the zero-bond. Thus, $R(t)$ represents the (positive or negative) risk that the zero-bond on the asset side will not exactly match the promised surrender value of the contract. But this risk only has to be taken into account for all insureds on a collective basis; hence the importance of $SP(t)$. Of course, $R(t)$ can be written as the difference of $R_+(t)$ and $R_-(t)$ where $R_+(t) = \max\{0, S(t) - ZB(t)\}$ and $R_-(t) = \max\{0, ZB(t) - S(t)\}$. These two expressions correspond to a long position in a call and a short position in a put on the zero-bond, both with strike equal to its book-value, which corresponds to the description of the surrender option given above for the case of the classical endowment. The evolution of $SP(t)$ over time is summarized in Table 12–3.

Note that this cash flow depends on interest rates through the market value $S(t)$ of the zero-bond. So the task of valuing the surrender option will have been accomplished if we are able to have present-value of interest-rate-sensitive cash-flows consisting of payments that may be either positive or negative.

Several approaches exist for doing this. We mention here the articles by P. D. Noris and S. Epstein (1989); M. Asay, P. Bouyaoucos, and A. Marciano (1989); and L. Miller, P. A. Shimpi, and U. Rajan (1989) on the more practical side. More satisfying also from a conceptual point of view and in terms of consistency with general

T A B L E   12–3

t	0	1	2	3	4	5
$SP(t)$	0	$D(1) \cdot R(1)$	$D(2) \cdot R(2)$	$D(3) \cdot R(3)$	$D(4) \cdot R(4)$	0

option theory, is the method due to H. Geman (1989)[6] based on the concept of the *forward neutral probability.*

THE SURRENDER OPTION: THE GENERAL CASE

We continue to describe the approach proposed by M. O. Albizatti and H. Geman (1994). The policyholder of a GIC will surrender the contract in other instances besides death. However, the motive for the exercise of the surrender option will not always be that of a rational investor. Here, as in the case discussed in "Targeting a Zero-Bond" above, we may resort to the smoothing effect of pooling risks. In the sequel, we shall stick to the notation of the previous section.

We first model the behavior of a rational policyholder. We assume that a rational policyholder will compare the benefit of holding onto the contract until maturity to the result of surrendering the contract and reinvesting it in a similar policy with the same investment horizon. The reason for this assumption is that the investor will try to remain in the same investment class in order to profit from tax privileges. The surrender value of the contract at time t is $ZB(t)$. Assuming that the new crediting rate is r percent, reinvesting in a new GIC with maturity $T - t$ will yield the final value $FV(t, r) = ZB(t) \bullet (1+r\%)^{T-t}$. Hence, *neglecting all transaction costs and tax issues* the rational investor will surrender the policy if $DC(t, r) > 0$ where $DC(t, r) = FV(t,r) - ZB(T)$. This is the investor's decision criterion: the potential risk-free profit resulting from switching to a new GIC.

The idea now is to have a function similar to that in the case of exercise by death, a function $p(t, r)$ that represents the frequency of surrenders in the pool of insureds at time t. The frequency $p(t, r)$ will account for surrenders due to death, rational behavior (hence the dependence on r, which enters through the decision criterion) and other various reasons. The evaluation of the surrender option now proceeds exactly as in the case of exercise by death where we only have to replace the function $p(t)$ by $p(t, r)$. Of course, in this case $D(t)$ will not represent the number of deaths at time t among the pool of insureds but the number of surrenders due to all of the aforementioned reasons.

Note that the fact that not all of the policyholders will exercise the surrender option rationally implies that $p(t, r)$ will be generally

---

6 See also Jamshidian (1989) for a PDEs approach and El Karoui and Geman (1991 and 1994).

strictly greater than zero even if $DC(t) \leq 0$ holds. However, for the same reason, $p(t, r)$ also will be strictly smaller than one in the case that $DC(t) > 0$.

The definition of $p(t, r)$ is the main issue when implementing this method. It will be based on a careful specification of the decision criterion (more realistic than that described here) and a reliable set of historical data on the behavior of the type of individuals investing in GICs. Note that experience in modeling the behavior of early repayments of mortgages will be of great use when addressing this issue.

INTEREST RATE MODELS

Since the term structure of interest rates moves randomly over time, making interest rate instruments accessible to a quantitative analysis entails modeling it by a suitable stochastic process. In particular, interest rate dynamics should be modeled so as not to admit arbitrage. But even when working with scenarios, an appropriate process is necessary to generate them. Specifying scenarios arbitrarily could result in inconsistencies.

The right choice of a stochastic process describing interest rate dynamics is a difficult matter. The question of whether to choose a one- or a multifactor model is not free of controversy. We shall not dwell on these issues here, referring the reader to the relevant chapters in this volume.

CONCLUDING COMMENTS

We have seen that life insurance policies can contain a variety of options that we have summarized under the name *surrender options*. In the case of the classical endowment, we saw that determining the value of this option has some problems. We also showed that index-linked products could prove to be a good surrogate for the classical endowment. For GICs or index-linked insurance products, we sketched a methodology for the valuation of the surrender option that is consistent with a general option theory approach. The reliability of the method depends crucially on the quality of the historical data used to model the behavior of policyholders with respect to lapses. Moreover, the implementation of the method also calls for a specification of a stochastic model for the dynamics of interest rates.

Insurance regulation in many countries enforces an artificial valuation approach on the asset as well as on the liability side. This constitutes a major drawback when trying to determine the true economical value of life insurance products. One additional comment on insurance regulation: In light of the fact that most life insurance products have a variety financial options embedded in them, it is surprising that in most of countries insurers are limited by regulation in their use of options on the asset side.

All in all, it can be said that if life insurers are to correctly assess and manage the incurred financial risks in their companies, it becomes necessary to acquire the appropriate know-how and to learn how to adapt it to their particular needs. This is probably one of the major challenges for the insurance industry in the years to come.

REFERENCES

Albizatti, M. O., and H. Geman. "Interest Rate Risk Management and Valuation of the Surrender Option in Life Insurance Policies." to appear in *Journal of Risk and Insurance*.

Asay, M.; P. Bouyaoucos; and A. Marciano. "An Economic Approach to the Valuation of Single Premium Deferred Annuities," issued by Goldman Sachs, *Financial Institutional Research*, April 1989.

El Karoui, N., and H. Geman. "A stochastic approach to pricing FRNs," *Risk* 4, no. 3 (March 1991).

El Karoui, N., and H. Geman. "A Probabilistic Approach to the Valuation of Floating Rate Notes with an Application to Interest Rate Swaps." *Advances in Options and Futures Research*, 1994.

Fabozzi, F. J. *Bond Markets, Analysis and Strategies.* 2nd ed. Englewood Cliffs, NJ: Prentice-Hall, 1993.

Geman, H. "L' Importance de la Probabilité 'Forward Neutre' dans une Approche Stochastique des Taux d' Intérêt." ESSEC Working Paper, 1989.

Hunziker, J. P, and P. Koch-Medina. "Swiss Way of Life." *Risk*, 7, no. 11 (November 1994).

Jamshidian, F. "An Exact Bond Pricing Formula." *Journal of Finance*, no. 44, 1989.

Leibowitz, M. L. Bond Immunization: A Procedure for Realizing Target Levels of Return." *In Investing: The Collected Works of M.L. Leibowitz*, ed. F. J. Fabozzi., Burr Ridge, IL: Irwin Professional Publishing, 1992.

Miller, L.; P. A. Shimpi; and U. Rajan. "Funding SPDA Liabilities: An Application of Realized Return Optimization. In *Fixed Income Portfolio Strategies*, ed. F. J. Fabozzi, Burr Ridge, IL: Irwin Professional Publishing, 1989.

Noris, P. D., and S. Epstein. "Finding the Immunizing Investment for Insurance Liabilities: The Case of the SPDA." In *Fixed Income Portfolio Strategies*, ed. F. J. Fabozzi, Burr Ridge, IL: Irwin Professional Publishing, 1989.

Williams, C. A. Jr.; M. L. Smith; and P. C. Young. *Risk Management and Insurance.* 7th ed. New York: McGraw-Hill, 1995.

Witzel, R. "Versicherung." in *Kleiner Merkur, Betriebswirtschaft*, 5. Auflage, Schulthess, Zürich, 1995.

13

⑥ OPTIONS ON VOLATILITY

Menachem Brenner, Professor
New York University, New York

Dan Galai, Professor[*]
The Hebrew University, Jerusalem

The concept of a volatility index and the idea of introducing options and futures on the volatility index was initially presented in our paper "New Financial Instruments for Hedging Changes in Volatility" (1989). The basic ideas were presented to the American Stock Exchange in June 1986 and to the Chicago Board Option Exchange in August 1987. Though the Crash of 1987 substantially increased the level of volatility, it reduced the activity in the derivatives market and all plans to introduce new instruments were postponed.

The concept of volatility has attracted the attention of academicians, especially since 1973, with the introduction of standardized options trading by the Chicago Board Options Exchange. Research has spanned a wide range of topics, including measurement and estimation methods of volatility, application of volatility in various investment strategies, and the pricing of financial instruments affected by volatility.

Traditional pricing models assume that volatility remains constant over the life of the financial instrument. This is the basic assumption behind the portfolio selection model of Markowitz, as well as behind the capital asset pricing model of Sharpe and Lintner. A major assumption of the Black-Scholes model to price European

[*] Financial assistance for this research was provided by the Zagagi Center and by the Abe Gray Chair.

options is that the standard deviation of the rate of return on the underlying asset is constant over the life of the option. This presumption has been challenged in the finance literature by many authors for different segments of the market. (See, for example, the survey paper of Bollerslev, Chou Ray, and Kroner [1992], especially for the equity market, and Tucker and Scott [1987] for foreign exchange rates). The evidence for the equity, bond, and foreign currency markets indicates that estimated volatility is nonstationary and the standard deviation tends to fluctuate.

The historical behavior of equity and bond volatilities in different countries is provided in Tables 13–1 and 13–2. The calculations are taken from a recent publication of Goldman Sachs ("Equity Derivatives Research," December 1994).

In the United States, the annual volatility of the S&P 500 Index fluctuated in the range of 5.33 percent to 35.78 percent during the last 50 years. In 1994, up to the end of October, it was 10.04 percent, up from 8.67 percent in 1993, compared to a 50-year average of 13.70 percent. The 10-year current coupon U.S. government bond had volatility of 6.52 percent in 1993, and it has moved higher to 9.12 percent during the first 10 months of 1994, compared to a 7-year average of 7.04 percent.

T A B L E   13–1

Historical Volatility Statistics for Seven World Equity Markets[*]

				Long-Term Volatility		
Market	Index	1994 YTD Volatility[**]	1993 Volatility	Entire Period	Volatility Range	Start Date
United States	S&P 500	10.04	8.67	13.70	5.33–35.78	July 1944
Japan	TOPIX	15.06	19.20	13.77	4.87–28.99	May 1949
United Kingdom	FT-SE All Share	12.40	8.60	15.88	8.12–37.76	Jan. 1965
France	Datastream Total Market	14.89	12.34	17.66	10.30–29.24	Jan. 1973
Germany	DAX	17.58	13.91	16.06	7.87–31.14	Jan. 1965
Switzerland	SBC General	14.46	9.63	13.44	6.70–27.45	Jan. 1969
Netherlands	CBS All Share	12.25	9.19	15.42	6.96–31.72	Jan. 1965

[*] Volatility calculations based upon daily data; "rolling" one-year volatility sampled quarterly.

[**] Through 10/31/94.

TABLE 13–2

Bond Volatility: Comparison across Periods and Markets*

Country	1994 YTD**	1993	2/1/88 YTD**
United States	9.12	6.52	7.04
Japan	7.20	4.73	5.60
United Kingdom	13.05	6.26	8.11
France	10.01	5.10	6.32
Germany	8.44	4.18	5.44
Netherlands	8.04	4.91	5.08

* Volatilities based upon daily prices of 10-year current coupon government bond.
** Through 10/31/94.

The tables illustrate the global phenomena of wide changes in estimated volatility from year to year for both stocks and bonds. This can be further described in Figure 13–1, depicting quarterly and annual "rolling" volatility estimation based on daily data for the S&P 500 Index. This figure also emphasizes the wide fluctuation in volatility from period to period. The shorter is the estimation period, the more "noisy" is its graph, which has more "spikes."

Many papers try to explain the sources of volatility changes. For example, in the foreign currency market Ito and Rolly (1987) showed that the volatility of the dollar/yen exchange rate is affected by U.S. money supply changes, and Johnson and Schneeweis (1992) showed that macroeconomic information releases affect volatility for several currencies. In the equity market, Schwert (1989) has tested the relationship between various macroeconomic variables and volatility.

While there are efficient tools for hedging against general changes in overall market direction, so far there are no effective tools available for hedging against *changes* in volatility. The creation of volatility indexes for various instruments, on which cash-settled options and futures can be traded, would expand the investment opportunities available to investors and provide efficient means to hedge against changes in volatility.

THE NEED FOR VOLATILITY OPTIONS AND FUTURES

Traders and investors who use option strategies find themselves exposed to volatility risk. For example, investors engaged in covered-

FIGURE   13–1

Historical Equity Volatility in the United States from 7/44 to 9/94 for the S&P 500 Index (daily rates of return, sampled quarterly)*

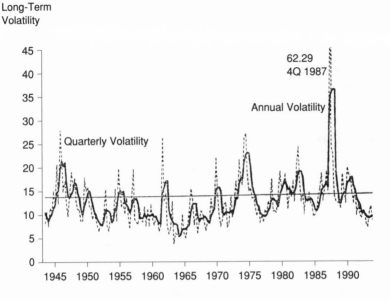

* From Goldman Sachs' "Equity Derivatives Research," December 1994, p. 5.

call strategies are subject to risk associated with changes in volatility. Being delta-neutral means that the writer of a covered call is not exposed to risk associated with a relatively small change in the price of the underlying instrument; however, he may lose money if volatility increases.

When volatility reaches relatively low levels, investors may speculate on an increase in volatility. Usually periods preceding elections, crucial meetings of the heads of central banks, and expected announcements of policy changes are characterized by increased volatility in financial markets. Buying a call option on volatility allows the investor to participate in increased market volatility while limiting risk to the buyer's initial investment. The proposed volatility options and futures provide an efficient and less costly alternative trading in volatility than purchasing or selling straddles.

Current asset-allocation models are based largely on the volatility of each asset and the correlations between pairs of assets. A change in volatility of a certain asset may lead to a change in the portfolio allocation. Volatility options and futures provide a means of protection against adverse changes in the portfolio. This approach should be further explored both on theoretical and practical grounds.

Volatility options and futures should be found useful in dynamic strategies for portfolio-protection and guaranteed capital funds schemes. To implement these strategies, synthetic puts are created from futures, using models such as Black and Scholes (1973) or Garman and Kohlhagen (1983), which assume that volatility is constant. Dynamic strategies adopting these assumptions are vulnerable to major losses and gains as a result of fluctuations in volatility. A volatility option could substantially reduce the risk of employing dynamic strategies; it will cost only a fraction of the potential change in the insurance premium.

The market for volatility options and futures will be mainly an institutional one. Institutional investors engage in dynamic strategies involving options as well as in asset allocation mechanisms. However, it can be expected that individuals will be attracted to this market both for speculation and for hedging positions that are exposed to volatility risk.

A major problem in creating a market for volatility options is in constructing an appropriate volatility index. There is no universally accepted method to measure the volatility of equity, bond, or currency markets. Moreover, no single index can reflect the volatility changes for all components in a given market (e.g., different currencies have different volatilities). Also, traders hold different positions, and no index can satisfy the hedging needs of all traders.

It is clear that a volatility index based only on one segment of the capital market (e.g., the computer industry) will provide a measure that is specific to that segment but may not provide a good indication of the volatility of another industry or of the market as a whole.

A volatility index must be updated constantly so historical volatility is not a good candidate for our index. Neither would volatility models of the ARCH family provide adequate estimates to track changes in volatility.

A natural candidate is an index based on the series of implied volatilities from options frequently traded. Even then, statistical procedures must be applied in order to smooth the noise element and achieve a reliable estimate of volatility changes. The index should reflect expected volatility, a factor that is not affected with each trade, and therefore, can be measured by some average of implied volatility. The CBOE volatility index (VIX), by our judgment, is too volatile since it does not neutralize the noise that is present in the trading of any security. An index that is too "noisy" will not appeal to investors and traders since it will not accurately reflect underlying volatility, and hence, options on such an index will not provide a good hedge against volatility changes.

One way to reduce noise in the estimation is to infer the volatility from options traded in different markets, such as options on the S&P 500 Index (SPX) and options on SPX futures for the stock market or, in the case of currencies, spot options traded on the Philadelphia Exchange (PHLX) and futures options traded on the International Monetary Market (IMM).

Another possibility is the creation of a volatility index for developed markets. This index will be based on volatilities of the major economies such as the United States, Japan, United Kingdom, France, and Germany. These countries have developed options markets, and their implieds could be used to create a volatility index for fund managers who diversify globally in these major markets.

It is also feasible to create an overall volatility index for, say, the U.S. dollar against all the other leading currencies. Such an index is useful especially when changes in dollar volatility spill over to other major economies. For example, the FINEX in the United States trades derivative contracts based on a dollar index representing the weighted-average dollar price of a basket of currencies used by U.S. corporations. The volatility of this dollar index may be of interest to many internationally traded American companies. A similar currency basket index could be constructed for the deutsche mark (DM) or the British pound. The volatility of such a currency index could be a useful vehicle for hedging the positions of those who have portfolio commitments in multiple foreign currencies.

CONSTRUCTING A VOLATILITY INDEX— THEORETICAL CONSIDERATIONS

Our research on equity volatility supports a volatility index based on implying the volatility from a synthetic 30-day, at-the-money, call option. By using a standardized option, problems associated with both the time to maturity bias and the "moneyness" bias in the estimation of volatility are avoided. In addition, short-term, at-the-money options provide the most liquid market and, therefore, data are more reliable. The value of the synthetic option should be calculated every few minutes, based on actual prices of traded calls, say, on the SPX. Only short-term and next-term options, and only series that are close-to-the-money, should be involved in the calculation. The 30-day at-the-money synthetic call will be interpolated from prices of calls from four series, with weights based on a pricing model for calls, whether stock index calls or currency calls.

First, the two slightly-in-the-money, short-term, and next-term series will be interpolated to yield a 30-day slightly-in-the-money synthetic option. Second, a 30-day slightly-out-of-the-money synthetic option is calculated. Third, the two 30-day synthetic calls are combined to yield the 30-day at-the-money call.[1]

Let us denote the currency spot-exchange rate by S, and the two closest-to-the-money striking prices by K_1 and K_2, so that $K_1 < S < K_2$. C^A_1, C^M_1, and C^A_2, C^M_2 denote the actual (A) and model (M) call prices for the current month (1) and the next month (2), respectively.

The first step is, therefore, to calculate

$$C(\tau = 30, K_1) = C_1^A(K_1)W + C_2^A(K_1)(1-W)$$

where

$$W = \frac{C^M(\tau = 30, K_1) - C_2^M(K_1)}{C_1^M(K_1) - C_2^M(K_1)}.$$

The same procedure is applied to calculate $C(\tau = 30, K_2)$. The third step is to calculate the synthetic at-the-money 30-day call, to be denoted by C^*, and

$$C^* = C(\tau = 30, K_1)V + C(\tau = 30, K_2)(1-V)$$

where

$$V = \frac{C^M(\tau = 30, K = S) - C^M(\tau = 30, K_2)}{C^M(\tau = 30, K_1) - C^M(\tau = 30, K_2)}.$$

C^* now reflects actual prices of traded options and provides information on the volatility of, for example, a stock market index. The pricing model can be used once more to calculate the implied standard deviation for C^*.

---

1 A similar procedure for a synthetic call is suggested by Galai (1979).

In order to reduce the noise in this estimation procedure, a combination of implied volatilities from synthetic call and put options should be considered. A moving average procedure over the latest estimates can also be used to reduce the noise further without affecting the basic changes in volatility.

CONSTRUCTING A VOLATILITY INDEX— AN APPLICATION

While the concept of interpolating a standardized 30-day, at-the-money option from traded options is simple, the implementation can be quite complicated. For example, the four options used in the interpolation should be traded simultaneously. Nonsimultaneous trading can introduce noise in estimating C^* and hence an error in the implied standard deviation. Another issue that should be dealt with is the possible noise in observed prices due to discrete changes in prices as well as transactions executed at either the bid or ask prices (and often inside the price spread).

Therefore, in order to implement the concept, additional working assumptions should be introduced. These should depend on the nature of the underlying instrument, the frequency of trading in the different series, the procedure for price changes, and more. The adjustments should be determined empirically, after studying the data and simulating alternative volatility indexes. Still, while a "well-behaving" index is the objective—one that will track true changes in volatility—it should not be complicated to calculate and update the index. Since "true" volatility is unobservable, the procedure employed in calculating the index cannot be perfectly verified.

Figure 13–2 depicts a volatility index that we calculated based on data for the period April 1991 to July 1991 for options on the Major Market Index (MMI).[2] The options were traded on the American Stock Exchange and their symbol is XMI. Our data consisted of all transactions that took place during the period in all series of XMI.

Since the XMI options are not heavily traded, with only a few thousand contracts changing hands daily, there are gaps in trading some series during any given day. To overcome this problem, we cal-

---

2 The MMI tracks the Dow Jones Index (DJI) very closely. Almost all the 20 stocks in the MMI are also contained in the 30 stocks of the DJI. In addition, the weighing procedure of the DJI is followed by the MMI.

FIGURE   13-2

Volatility Index for MMI and the MMI for the Period April 91–July 91
(15-minute intervals combining calls and puts)

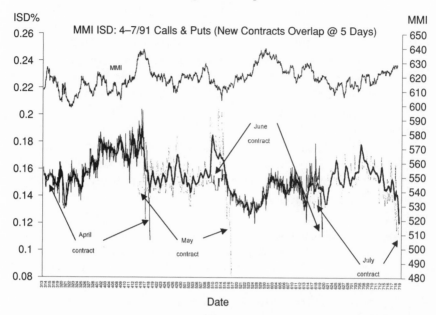

Date

culated the average price for each options series involved in calculating
the 30-day, at-the-money synthetic option during a 15-minute interval.
Therefore the calculation of implied volatility for the XMI options is
updated every 15 minutes.

In addition, we deleted the first 30 minutes of each trading day
because prices vibrate wildly at the beginning of trading. The
implied volatility calculated from prices during that time interval
are usually significantly higher than volatilities estimated during the
rest of the day.

To add more information, we calculated both the synthetic calls
(C^*) and puts (P^*) and implied the volatilities for each option separately, and then averaged the two during each time interval. While it
is frequently found that implied volatilities from puts are higher
than those calculated from calls, averaging the two provides a more
stable series while using more information.

If in a given series no trade took place during the 15-minute interval, the last available price was used. Though using stale information

does not introduce a systematic bias, its potential error is reduced by the averaging procedure behind the interpolation technique.

The interpolation to derive C^* and P^* involves the shortest term options and the next shortest. However, when the short maturity options approach their expiration date, the prices become more erratic. In the example for the XMI options, we switched from the shortest term options to the two other series, which are one and two months away from the shortest, when the shortest was five days to expiration. In such a case, C^* and P^* are calculated by the same formula as in the section above on constructing a volatility index, but by means of extrapolation.

The bold line for the implied volatility is a moving average over the last 20 15-minute intervals. Moving average reduces the noise in the index without significantly altering the pattern of volatility changes. The new implied volatility series are also depicted in the graph in lighter lines.

Implied volatility during the four-month period from April to July 1991 showed implied volatility moving in a range of 12 to 18 percent on an annual basis, with an average around 16 percent. The MMI moved between 600 to 640. The negative correlation between the price level and volatility can be noticed by comparing the behavior of the two series simultaneously.

VALUATION OF VOLATILITY OPTIONS

Valuation models for options on volatility indexes are not simple to derive. The no-arbitrage approach may be useless since a riskless hedge, that simultaneously takes care of both stochastic prices or rates and stochastic volatility, cannot be constructed.

In order to illustrate how volatility options can be valued, we assume that investors are risk-neutral and apply a risk-neutral valuation approach. The model described in this section for pricing call options on volatility of foreign currencies is taken from our paper (Brenner and Galai 1993).

Let us assume that a G-7 meeting is expected to be held next month (time 1), and that one month later (time 2) an OPEC meeting will take place. If the G-7 meeting is "successful," the dollar is expected to appreciate against the deutsche mark from 1.50 to 1.55, and its volatility is expected to be 10 percent (on an annual basis). If the meeting is "unsuccessful," we expect the exchange rate to be 1.47, and the volatility to be 14 percent. In this example, we expect one of two outcomes to take place, with each outcome characterized by two parameters: the exchange rate, and the volatility of the subsequent exchange rates.

The OPEC meeting the following month, can also result in two outcomes: the price of oil increases or decreases. If the G-7 meeting at $t = 1$ is successful, and the price of oil increases, we may expect a further strengthening of the dollar, to 1.60, and no change regarding future volatility, $\sigma_{11} = \sigma_{21} = 10$ percent. If, however, the OPEC meeting results in a decrease in the price of oil, we would observe a decline in the exchange rate to 1.50, but volatility may either be 12 percent or 16 percent, with equal probability.

Similarly, if the G-7 meeting is unsuccessful, and the price of oil increases, the exchange rate will increase to 1.50 (from 1.47), and volatility may assume one or two values, 12 percent or 16 percent. If, however, the price of oil decreases, the dollar will slip further to 1.35, and volatility will have a wider distribution: it will be either higher at 18 percent or lower at 10 percent with equal probability. All possible outcomes are described in Figure 13–3.

To value a volatility option, using a 12 percent strike price, we make some additional simplifying assumptions. The option is European, and the domestic and foreign interest rates are the same at 0.5 percent per month. Using the binomial tree in Figure 13–3, we show in Figure 13–4, the payoffs of the volatility call option at time 2.

At time 1, however, we have two uncertainties: first, the uncertainty of the exchange rate (e.g., moving from 1.47 either to 1.50 or to 1.35), and then the uncertainty about the level of volatility at either of the exchange rates. For example, if we get to $F_{22} = 1.50$, we may have a volatility of either 12 percent or 16 percent. Thus, to value the option at time 1, we use a 0.5 probability that σ_{22}, for example, will be 16 percent. We then use the probability of getting to node (2, 2) from node (1, 2), that is the same as the risk-neutral probability of getting from F_{12} to F_{22}.

Hence, the value of the volatility call at time 1, state 2, C_{12} is given by:[3]

$$C_{12} = \left[C_{22}P + C_{23}(1 - P)\right]/(1 + 0.005)$$

where

---

3 This is based on the binomial valuation model for foreign currency options given, for example, in Bodurtha and Courtadon (1987).

F I G U R E   13–3

Exchange Rates F_{ij} and the Standard Deviation σ_{ij} at Time I ($I = 1,2$) and State j ($j = 1, 2, 3$)

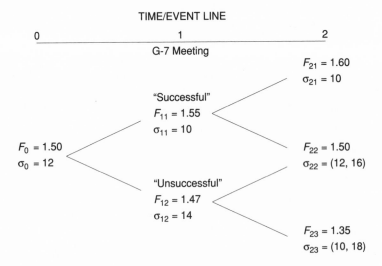

Notes: σ_{ij} is in annualized percentage points. σ_{22} and σ_{23} assume two possible values each (numbers in parentheses).

$$P = \frac{(1+0.005-0.005)-(1.35/1.47)}{(1.5/1.47)-(1.35/1.47)} = 0.8.$$

Thus,

$$C_{12} = \left[(2\times0.8)+(3\times0.2)\right]/1.005 = 2.19.$$

Similarly:

$$C_{11} = \left[(0\times0.5)+(2\times0.5)\right]/1.005 = 0.995.$$

Using C_{11} and C_{12}, the value of the option at time 0, C_0 is given by:

$$C_0 = \left[(0.995\times0.375)+(2.19\times0.625)\right]/1.005 = 1.73$$

The value of the volatility option is about 1.73 pfennings. It provides insurance against changes in volatility above 12 percent.

CONCLUSIONS

The large swings in volatility in all markets for stocks, bonds, and foreign exchange (FX) in the past few years demonstrate the need for

FIGURE   13-4

Value-Tree for a Two-Period Call Option on Volatility with a Strike Level of 12 percent.

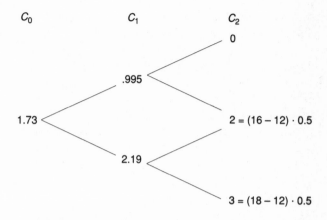

financial instruments for hedging changes in volatility. The recent fluctuations in FX volatility have affected the willingness of FX options traders to take positions, especially in writing options that result in higher bid/ask spreads in the options market and probably in a smaller volume of trading.

Generally, options on volatility would have contributed to more trading in options and thereby expand the insurance provided in the financial markets. Options would increase the potential for hedging and risk management, and for new investment strategies.

REFERENCES

Black, F., and M. Scholes. "The Pricing of Options and Corporate Liabilities." *Journal of Political Economy,* 3 (1973), pp. 637–54.

Bodurtha, J., and G. Courtadon. "The Pricing of Foreign Currency Options. *Monograph Series in Finance and Economics* 4, no. 5 (1987), pp. 1–87.

Bollerslev, T.; Y. Chou Ray; and K. F. Kroner. "ARCH Modeling in Finance: A Review of the Theory and Empirical Evidence." *Journal of Econometrics* 52 (1992), pp. 5–59.

Brenner, M., and D. Galai. "New Financial Instruments for Hedging Changes in Volatility." *Financial Analysts Journal,* (1989), pp. 61–5.

——— "Hedging Volatility in Foreign Currencies." *The Journal of Derivatives,* Fall 1993, pp. 53–9.

Galai, D. "A Proposal for Indexes for Traded Call Options." *Journal of Finance,* 1979, pp. 1157–72.

Garman, M., and Kohlhagen. "Foreign Currency Option Values." *Journal of International Money and Finance* 2, 1983, pp. 231–7.

Goldman Sachs. "Index Volatility in Global Options Markets." *Equity Derivatives Research,* December 1994.

Ito, T. and V. Rolly. "News from the U.S. and Japan: Which Moves the Yen/Dollar Exchange Rate?" *Journal of Monetary Economics* 19, (1987), pp. 255–77.

Johnson, G, and T. Schneeweis. "Trading/Non-Trading Time and Information Effects in Foreign Currency Markets." Working paper, University of Massachusetts, 1992.

Schwert, G.W. "Why Does Stock Market Volatility Change over Time?" *Journal of Finance* 44 (1989), pp. 1115–53.

Tucker, A., and E. Scott. "A Study of Diffusion Process for Foreign Exchange Rates." *Journal of International Money and Finance,* 1989, pp. 465–80.

Software Installation Guide
User's Manual for the Excel Interface

CONVERTIBLE BOND SAMPLE DISK
INSTALLATION GUIDE (EXCEL VERSION)

Thank you for your purchase of *Option Embedded Bonds.** Here is a demo of ConvB, our Convertible Bond Evaluation System. Enclosed please find a free sample disk. This disk lets you explore and experiment with our system. The only restriction is that it can only price bonds with 10-year maturities, 30 percent stock volatilities and 15 percent rate volatilities. To order the complete, unrestricted system, please call phone number given below.

Obviously, Excel must be installed on the computer system running this program.

This package contains:

1. A free sample disk.
2. These installation notes.
3. A program manual.

Please look for our papers "Costing the Converts," *Risk* magazine, July 1994; and "The Fervor of the Convert," *AsiaRisk* magazine, April 1996. Reprints are available upon request. Chapter 8 of this book is also relevant.

INSTALLATION

To install the program on your PC, perform the following steps:

1. Insert the floppy disk into your computer.
2. Create a directory called "convb" on your system by typing the command
   mkdir convb.

---

* Super Computing Consulting Corporation, 440 North Wabash Ave. Suite 4909, Chicago, IL 60611 USA; Phone/fax: (312) 527-6127; e-mail: iamizzy@ix.netcom.com; WWW home page: http://www.miint.net/~sccc; Copyright: Dr. Izzy Nelken, President.

3. Copy the spreadsheet file from the floppy into your system
   by typing the command
   copy a:\convb.xls c:\convb.

4. Do you have a 16-bit system or a 32-bit system?
   a. If you have Excel version 7.0 or higher and a 32-bit
   system, type
   copy a:\bit32\convb.dll c:\winNT\system32.
   copy a:\convb.key c:\winNT\system32

   Note that **c:\winNT\system32** might have another name
   on Windows 95 systems (e.g., it may be called c:\windows\
   system). Check with your systems person for more details
   or call us at the number below.

   b. Otherwise, for the 16-bit program, type
   copy a:\bit16\convb.dll c:\windows\system
   copy a:\bit16\sswin.dll c:\windows\system
   copy a:\convb.key c:\windows\system.

This concludes the installation part of the program. To run the
program, start up Excel and open the spreadsheet

c:\convb\convb.xls

Caution

This free sample disk will only evaluate convertible bonds with 10-
year maturities, 30 percent stock volatilities and 15 percent rate
volatilities. Any attempt to evaluate bonds with other parameters
will result in a warning message.

Notes

(1) We also have more complete demos available. Please
    contact us for more details.
(2) We are constantly improving our software. Please contact us for
    up-to-date versions.

Call Us

If you have any problems with the install procedure, questions, or
comments please call us at (312) 527-6127 or e-mail to: **iamizzy@ix.
netcom.com.** Visit our site at the World Wide Web at http://www.
miint.net/~sccc.

USER'S MANUAL FOR THE CONVB EXCEL INTERFACE

INTRODUCTION

ConvB is a program designed to price and hedge portfolios of convertible bonds, preferred shares, or both. The program is designed around the quadranary tree approach developed by Super Computer Consulting Corporation (see our papers in *Risk* magazine and *Asia-Risk* magazine).

The program has very many features and can handle bonds with a variety of features. These include:

- Call options.
- Put options.
- Conversion into stocks, shares, or a combination of both.
- Dual currency convertibles.
- The dilution effect.
- Step up, step down or changing coupon.
- The phenomenon under which corporate spreads usually rise when shares fall to really low levels.
- Complete hedging parameters: duration, convexity, and functional (key-rate) duration and convexity.

ConvB also computes delta, gamma and the various vega sensitivities. It can account for dividends as a cash amount, a percentage rate, or a combination of both, and it can connect to various convertible databases, including ValueLine.

EXAMPLE

Open the Excel spreadsheet and the file CONVB.XLS. This file contains two sample bonds called Example1 and Example2. In the next few pages, we will show how the data for this bond was entered. The spreadsheet also contains other examples such as preferred shares, dual currency convertibles, and various other bonds.

COMPUTATION

In the Excel spreadsheet top menu you will find a pull-down item called ConvB. The item Compute Bond computes the value of the current bond (the one that is indicated by the cursor). The item Compute All will compute the value of all bonds.

Settlement Date

This is given in the third row. Enter the settlement date, or the date at which the portfolio should be evaluated.

Settlement Date: 1-Jan-1996

Bond Identifier

This could be a ticker symbol or the CUSIP of the security.

Bond
Identifier

Example1
Example2

Comments

An additional column is included in the spreadsheet for comments. These could be anything the user desires (e.g., rated a "Buy" by Merrill Lynch).

Face Value

In this cell, enter the face value of the instrument. For most convertible bonds, this should be $100 (par). However, for preferred shares or other structures, the face value may be different.

Face
Value

$ 100.00
$ 100.00

Maturity Date

In this field, enter the final maturity of the bond.

Maturity
Date

1-Jan-2006
1-Jan-2006

Coupon Payment Frequency

This is a code for how often the coupon is paid out.

A—Annual

S—Semiannual (for most U.S. convertibles)

Q—Quarterly

M—Monthly

W—Weekly

**Frequency
(A/S/Q/M/W)
S
S**

Stock Price

This is the share price of the underlying stock. Note that this field could be tied in to a real-time feed.

**Stock
Price

$ 20.00
$ 21.25**

Volatility of Stocks

The user enters the volatility of the underlying shares in this field as a percentage. For example, a volatility of 30 percent would simply be entered as 30.00. In this example, the first convertible has an underlying stock whose volatility is 30 percent and the second also has an underlying stock with a volatility of 30 percent.

**Stocks
Volatility

30.00
30.00**

Rate Volatility

In this cell, the user types in the volatility of interest rates. This is the volatility of the corporate rates the issuer pays. A volatility of 20 percent is input as 20.00. In both examples, the volatility levels are 15 percent.

Rates
Volatility

    15.00
    15.00

New Bond

In this field, the user enters Y for a new bond or N for a bond that has already been issued and is being traded on the secondary market. The difference between them is in the way the coupon payments and accrued interest are computed. A new bond will not pay interest until the coupon payment period has passed. However, a bond that has already been issued is already paying interest and we are already evaluating it in the midst of the coupon payment stream.

Dual Currency

A dual currency bond is a bond that is denominated in one currency (the domestic currency) whose underlying stock is denominated in a different currency (the foreign currency). For example, the Bangkok Land 4.50 percent of 12/97 are denominated in Swiss francs but the underlying shares are denominated in Bangkok baht.

In this cell is a switch that should be switched to Y or N for yes or no. If the bond is dual currency, the user should enter a Y, otherwise the user must enter N.

For dual currency bonds, we assume that the bond, its coupons, and its call and put features are all denominated in the domestic currency. The share and its dividends are denominated in the foreign currency.

Dual Currency?
(Y/N)

    Y
    N

Domestic Yield Curve

The domestic yield curve is to be found under the Yields sheet.

Domestic
Yield Curve

DOM1
DOM2

Our first example uses a curve called DOM1, and the second example uses a curve called DOM2. For all practical purposes, we can name these curves after the credit ratings they refer to (e.g., FINAA could refer to AA rated financials).

Foreign Yield Curve

This field is only used in the case of dual currency bonds. In other cases, it could have a dummy entry. It refers to the foreign currency yield curve shown under the sheet Foreign.

Foreign
Yield Curve

FOR1
FOR1

In this case, both foreign curves refer to FOR1; however, only the first bond is of dual currency. The foreign curve is ignored in the case of the second bond.

Accrued Interest on Calls

When bonds are called, do they pay the accrued interest on top of the call price?

If the answer is yes, type a Y. Otherwise, type an N.

Calls Acc.
Interest (Y/N)

Y
Y

Accrued Interest on Puts

When a bond is put back to the issuer, does the issuer also have to pay the accrued interest?

Puts Acc.
Interest (Y/N)

Y

Y

Accrued Interest

The program computes the "full price" of the security (including accrued interest). To get a market price, the accrued interest must be subtracted. There are several methods of computing accrued interest. Choose the most applicable method.

1 = act/act, 2 = act/360
3 = act/365

Acc. Interest
Type?

3

2

Time Step

This parameter determines the distance (in time measured in years) between successive levels of the tree. Therefore, it controls the speed and accuracy of the algorithm. When the time step is small, the pricing algorithm is more precise but it requires more resources (memory and CPU time). With large coarse time-steps, the algorithm slightly loses in accuracy but gains much in speed. We recommend that the choice of time step be governed by the final maturity of the bond.

Final Maturity	Time Step
More than 30 years	1 year
15–30 years	0.5 years
5–15 years	0.25 years
less than 5 years	0.1 years

The idea is to have a tree that is rich enough in nodes to catch the various possible states of the world with reasonably accurate probabilities.

Time
Step

0.5
0.5

In our example, we used 0.5 years for both bonds.

Percent Change for Delta

The program automatically calculates not only the price of the bond but also its sensitivity to price movements in the underlying stock. It does this by moving the price of the stock by a certain increment, rerunning the algorithm, and recomputing the result. The increment by which the stock price moves is computed as a percentage of the current share price.

For example, if the stock price is $20 and the percentage is 10, the increment is determined as 10% * $20 = $2.

The program would compute the bond price when the share is priced at $20 and this will be the price that will be displayed. The program also computes the bond price when the share is priced at $18 and also at $22. These two numbers are used to compute Delta, as shown below.

Delta %
Change

10
10

In most cases, a 10 percent figure is reasonable. However, this could be increased for highly volatile stocks and decreased for low volatility shares.

This percentage change also applies to the computation of gamma.

If you are not interested in delta or gamma, set the percentage change to zero. This will improve the run time of the program.

Percent Change for Vega1 and Vega2

In these fields we enter the percent change of volatility, which is used to compute Vega1 (the sensitivity to the volatility of the stock) and Vega2 (the sensitivity to the volatility of the rates).

If you are not interested in Vega1 or Vega2, set the appropriate percentage change to zero.

Additional Inputs

The remaining columns in the "main" sheet are used to display the output of the algorithm. Before describing them, we continue to describe the additional inputs in the succeeding sheets.

Coupon Schedule

The user needs to input the coupon rates. Rates should be entered in the sheet marked Coupons. For normal bonds, this entry would be a single number. However, some bonds have step-up, step-down, or a varying coupon. For these, a coupon schedule is required. In our example, the first bond is a step-up bond. The coupon level starts out at 7 percent but after about four years it increases to 8 percent. The second bond has a coupon of 5 percent until maturity.

Example1		Example2	
term	rate (%)	term	rate (%)
1-Jan-1995	7.0	1-Jan-1995	5.0
1-Jan-2002	8.0		

Call Schedule

The next item is the call schedule for the bond. There are two types of calls: protected calls and unprotected calls. A protected call allows the issuer to call the bond only if the underlying stock has risen to above a predetermined level. An unprotected call allows for an unrestricted call option. If the issuer utilizes the call option, the investor may convert the bond into common shares. This is known as *forced conversion*. Of course, the program takes this into account.

Example1			Example2		
term	**price**	**min.stock**	**term**	**price**	**min.stock**
1-Jan-1997	**$100.00**	**$30.00**	**1-Jan-2000**	**$100.00**	**$31.82**
1-Jan-1998	**$100.00**	**$40.00**			

Bond Example1 is callable at par beginning January 1, 1997, but only if the stock price is above $30. This call option lasts until January 1, 1998. Beginning on January 1, 1998, the bond is callable at par but only if the stock price has climbed above $40.

The bond labeled "Example1" is callable at par beginning in January 1, 2000, but only if the share price is greater than $31.82. If we were to change this to an unprotected call, our input section would be:

Example1		
term	**price**	**min.stock**
1-Jan-2000	**$100.00**	**$0.01**

That is, the bond is callable at par if the share price is above $0.01, which is virtually guaranteed.

Put Schedule

The bond's put schedule is entered in this sheet. If a bond is puttable, enter the put date and the put price.

Example1		Example2	
term	**price**	**term**	**price**
1-Jan-1998	**$120.01**		
1-Jan-1999	**$100.00**		

The bond labeled Sample is puttable on January 1, 1998, for $120.01 and on January 1, 1999, for $100.00. The bond Example 1 is not puttable at all.

Dividends

This is the place to enter the dividend stream enjoyed by the shareholder. Dividends may be fixed or there might be precise projections for them. There are two conventions for dividends:

A cash dividend on a specific date. This will be paid out regardless of the share price.

A dividend yield expressed as a percentage of the share price.

Example1			Example2		
term	cash	rate(%)	term	cash	rate(%)
4-Jan-1996		2.00	4-Jan-1996		5.00
1-Jan-2002		3.00			

Bond Example 1 will pay a 2 percent dividend for the four years. Thereafter, the dividend rate will increase to 3 percent. Bond Example 2 will pay a dividend rate of 3.012 percent for its entire life. In this case, the dividends are assumed to be paid out continuously and they are quoted as a percentage of the underlying share price.

In other cases, the user may input the dividend as a cash amount (e.g., 0.25 for a 25 cent dividend).

Conversion Schedule

Bonds may be converted into

1. Shares.
2. Cash.
3. A combination of shares and cash.

The user should enter the date at which the conversion options begin and then the number of shares and cash amount to which the bond may be converted. If the bond is convertible to shares only, the cash amount should be entered as zero.

Example1			Example2		
term	shares	cash	term	shares	cash
4-Jan-1996	3.00	$2.00	4-Jan-1996	3.8554	0.00
1-Jan-1997	4.00	$1.00			

The bond Sample is convertible to a combination of three shares and $2 in cash beginning on January 1, 1995. This conversion option lasts for two years. On January 1, 1997, the bond may be converted to four shares and $1 in cash. The bond Example 1 is convertible to 3.8554 shares (and no cash). The holder has the right to convert throughout the life of the bond.

Domestic Yield Curve

Next, the program needs the domestic yield curve. This is entered as the risk-free par bond curve and a corporate spread component. One source of par bond yield-curves is the Bloomberg system.

So for each benchmark government bond, enter its maturity date, the equivalent par bond yield, and the corporate spread for this maturity. Note that you must give each yield curve a specific name. This could be USAA for United States AA rated bonds. This name is used in the Main sheet when the bond is being described. Note that many bonds can refer to the same yield curve.

DOM1				DOM2		
perturb = what? (Y/S)	Y			perturb = what? (Y/S)	Y	
=				=		
perturb = amount	20.0	bps		perturb = amount	10.0	bps
term	yield	spread	pert?	term	yield	spread	pert?
1-Mar-1996	4.676%	400.0		1-Apr-1996	5.469%	100.0
1-Jun-1996	5.114%	400.0		1-Jul-1996	5.950%	100.0
1-Jan-1997	6.192%	400.0	Y	1-Jan-1997	6.434%	100.0
1-Jan-1998	6.540%	400.0	Y	1-Jan-1998	7.652%	150.0
1-Jan-2000	6.908%	400.0		1-Jan-1999	8.098%	150.0
1-Jan-2005	7.261%	400.0		1-Jan-2000	8.430%	150.0
				1-Jan-2002	8.688%	200.0
				1-Jan-2005	8.623%	200.0
				1-Jan-2015	8.580%	250.0
				1-Jan-2025	8.544%	250.0

The yield curve DOM1 is composed of six benchmark bonds. For example, the five-year bond matures on January 1, 2000, and yields 6.908 percent. The corporate spreads are 400 basis points across the board. This means that a four-year corporate bond would yield 10.908 percent.

The yield curve DOM2 is composed of 10 benchmark bonds. The 30-year (actually 29-year) benchmark, for example, yields 8.544 percent. The corporate spreads vary along the curve. At the short end of the curve they are 100 basis points, and at the long end they are 250 basis points. So the 30-year corporate bond would yield 8.544% + 250/100 = 11.044%.

This is also the place to indicate how the duration and convexity are to be computed. If these are computed with respect to the yield curve, place a Y. If they are computed with respect to spreads, place an S. Also, we place the perturbation size appropriate to the computation.

If a functional (key-rate) duration and convexity is desired, place either a Y or an S next to the benchmark bond that pertains to that key rate duration and convexity.

Foreign Yield Curve (Optional)

This input is only required only when pricing dual currency bonds. We distinguish between two currencies:

- The domestic currency that pertains to the bond, its coupon, and any embedded features such as call, put, or conversion options.
- The foreign currency that pertains to the share price and any dividends received from the stock.

The user needs to enter the spot exchange rate between the two currencies. Our convention is easy to remember:

one unit of domestic currency = X units of foreign currency.

The curve itself is entered in a format similar to that of the domestic yield curve. That is, the user should enter the foreign par bond yield-curve. In this case, the program does not need the corporate spreads and only the yield curve should be entered.

1 domestic unit = x foreign units.

FOR1

x =	2.00
term	yield
1-Mar-1996	0.0468
1-Jun-1996	0.0511
1-Jan-1997	0.0619
1-Jan-1998	0.0654
1-Jan-2000	0.0691
1-Jan-2006	0.0726

Note that the four-year benchmark par bond would mature on January 1, 2000, and would yield 6.908 percent.

Dilution Effect

For some convertibles, when the holders choose to convert, the issuer simply issues more stock and gives it to the bond holders (in exchange for their bonds, of course). This causes an increase in the number of shares outstanding and a corresponding drop in the price per share.

If a bond exhibits the dilution effect, the algorithm expects to know the number of bonds outstanding as well as the number of shares outstanding. In addition, not all retail clients exhibit "rational" behavior. That is, even when it makes economical sense to convert, some holders may choose not to (e.g., for taxation reasons). So the user should also input the percentage of holders that would convert when it makes economical sense to do so.

Bond Identifier	Dilutions? (Y/N)	# Outstanding Shares	# Outstanding Bonds	Conversion Percentage (%)
Example1	Y	1000000	10000	50
Example2	N			

The bond Example1 exhibits the dilution effect. So the corresponding column is marked Y. There are 1 million shares outstanding and 10,000 bonds outstanding. The conversion ratio is 50 percent. That is, when it makes sense to do so, 50 percent of the 10,000 outstanding bonds will be converted. When 5,000 bonds are converted, the issuer would issue more shares. This would increase the amount of outstanding stock to 1 million plus 5,000 times the conversion ratio.

The bond Example2 does not exhibit the dilution effect.

Stock Price Drops

If share prices drop to very low levels, bond investors may fear increased risk of bankruptcy. Therefore, corporate spreads would rise. This, of course, would have an adverse effect on the price of the bond. The information has the following format:

If share prices dip below xxx, spreads increase by yyy basis points.

Of course, the more share prices drop, the higher the spread increase.

Example1		Example2	
if stock falls below	spread rises by		
19	400	5	10
15	800		

For bond Example 1, if share prices drop below $19, spreads would rise by 400 basis points. Further, if the share price dips below $15, spreads would increase to a level 800 basis points above where they originally were. The original spreads were given in sheet Yields.

Bond Example 2 suffers much less from this effect. If share prices dip below $5, spreads only rise by 10 basis points. Given that the spot price of the share is currently $20, there is only a low probability of a drop to below $5. Even if such a drop were to occur, spreads would rise by only 10 basis points.

Note

When the pertinent details of a bond are changed, the output related to the bond is no longer correct. The output changes color to Red. This is a sign that the bond must be recomputed.

INDEX

A

Asset swaps, 207-209, 222-223
  amortizing, 220-221
  convertible bond, 218-219
  cross-currency, 213-215
  mortgage, 221-222
  par versus market value, 210-213
  structured note, 215
  structuring, 210
  tax-immunized, 215-218

B

Back, Kerry, 3
Benoussan, Alain, 127
Black-Scholes
  application to pricing compound call
    options, 132-134
  application to pricing equity warrants,
    134-144
  approximation of complex option val-
    ues, 127-130
  beyond default-adjusted, 250-254
  preliminary technical properties of,
    130-132
  valuation of complex contingent
    claims and, 144-147
Brenner, Menachem, 273

C

Calderini, P., 231
Cheng, Daizhan, 171
Clewlow, Les, 37
Convertible bonds and preferred shares
  case study of pricing, 167-169
  primer on, 155-162
  modeling of, 162-167
Credit risk; see Default risk; Graver risk
  measure
Crouhy, Michel, 127

D

Default risk
  data analysis and, 96-106
  market-based measure of, 92-95
  market versus accounting-based mea-
    sures of, 89-91
  overview of, 91-92
  private borrowers and, 106-108
Deutsche mark yield curve, 69-75
Dunis, Christian L., 59

E

Efraty, Ravit, 197
Emerging market debt
  Brady bond market and, 232-233
  mathematics for, 235-239
  modeling derivatives on, 239-250
  options market and, 233-234
  pricing derivatives on risky, 231-232,
    234-235, 250-254
Equity warrants, 127-130
European compound call options, 127-
  130

F

Finkelstein, V., 231
Fong, Gifford, 171
Forecasting interest rates, 59; *see also*
  Deutsche mark yield curve
  empirical research on, 64-68
  theoretical considerations for, 60-64

G

Galai, Dan, 127, 273
Gelfand, B.Y., 231
Graver, Paul, 79
Graver risk measure, 79, 85
  credit risk and, 81-83

303